WHAT YOUR COLLEAGUES ARE SAYING . . .

"How do we empower our students as learners? How do we ensure that every teacher receives the guidance to deliver powerful instruction, particularly to the students who are most often underserved? These and other critical questions are addressed in this important new book by Jeffrey D. Wilhelm and his colleagues Rachel Bear and Adam Fachler. Under NCLB, we've spent too much time on testing and not enough time focused on how to provide all students with the opportunity to learn. This book moves us in this direction with thoughtful guidance and helpful strategies."

—Pedro A. Noguera, Distinguished Professor of Education and
Faculty Director of the Center for the Transformation of Schools, UCLA

"What does it mean to empower? The answer is here, in Wilhelm, Bear, and Fachler's practical, step-by-step guide. Giving students agency and making learning happen can feel elusive. This book erases the fuzziness and makes smart planning doable. I feel empowered to empower others after reading it! I wish I had this book years ago in my teaching. This is a doable and replicable model that takes the guesswork out of transformative teaching. It unravels the mystery behind expert teaching, planning, and assessment. The reader just needs to bring passion for teaching and caring for kids, which every teacher I know has in spades! The book will do the rest—leading you to transformational teaching. Great teaching doesn't just happen. We might know what works, but translating that into everyday practice is hard. There are deliberate, specific moves we can make, and this book walks us through them, step by step."

—Berit Gordon, author of *No More Fake Reading*

"This book is built upon a premise many of us have dedicated our lives to: 'teaching is the most noble . . . and transformative pursuit that exists in the world.' From its earliest pages, teachers like me will be nodding their heads and pumping their fists. But then the authors go on to lay out a model for *doing* the work that has the potential to sharpen secondary classroom practice around the world. The EMPOWER method is the kind of tool that earnest teachers yearn for: simple enough to understand in a day, deep enough to explore for a career. When it comes to teaching students toward expertise, I can't recommend *Planning Powerful Instruction, Grades 6–12* enough. My own copy will quickly earn the wear and tear of usefulness."

—Dave Stuart Jr., author of *These 6 Things: How to Focus Your Teaching on What Matters Most*

"What a profound and daring aim: to help teachers transform their teaching so that they can, in turn, transform their students' lives—both in and out of school. *Planning Powerful Instruction, Grades 6–12* provides a framework to help teachers across disciplines plan units and lessons that will make their classrooms places that they and their students will want to be: caring communities in which all of the members engage in the kind of thinking, talking, reading, and writing that motivates genuine engagement and that develops and rewards expert strategies and habits of mind. I'll admit to some acronym envy: Wilhelm, Bear, and Fachler demonstrate the power of EMPOWER, a model of instructional planning that will surely invigorate the work of any teacher."

—Michael Smith, co-author of *Developing Writers of Argument*

"Wilhelm, Bear, and Fachler's *Planning Powerful Instruction, Grades 6–12* is an essential text for every secondary educator who has inquiry at the heart of learning. The authors describe teaching as an act of both love and social justice. Yet, knowing how to transform teaching in order to put this mission at the center can seem daunting at times. This book introduces a planning structure (EMPOWER) that can be used across curricular models, such as UbD, to support young learners in their thinking—encouraging discussion, well-crafted argument, and more. It is a treasure chest of strategies and examples for teachers to utilize to make a difference in their classrooms. The thinking that is encouraged in planning will break through the walls of the classroom into the community to impact our world."

—Jennifer Wheat-Townsend, Director of Learning, Noblesville Schools

"In *Planning Powerful Instruction*, Wilhelm, Bear, and Fachler offer us the best of their thinking in a book we can all put to use right away through practical but deeply examined ideas that will EMPOWER us all as teachers as much as our students. This is the culmination of years of careful study of their own instructional practices in an effort to help us improve ours."

—Jim Burke, co-author of *Your Literacy Standards Companion* and *Academic Moves for College and Career Readiness*

"*Planning Powerful Instruction* weaves the most important ideas in education into one beautiful package. The authors show through examples, models, and scenarios what deep, meaningful, engaging instruction looks like. Their specific, doable practices—all backed by current and compelling research—affirm their belief that teaching is 'an act of love.' Read this book once for the sheer pleasure of it, and then grab a few colleagues, pass out the highlighters, and begin a book study that will transform learning for every student in your class."

—ReLeah Lent, author of *This Is Disciplinary Literacy* and *Disciplinary Literacy in Action*

PLANNING POWERFUL INSTRUCTION

GRADES 6-12

Jeff dedicates this book to his daughter, Jasmine Marie Wilhelm, who is just entering the exciting and empowering career of teaching, although she has already been Jeff's teacher since the day she was born!

Rachel dedicates this book to her husband, Phil Bear, who supports her in all things, including countless evenings and weekends spent grading papers, planning lessons, and writing this book.

Adam dedicates his first book to his parents, Bonnie and Jeff, his original teachers, who taught him how to challenge ideas, ask questions, and find answers; to his sister, Amanda, who was first in the family to publish and showed him it was possible; and to his wife, Liz, who has endured more brainstorming sessions than she ever signed up for, who has supported every creative endeavor without question, and whose love makes all this possible. Thank you; I love you all.

PLANNING POWERFUL INSTRUCTION

7 Must-Make Moves to Transform How We Teach—and How Students Learn

Grades 6-12

Jeffrey D. Wilhelm, Rachel Bear, and Adam Fachler

CORWIN Literacy

FOR INFORMATION:

Corwin
A SAGE Company
2455 Teller Road
Thousand Oaks, California 91320
(800) 233-9936
www.corwin.com

SAGE Publications Ltd.
1 Oliver's Yard
55 City Road
London EC1Y 1SP
United Kingdom

SAGE Publications India Pvt. Ltd.
B 1/I 1 Mohan Cooperative Industrial Area
Mathura Road, New Delhi 110 044
India

SAGE Publications Asia-Pacific Pte. Ltd.
18 Cross Street #10-10/11/12
China Square Central
Singapore 048423

Acquisitions Editor: Tori Bachman
Editorial Development Manager: Julie Nemer
Senior Editorial Assistant: Sharon Wu
Production Editor: Tori Mirsadjadi
Copy Editor: Melinda Masson
Typesetter: C&M Digitals (P) Ltd.
Proofreader: Lawrence W. Baker
Indexer: Mary Mortensen
Cover and Interior Designer: Scott Van Atta
Marketing Manager: Deena Meyer

Printed in the United States of America

ISBN 978-1-5443-4286-3

This book is printed on acid-free paper.

SUSTAINABLE FORESTRY INITIATIVE   Certified Sourcing
www.sfiprogram.org
SFI-00756

19 20 21 22 23 10 9 8 7 6 5 4 3 2 1

CONTENTS

Visit the companion website at
http://resources.corwin.com/EMPOWER-secondary
for downloadable resources.

ACKNOWLEDGMENTS

We all want to thank Lisa Luedeke and Tori Bachman, our most dedicated and wonderful editor, and Chris Downey, our developmental editor. We are doing something totally new in this book, and this team helped us navigate that territory. Thanks, too, to the entire design team at Corwin for making our work look so good. Finally, a team of teacher reviewers provided very valuable feedback on our proposal and as we were working on our final revisions. Thanks to all of you.

We tried our ideas in collaboration with the fellows of the Boise State Writing Project, in their classrooms, and through the Idaho Coaching Network, as well as through Jeff's work with the coaches from the American Reading Company. Our thanks to Scott Cook for all his support over many years.

Jeff would like to especially thank Rachel and Adam for undertaking this significant and very exciting project as a true team of thinking partners. He appreciates their hard thinking, good humor, and constant collegiality. Jeff also wants to give a 21-gun salute to his wife, Peggy Jo, and to all his colleagues and students with whom he has taught and learned over the course of his career. Thanks to so many Boise State Writing Project fellows for their collegiality and support over many years, especially Chris Butts, Jerry Hendershot, Jackie Miller, Karen Miller, Cecilia Pattee, Laurie Roberts, Paula Uriarte, Ramey Uriarte, and so many more too numerous to mention.

Rachel would like to offer a special thanks to Jeff for being a constant mentor throughout all phases of her career, beginning after her first year of teaching and leading up to inviting her to partner with him on this book. Rachel also wants to thank Adam for all his hard work, his thoughtful planning, and his constant ability to see the big picture. She would also like to thank all the thinking partners who have co-planned and reflected with her on lessons and professional development, especially Cecilia Pattee, Chris Butts, Jackie Miller, Laurie Roberts, Rhonda Urquidi, Paula Uriarte, and Amber Tetrick. Finally, Rachel wants to thank all her Writing Project colleagues in the national network and all her students who have stuck with her through her messy, challenging, and successful teaching moments.

Adam would like to thank Jeff and Rachel for being the best thought partners possible and helping bring EMPOWER to life. Adam would like to thank Jeff especially for his commitment to the profession, constantly pushing it forward and creating new pathways for teachers to learn. Adam also graciously acknowledges the contributions of the following educators, leaders, and thought partners who helped develop EMPOWER from an insight into an actionable idea: Alex Corbitt, Lucas Cittadino, Julie Conason, Serapha Cruz, Chris D'Ambrosio, Dr. Elizabeth Dellamora, Michael Devlin, Norman Eng, Jennifer Haig, Evan Meyers, Grace Omorebokhae, Emily Puccio, Joshua Russo, Adam Sarli, Melissa Szymanski, Maria Vera-Drucker, Katie Zingaro, and Grant Wiggins (of blessed memory).

PUBLISHER'S ACKNOWLEDGMENTS

Corwin gratefully acknowledges the contributions of the following reviewers:

Lydia Bowden
Assistant Principal, Language Arts
Berkmar High School
Lilburn, GA

Jennifer Wheat-Townsend
Director of Learning
Noblesville Schools
Indianapolis, IN

ABOUT THE AUTHORS

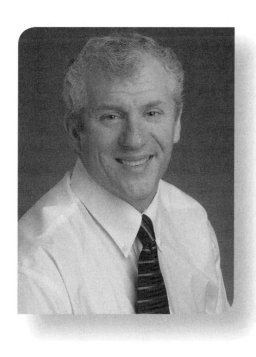

Jeffrey D. Wilhelm is Distinguished Professor of English Education at Boise State University. He is the founding director of the Maine and Boise State Writing Projects. He is the author or co-author of 39 books about literacy teaching and learning, and he has won NCTE's Promising Research award for *You Gotta BE the Book* (1997) and the David H. Russell Award for Distinguished Research in the Teaching of English for *"Reading Don't Fix No Chevys"* (2003) and for *Reading Unbound* (2016). Jeff has devoted his professional career to helping teachers help their students. He is particularly devoted to assisting students who are considered to be reluctant, struggling, or at risk. He is a passionate advocate for teachers and for students. He is committed to teaching for wholeness and well-being. He is an ardent Nordic marathon skier, mountain biker, and backpacker. He lives with his wife, Peggy, in Boise, Idaho.

After eight years as a classroom teacher, Rachel Bear spent two years as co-director of the Idaho Core Coaches for the Idaho State Department of Education, supporting teachers in implementing the Next Generation Learning Standards. She currently is a senior program associate for the National Writing Project (NWP). Her work at NWP involves supporting the College, Career, and Community Writers Program (C3WP), which focuses on improving academic writing in rural school districts. Rachel believes strongly in honoring the expertise of teachers as reflective practitioners, professional development providers, and advocates for students. Rachel lives with her husband, Phil, their son, Bodhi, and their three dogs in Boise, Idaho.

Adam Fachler is a strategist, coach, and consultant for pre-K–12 teachers and educational leaders throughout New York. Formerly a middle school teacher, staff developer, and intern principal, he left the classroom in 2014 to co-found the School in the Square, a public charter school in Washington Heights. Adam believes all educators deserve a coach in their corner and strives to provide them with the highest caliber of professional support they have ever received. In addition to creating the EMPOWER framework, Adam is a leading expert in Thinking Maps®—a visual language for learning—and a StoryBrand Certified Marketing Guide. Adam lives with his wife, Liz, in Brooklyn, New York.

Introduction

Education is an act of love, and thus an act of courage.
—Paolo Freire (2013, p. 34)

Teaching well is an act of love for our students. It is also an act of love and respect for ourselves; for knowledge that has been developed over time in the disciplines; for reading, composing, and problem solving; and for all significant learning that makes a difference to the quality of our personal and shared human experiences. It is an act of love for the world and for the future, and an act of faith in our capacity to better ourselves and our world. Teaching well is often a kind of loving rebellion, because it requires going beyond the status quo; caring for what is yet uncared for; and working for justice, for new knowledge, for new ways of knowing and being, and for what is in the act of becoming and yet to be (Wilhelm & Novak, 2011). Teaching well is all about *transformation*.

Teaching well is an act of social justice. In America today, demographics often determine destiny. Parents' socioeconomic status and educational attainment are the primary predictors of a learner's later success. But it does not have to be this way. When we *cognitively apprentice* students into the joy and the capacity of greater expertise, social barriers to success can be overcome. Research on human potential stretching from Vygotsky (1978) in the 1920s to Benjamin Bloom (1976) to the recent work of Anders Ericsson (e.g., Ericsson & Poole, 2016) demonstrates the liberating finding that *all students* are capable of learning the next available concept or process if they get the proper assistance in a meaningful context of use—if they are apprenticed.

Teaching—as an act of love and for social justice—is the most noble calling and transformative pursuit that exists in the world.

Teaching for deep understanding and growth requires passion, purpose, and dedication, but more than that: Teaching well requires expert practice in the use of scaffolds, structures, and strategies to activate and enliven the passion and purpose; to operationalize the dedication; and to make the learning happen, now and into the future. These scaffolds, structures, and strategies move from providing models and guided support to promoting self-regulation and self-direction, and move the learners into independence, into the full flowering of their human potential. Teaching well is about inducting students into meaning-making power; it is about sharing the persuasive power of expertise *with* students, not having authoritative power *over* students.

THE TRANSFORMATIVE POWER OF GUIDED INQUIRY

This book is about using a specific form of guided inquiry (known as inquiry as cognitive apprenticeship or ICA) to teach in ways that develop passion, purpose, and independent expertise in learners. We use guided inquiry to transform literacy to transform learning across disciplines to transform lives, and to work toward deeper learning, equity, and social justice.

The EMPOWER model we introduce in this book is a map that guides instructional planning of guided inquiry at both the unit and day-to-day instructional levels. EMPOWER names the "must-make moves" of teaching through guided inquiry and apprenticeship:

> E = Envision a lesson or unit's bottom-line goals for student learning
>
> M = Map out the steps of the learning journey for moving to a new destination
>
> P = Prime learners by activating their prior knowledge and interests
>
> O = Orient learners to the goals, purposes, and payoffs of the learning
>
> W = Walk through the process of achieving expertise through modeling, mentoring, and monitoring learner performance, gradually releasing responsibility to the learners through the process of apprenticeship
>
> E = Extend and explore new territory as learners personalize and transfer what has been learned
>
> R = Reflect through the process to name what was learned, how it was learned, and ways to continue growing, applying, and transferring what has been learned

EMPOWER is a model for systematic instructional planning that uses backwards design and captures current research into motivation, engagement, optimal experience, cognition, development of expertise, understanding and transfer, and more. This kind of planning is the central domain of a teacher's professional knowledge. In the chapters that follow, we first share the research and general principles behind EMPOWER and then proceed to the specific must-make moves necessary to enact the transformational teaching of guided inquiry as we plan units, plan lessons, and then implement and hone them with our students. The strategies in this book are the concrete practices that put the must-make moves of the EMPOWER model into our teaching practice.

When we learn how to plan and then teach with EMPOWER, we focus on learners and the highest goals we have for them. We use and adapt the must-make moves flexibly and in service of learners' deepened engagement and learning. Teaching begins and ends with attentiveness and responsiveness to students and their learning: teaching them from where they are and moving them toward where they could be. The teaching itself requires knowledge of planning and the use of strategies that scaffold and support new ways of expert learning and being, and new kinds of knowledge that can be transferred and performed.

If we have a planning process and a repertoire of strategies to model reading and composing and problem solving in new ways *for* students, then we can ask them to use these processes *with* us, then *with* each other, and finally on their own *by* themselves. This is the process of cognitive apprenticeship, also known as the gradual release of responsibility. Our approach works toward *total engagement* and *total participation* on the part of each student and in ways that develop generative strategic and conceptual expertise that can be used and honed throughout a lifetime.

Our colleague Pedro Noguera (2018) has stressed that as a culture we typically ask the wrong question: *How can we raise achievement?* Instead, what we should ask is this: *How can we engage, challenge, stimulate, and deepen the learning of our students, those specific human beings who enter with us into our learning environments?*

Noguera's question is one we take on in this book. To undertake it, courage will be more important than caution. Improvement requires building on what we already know and do to move into new ways of knowing and doing. This book is about transforming how we teach so we can transform why, and how, and what our students learn. The ultimate goal is for students to be transformed through deep understanding and the achievement of conscious competence—the capacity to monitor, justify, reflect on, and transfer what they've learned, and the ability to extend and adapt their knowledge to solve future problems. But how do you *do* it? What is the *process* for getting the results you're seeking in your classroom?

Before we move further, let's be clear: *Guided inquiry is not an extra or an option.* It is the work of truly teaching. It is the necessary process for achieving motivation, engagement, deep learning, practical and usable disciplinary expertise, and the capacity to meet all next-generation standards and assessments. It is a way to make your classroom into a caring community of practice, where everyone works together on common projects that mirror real-world expertise. It is what is necessary to move away from the shallowness of information-driven teaching with its recitation and retrieval and to move toward learning how to expertly construct and justify meaning and disciplinary knowledge for oneself. We are devoted to guided inquiry and our EMPOWER model for planning and teaching with it, because this process

1. Promotes, increases, and leverages the motivation, engagement, and even joy of learners (Smith & Wilhelm, 2002, 2006)

2. Prepares students for the intellectual and problem-solving demands of future education, work, citizenry, and personal affairs (Newmann, Carmichael, & King, 2016)

3. Significantly boosts achievement, understanding, and transfer of learning, including achievement on standardized tests (McTighe, Seif, & Wiggins, 2004; Newmann & Associates, 1996; Newmann & Wehlage, 1995; Smith & Wilhelm, 2006; Weglinsky, 2004)

4. Strengthens a sense of belonging and of community on many levels—the community of the classroom, and the connection between students, between students and teacher, and from the classroom to real-world communities of practice—and supports collaborative culture and powerful professional community among teachers (Wilhelm, 2012), which is consistent with and extends all other proven methods of guided inquiry, as shown in Figure I.1.

■ FIGURE I.1: CHART COMPARING EMPOWER TO DIFFERENT GUIDED INQUIRY MODELS

EMPOWER	SYSTEMS CONNECT	PROJECT-BASED LEARNING (PBL)	INTEGRATED INQUIRY (INTERNATIONAL BACCALAUREATE)	UNDERSTANDING BY DESIGN (UBD)	VESTED	SHELTERED INSTRUCTION OBSERVATION PROTOCOL (SIOP)	6 E'S	TEACHING FOR UNDERSTANDING
Envision	Topic selection and learning objectives	Key knowledge	Transdisciplinary theme	Stage 1: What is worthy and requiring of understanding?		Lesson prep	Engage	Use topics that engage and connect to other subjects
Map	Essential/driving questions; context; define issues and measurable changes		Tuning in		View	Building background		Create coherent goals
Prime		Challenging problem or question and student voice		Stage 3: What learning, experiences, and teaching promote understanding, interest, and excellence?				
Orient								
Walk Through	Plan and conduct investigations; analyze and interpret data; construct explanations; develop claims; informed action	Sustained inquiry, authenticity	Finding out, sorting out, going further, making conclusions		Experience / Speak	Comp. input strategies / Interaction	Explore / Explain	Create engaging learning experiences
Extend and Explore		Public product	Going further; taking action	Stage 2: What is the evidence for understanding?	Transform / Extend / Deliver / Perform	Practice/application / Lesson delivery / Review and assessment	Elaborate / Extend	
Reflect		Reflect					Evaluate	Develop formative and summative assessments that deepen understanding

MOVING FORWARD: TAKING THE JOURNEY TOWARD EMPOWERMENT

Be aware that this process and this book is not DFY (done for you), but instead DIY (you will learn how to do it for yourself, and to adapt and extend the model for your purposes with your students throughout the evolving challenges of your career). EMPOWER is not a script; it is a flexible framework and mental model of expert teaching. Your vision, energy, and commitment to improving your teaching and helping your students plays a major role in this process. If you bring the *passion*, we bring the *process* and *teaching strategies* to implement expert planning and teaching—a process that you will soon be able to make your own. You will be able to adapt our high-leverage apprenticeship strategies, extend them, and understand the principles behind each must-make move so you can come up with lessons and activities of your own. The model and principles support transfer: the capacity to use what you learn to plan and design lessons of your own, based on our models and the principles behind them.

As Jeff's dad used to say: If you always do what you've always done, then you'll always get what you always got. Our approach rejects the traditional and typical (so embedded in educational practice) and deepens many more progressive ways of teaching, to work for deep engagement and the development of deep and usable understanding, to help ourselves as teachers and all of our learners progress toward becoming our most powerful and best possible selves.

Teaching well is an act of love. And with love—and a teacher's mindful, planful instruction and support—all potential can be brought into being; all things can become possible.

An Introductory Activity: Getting in the Game of Guided Inquiry

What teacher has not struggled with planning curriculum that works for students? Or felt perplexed at how to help students develop the skills they need while still keeping the learning joyful? Maybe you know the feeling of giving up on creating a new unit of study (or even a lesson) because the task of putting it together and knowing if it would work was just too much. Perhaps, like your fellow teachers nationwide, you must face down a new set of standards requiring students to think at a deeper level than ever expected in the past. Or maybe you've just grown tired of hopelessly searching online for the "perfect" lesson or unit for your learners, only to be let down. If any of this sounds familiar, this book is for you. We intend it as a practical guide to creating curriculum and delivering instruction—units, modules, and lessons—to achieve three goals:

1. Unlock the motivation and engagement in classrooms of diverse learners

2. Maximize your students' chances of mastering desired learning outcomes

(Continued)

3. Position and help learners to think, understand, and act more like disciplinary experts and compassionate democratic citizens

We all want to make a positive impact in the lives of our learners and in the classrooms of our colleagues. In order to do that, we need a consistent, reliable way to design and deliver instruction that works. But that leads to another question: What works? Consider the four teaching vignettes below. Because we want the focus to remain on the pedagogy—the teaching moves, not the subject area—we designed scenarios around a subject we're fairly confident few of our readers teach: rock climbing. After reading the scenarios, try to determine which one will most likely lead to the highest degree of climbing independence and expertise, and be able to explain why you think so.

Vignette 1: The unit begins with the teacher explaining why people climb mountains and how the class will climb one. Every day, the teacher models a new skill on a section of terrain for students, guides practicing the new skill for a brief while, then facilitates their independent practice. "I do, we do, you do" is practiced with each new skill each day, until the class collectively reaches the top of the mountain, with the teacher providing copious feedback along the way. At the end of the unit, students put all the skills together and climb a new mountain independently. After the climb is complete, the teacher creates a gallery of photos from certain students' climbs and writes "a glow and a grow"—a point of praise and a suggestion for improvement—next to each photo.

Vignette 2: How do *you* think we should climb this mountain? Not wanting to stifle students' creativity, the teacher invites students to discover their own strategies for climbing and presents them with various tools they might need. Documenting their own trial and error, students create a notebook full of personal climbing strategies. Not only do they create their own styles of climbing, but they also all climb different mountains tailored to their interests. The more naturally gifted student climbers help and give feedback to the less gifted climbers during group work. At the end, the students all climb different mountains independently using their own unique styles and give a presentation based on their climb to the community.

Vignette 3: The teacher opens the unit by asking students what strategies they already know for climbing and then assesses their use of these strategies on a climbing wall. The teacher identifies a mountain off in the distance as the end destination of the unit and poses a guiding question: Why and how do experts climb mountains? After exploring a few stories and strategies of expert climbers, the students create a basic checklist of moves for their first climb, a molehill. With a "quick win" under their belts, the students scale two progressively higher mountains with the teacher's coaching, using and extending their "expert move" checklist after each climb. They then tackle two even higher mountains in groups, relying almost entirely on their peers' feedback and support. By now, they have outgrown the checklists, are using more developed scorecards, and are keeping process journals. The students' final task is twofold: (1) climb a new mountain independently and (2) teach a group of local kids who have never climbed before how to tackle their first mountain. Afterward, there is a debrief where students share their experiences and brainstorm a plan to climb another mountain or a way to transfer their skills to a new pursuit.

Vignette 4: A new unit called "Mountains and Molehills" begins. The teacher assigns worksheets about the process of climbing, multiple-choice questions about different kinds of mountains, and matching tasks relating climbing tools to their purpose (a chisel breaks rock; a rope holds the climber; a helmet protects the head). Sometime toward the end of the year, students climb a mountain on the same day as all the other kids in their state. Afterward, students watch many, many movies about climbing.

ANALYSIS OF THE VIGNETTES

Vignette 4: Educational Malpractice

The learning activities in the worksheet-driven classroom do not correspond to how real-world climbing experts train, plan, or climb, so this approach fails to translate into gains in rock climbing expertise. Nobody wants or argues for teaching this way, but it still tends to dominate American education (see Chapter 2). Students in classrooms like these feel disengaged and grossly unprepared for their state test on "climbing" and for real-world applications.

Vignette 1: "Skill a Day" Learning

While this vignette presents many elements that *appear* sound, upon closer inspection, it appears the teacher misunderstands the gradual release of responsibility—the process of transferring ownership of a task from the expert to the learner over time—as something that happens over a day, instead of over weeks, months, or even years. While this teacher values the consistency and structure of having an "I do, we do, you do" element in every lesson, the unintended consequence of this is students becoming dependent on *daily teacher assistance*. There is always a "we do," but never a period for students to just consolidate and extend their previous learning. The teacher's removal of all scaffolding for the final task can be abrupt and jarring for students. One final point: By breaking down the climbing into a series of subskills and only focusing on one at a time, students never get the experience of linking moves to climb a whole mountain, even a miniature one, making success on the final task highly unlikely for many students.

Vignette 2: Discovery-Based, or "Choose Your Own Adventure," Learning

While allowing students to wrestle with open-ended challenges has a role, exclusive reliance on this strategy is unsound pedagogy, abruptly releasing responsibility to unready learners. In this totally unscaffolded, discovery-based environment, the climbers climb, and the nonclimbers roll down the mountain. Students almost certainly will not develop real expertise because real expertise is passed down through communities of practitioners studying up on their predecessors, comparing notes, and making connections to new challenges, not by simply holing one's self off and tinkering. We admit this vignette presents a rosy if not romantic vision of learning, but ultimately, it is a misguided and unrealistic one. Furthermore, as the description of the final task suggests, learners in classrooms like these end up "all over the map" (in this case, both literally and figuratively) as a result of uneven skill development and unclear direction. Students who never learn the practices of experts cannot be expected to independently navigate an open-ended challenge.

ANOTHER WAY?

Insightful readers may notice somewhat exaggerated parallels (though not by much) between the vignettes provided here and the most common instructional approaches employed by schools nationwide. The pedagogical issues enumerated above abound in even the most popular publishers' curricula. So, if Vignette 1 is too scaffolded, and Vignette 2 is too unscaffolded, what is the alternative? What would such a pedagogy

(Continued)

present? Ideally, such an approach would balance the need for explicit instruction with the need for student autonomy, infuse rigor with meaning, and serve learners now and in the future.

Vignette 3: EMPOWERment Pedagogy

In this vignette, the teacher *primes* learners for the new challenge by tapping into their prior knowledge and skill. She then *orients* them toward a new destination and asks a compelling, framing question. From there, it's classic apprenticeship: She *walks through* some expert approaches to the task, inviting students into a community of experts, and helps students get a quick win. Over time, the teacher *extends expertise* in learners by challenging them to take on progressively harder climbs with less assistance from her and more assistance from their peers. Finally, the teacher calls on learners to *explore new territory*, climbing the mountain independently and teaching someone else how. Both the teaching task and future climbs are made possible by students' having developed an evolved mental model of climbing expertise from ongoing opportunities to *reflect* on their process through checklists, scorecards, and process journals.

These five elements (whose initial letters spell P-O-W-E-R), in addition to two "behind the scenes" teacher moves, *envision* and *map* (giving us E-M), "spell out" the pedagogy of EMPOWERment: the subject of this book.

While other pedagogies impose artificial form and vocabulary onto learning, EMPOWER does the opposite: It distills the elements of real-world teaching and learning and codifies them into a replicable process. Far from formulaic, EMPOWER merely *describes* what happens when students and teachers engage together in highly relevant, highly authentic teaching and learning. EMPOWER leverages the power of two schools of thought:

1. Expert inquiry—the recursive process of developing and performing knowledge the way real-world experts do

2. Apprenticeship—the art of gradually releasing responsibility for task performance to learners by building their capabilities until they can "own" the whole endeavor themselves

Instead of treating relevance and authenticity as an afterthought, EMPOWER uses them as a starting place to explain real-world learning better than any other existing paradigm.

A MAP OF THIS BOOK

These vignettes attempt to answer timeless questions about teaching: What kind of teaching can actually achieve transformations in understanding, performance, and ways of being? Under what conditions are people guided to inquire and develop expertise that can be applied in the real world? In light of that, what defines excellent instructional design? What moves must educators make to guarantee that learners develop expertise, insight, and independence?

Like the students in our vignettes, as we explore how we came to EMPOWER and detail the shifts required to teach this way, you, too, will begin a journey, surveying your methods and engaging in reflective practice. If you put in the work, then your destination is assured: You will reach new heights as an educator. You may find, too, that you'll take on a new role as an instructional leader.

We frame each chapter with a guiding question and include illustrative examples, stories from the field, and actionable insights. Chapters 1 and 2 provide a "map of the territory" and necessary background for the EMPOWER framework. Chapter 1 explores how people get better and become experts, and how EMPOWER works as a model of guided inquiry and apprenticeship to help people achieve the capacity of experts. In Chapter 2, we look at how to make the shift from informational to transformational teaching. We describe the differences so you can monitor your own shift. We explain why even very accomplished and progressive teachers often revert to the "salience of the traditional" (Zeichner & Tabachik, 1981).

Then we get totally practical. Chapters 3 through 5 explore how to work offstage to plan your units and individual lessons through the techniques of envisioning and mapping (the E-M of EMPOWER). Chapter 6 is about how to prime the classroom culture and community necessary for guided inquiry. In Chapters 7 and 8, we explore how to prime students for success with specific conceptual and procedural learning targets through priming and orienting (the P-O of EMPOWER). Chapters 9 through 13 focus on how to use various scaffolds and supports to actually apprentice, or walk through, new complex learning with students in order to develop and then extend and explore new territory (the W-E of EMPOWER), and Chapters 14 and 15 explore techniques and assessments to help students reflect (the R of EMPOWER) on, name, transfer, apply, and move consciously into the future with their newfound expertise.

We feature a throughline unit on civil rights in each of the chapters so that you can see how each must-make move of guided inquiry can be used as a lesson that is part of an actual unit. The first strategy and the accompanying lesson canvas in each chapter come directly from this unit. The following strategies in each chapter demonstrate how the featured must-make move can work in other ways in the throughline unit as well as in any other units from other subjects across the curriculum.

For ongoing updates as well as additional resources complementing and extending those from this book, visit empoweryourteaching.com.

PART 1: TRANSFORMATIVE PLANNING AND INSTRUCTION

ENVISION   MAP   PRIME   ORIENT   WALK THROUGH   EXTEND/EXPLORE   REFLECT

Chapter 1

WHAT'S AT STAKE? TEACHING TOWARD EXPERTISE—WITH A SENSE OF URGENCY

> **ESSENTIAL QUESTION**
> How can we best support learners in developing usable real-world expertise?

If our goal is to transform learners' motivation and capacity into those of experts, *then we must apprentice learners* into this motivation and into this expertise. This is accomplished by meeting the conditions of motivation (Csikszentmihalyi, 1990) and through deliberate practice that develops mental models of expert practice and conscious competence, which allows for high-road transfer to new tasks and problems throughout one's lifetime.

The most effective way we have ever found to move away from deeply embedded educational practices and move to planning and implementing guided inquiry for this kind of transformational teaching and learning is EMPOWER. In this chapter, we explain the EMPOWER framework more fully, and show how it captures the research about creating the conditions of motivation; the research on developing expertise, especially through the use of deliberate practice; and the research on achieving transfer. This process is called 3D teaching and learning in which learners come to *know* (understand conceptually like an expert), *do* (perform and use knowledge more like an expert to get things done), and *think* (justify and explain what and how they know, monitor and self-correct performance, and adapt what has been learned for use in new situations). This promotion of knowing, doing, and thinking mirrors what cognitive scientists would call *understanding*.

What's in this shift for you? Becoming a more consciously competent and professional teacher who can more expertly motivate and assist your learners. What's in it for the learners? Everything! EMPOWER moves learners into the future with purpose, motivation, and expert tools that provide them with the deep understanding to make their way in the world as learners and as democratic citizens in ways rarely achieved by traditional instruction.

The mental model of EMPOWER, which helps teachers simplify the design and delivery of teaching with the lens of guided inquiry, honors and aligns with the cognitive science of *improving*. At every stage in the process, students actively engage in the "hard fun" of mastering new learning. There is much explicit and active teaching punctuated by periods of learners' deliberate practice, and then time to use and enjoy, make choices, consolidate, personalize, and extend their new competence. In other words, there is a balance of instructional work and independent work—of apprenticeship, practice, and then independent use.

Teaching requires adept decision making and intentional design. Every day, there are multiple decisions to make about how to plan, design, revise, differentiate, and implement instruction, not to mention managing your students' energy—which is best done through both caring relationships and engaging and assistive instruction. In our work with teachers, we have found that just getting *started* on planning can provide the biggest challenge. Pre-service teachers, and even many in-service teachers, face the challenge of knowing how to take the first steps. As a result, they often rely on textbook questions or turn to Pinterest or Teachers Pay Teachers to grab a lesson plan. Such lessons were not designed or differentiated for their own students' deepest felt needs and current challenges. The result is typically disappointing because it is not responsive to specific students and does not build the professional knowledge of the teacher.

The alternative is to develop a powerful mental model of expert planning and teaching based on what we know about our own students and their needs. After all, you are the world's only expert on *your* students. In line with this "filter," we develop a rich repertoire of strategies for delivering the assistance our students need *right now* to progress toward deep engagement, understandings, and use.

Expert teaching and deep learning do not happen by accident; they happen by *design*, through mindful planning and implementation. Teachers design classroom culture and learning experiences. We design learning experiences not just for our students but also for ourselves and even our school and local communities. We must ask: What kinds of experiences do we want to have with students? What kinds of papers do we want to read? What kinds of projects do we want to collaborate on and share with the community?

TEACHING TOWARD EXPERTISE

Expertise in teaching is knowing *how* to teach people *how* to do new complex tasks: to read, write, problem solve, and do math and science more like experts. We want our students to develop authentic, applicable, real-world expertise across all content areas and human pursuits. This is usable expertise that is "tool-ish" instead of "school-ish" (Newmann, Carmichael, & King, 2016; Smith & Wilhelm, 2002, 2006); it is learning that has value outside of school in a variety of contexts.

For example, when students really learn and internalize a mental model for logical argumentation, it helps them in many ways: They can advocate for themselves and for others, they can resolve conflicts more peacefully, they can identify "fake news," they can apply reasoning in their problem solving and evidence in their interpretations, and so on. Expertise in the whole enterprise of argumentation—from composing arguments developed from evidence to analyzing arguments to discovering compelling opportunities to use them, not to mention developing even *more* transferable skills such as deep and focused listening throughout the process—is representative of the kind of tool-ish learning we're talking about here and throughout this book. If our teaching does not lead students toward applicable expert practice, we are not teaching for understanding and use; we are in the realm of the school-ish, and kids are merely "doing school." Cognitive scientists call this authentic application of expertise *meeting the correspondence concept* (Bereiter, 2004). In other words, good teaching corresponds to what actual experts do. It meets the real reader test and the real writer or mathematician test.

Since the 1980s, data from the United States have demonstrated low average student competence in academic subjects, analysis and problem-solving skills, interpersonal relations, communication, technology use, and a wide variety of occupational skills (see, e.g., Autor & Price, 2013; Newmann et al., 2016). Further, there are major disparities in achievement along racial and ethnic lines, and by economic and disability status. The takeaway: We're generally not teaching for real-world expertise, and students who are marginalized in any way are especially endangered by standard teaching approaches. There is so much at stake for our students and for our world!

When we think of how little time during any given year we have to spend with our own students, and when we think of the momentous task of helping diverse learners to become more engaged and expert and to overcome social inequities, we feel a profound sense of urgency. After all, which one of our students doesn't need to be more engaged, more literate, more wide awake and aware, and more expert at reading, composing, critical thinking, and problem solving in every subject? Who does not need to be prepared to meet new and nonroutine challenges by drawing flexibly on what has been learned? These needs require us to be more consciously competent teachers, continuously improving and moving forward to teach in more wide-awake and powerful ways.

WHAT ARE THE PREREQUISITES TO ALL LEARNING? MOTIVATION AND ENGAGEMENT

The research is abundantly clear that motivation and engagement are prerequisite to learning. The research is also clear on the conditions that promote motivation and deep engagement that works toward expertise (Csikszentmihalyi, 1990; Ericsson & Poole, 2016). In other words, we need to develop both motivation, the *impulse* to do something new, and engagement, the behavioral and cognitive tools to *do* something new. Mihaly Csikszentmihalyi (1990) termed this experience of total motivation and engagement a flow experience. *Meeting these conditions is under the control of a teacher.* Here's how: First, we must plan to meet the conditions of flow experience, or the state of total immersion in a task or activity, which satisfies the basic human needs for motivation and for engagement. We must then plan for learners to deliberately practice the strategies of experts over time until they reach independence; Figure 1.1 shows how the conditions of flow correlate to the stages of the EMPOWER framework in a classroom. What kind of teaching and learning approach meets these demands? *Only* guided inquiry through cognitive apprenticeship: a learning-centered curricular

FLOW CONDITION	WHERE IT CONNECTS TO EMPOWER	WHAT IT LOOKS LIKE
A clear purpose, payoffs, goals, and immediate ongoing feedback	Envisioning Mapping Reflecting	Learning framed as a problem to be solved (e.g., with an essential question); goals clear to all; culminating projects identified that require meeting the goals; instructional path to develop student capacity in meeting goals clear to all
A focus on immediate experience	Priming Orienting Walking Through	Proactive preparation for success through frontloading; focus on current relevance; active involvement: making and doing; immediate function and applications; fun and humor; edginess and debatability
A challenge that requires an appropriate level of skill and active assistance to meet the challenge as needed to be successful	Priming Orienting Walking Through Extending and Exploring Expertise	Guided assistance and apprenticeship in the strategies of experts; plenty of time for deliberate practice and ongoing procedural feedback
A sense of control and developing competence	Walking Through Extending and Exploring Expertise Reflecting	Use of one's voice and cultural resources; justifying one's practice; the opportunity to stake and defend points of view; provision of meaningful choice; naming growing competence and ways forward (procedural feedback)
The importance of the social and reflection	Walking Through Extending and Exploring Expertise Reflecting	Collaborative group work; peer assistance including reflecting together and providing feedback to each other; social purpose for all learning and use of learning; social reflection on how the purposes are being met and used; negotiating and sharing what is learned; reflecting on learning

structure that assists students to ask their own questions, solve problems, and create knowledge artifacts that do "social work" (Csikszentmihalyi, 1990; Smith & Wilhelm, 2002, 2006). These research findings explain why those one-and-done activities from textbooks or Teachers Pay Teachers fall woefully short. EMPOWER reflects research on motivation, engagement, and the deliberate practice necessary to develop consciously exercised expertise.

HOW DOES SOMEONE BECOME AN EXPERT? APPRENTICESHIP TOWARD CONSCIOUS COMPETENCE

Expert teachers teach for *conscious competence* and *high-road transfer*, for the flexible application of what is learned in various future situations different from those in which the learning took place. They teach for transformational change as learners move into the future.

But *how* do we start to teach the *how* of becoming more expert with any learning process or performance?

Let's do a thought experiment. Think of something significant that you have learned to do, either in school or out. How did you progress toward and achieve competence and then expertise? How were other people implicated in your learning?

Also consider this: Was there something at stake? As in, why did you care about the learning in the first place? Did you learn to more efficiently exercise to lose weight, promote fitness, or finish a race? Did you pick up a new language because you planned to visit a different culture? Did you develop a new teaching strategy to solve a learning challenge, to engage students, and to stay current in our profession? Or did you simply have a deep "felt need" to explore some topic out of pure personal interest?

As a lifetime adrenaline junky and competitive athlete living in beautiful Maine, Jeff found learning how to white-water kayak was a natural fit. He was motivated to try a new sport, to go down rivers enjoying the outdoors, to paddle with friends and students, and to enjoy the excitement of white water. When he was first learning, he spent a lot of time learning how to roll his boat, a prerequisite skill for white-water kayaking. As Jeff improved, he watched kayakers roll in different situations (like in giant side waves or river holes) and tried to emulate them. He also watched slow-motion videos as an expert kayaker narrated her thought process while conducting an advanced rolling strategy, naming the moves and using prompts to guide practice, such as "Hand on your butt to save your butt!" when setting up to roll a boat in heavy roiling white water.

While practicing how to roll, a teacher helped Jeff place his hands (one hand on the butt!) and paddle in the right place (curl that wrist!), guiding his movements until he could execute the maneuver on his own. Jeff practiced another foundational move of rolling, the hip snap, while leaning against the side of the pool as well as in the gym with weights, ironing these muscular firing patterns into his mind until he mastered them. When he was competent enough, he went to increasingly challenging places in the river to practice rolling, using the cues and moves he learned from his teachers and paddling partners.

Over time, his confidence—and, more importantly, his *competence*—grew. And even more than that, Jeff grew increasingly conscious of *why* he was successful (or not), and was able to explain what contributed to his performance and to reflect on how he could improve. He became a *consciously competent* kayaker who understood the principles behind important practices, possessed *executive function*, and could *self-regulate* and self-correct his performance—and therefore teach others. From point zero (at first, he did not even know how to get into a kayak!), the process of apprenticeship is what helped Jeff become an accomplished kayaker (who has twice kayaked the Grand Canyon and even rolled his boat in the famous Lava Falls—and most definitely not on purpose!).

We wonder: How often does teaching and learning through this kind of apprenticeship happen in English language arts, math, science, or history class? How can we more mindfully enact this time-honored process of apprenticing learners into developing expertise in our own teaching?

HOW DOES SOMEONE IMPROVE?
BY DEVELOPING MENTAL MODELS AND MAPS

Throughout our careers, we have all been obsessed with answering this age-old question at the heart of the teaching profession: *How* does anyone get better at anything? How do people become competent and then truly expert—especially with complex repertoires like those required by reading, composing, and doing math or science?

What role does an educator, coach, or mentor play in that process? In other words: *How* can we most powerfully teach and assist learners to transformative capacity?

Cognitive science provides us with a clear answer (Ericsson & Poole, 2016): Like Jeff in his kayak, experts are those who have been apprenticed and mentored into *deliberately practicing* to approximate and then master the stances and the thinking, problem solving, and performance activity of established experts. This deliberate practice can often be playful and involve mindfully trying things out. Those who have achieved expertise have used mindful practice over time to develop a rich *mental model* of the specific tasks they must navigate. This rich mental model is a kind of *map*, typically including rich visualizations (like a flow chart), that guides and then extends continued development of expertise over time. This mental task representation is consciously held, revised, and developed over time, and can guide us to create new kinds of knowledge. *Possession of such a mental model is considered to be the hallmark of expertise* (Ericsson & Poole, 2016). EMPOWER is such a map for planning and teaching. Throughout this book, you will experience mental maps for pursuing many specific kinds of teaching and learning performances.

Our careers as teachers and researchers have been about articulating mental models: making the stances, strategies, and processes of expert performances visible and available to teachers and to students. These elements of expertise become a model and a source of mentoring to students. Visible representations of expertise make critical standards clear, providing both a mirror and a measure of success. As one example, in *You Gotta BE the Book* (Wilhelm, 2016), Jeff presented a rich mental model of engaged reading and a map for how to help learners develop the strategies of engaged reading. The possession of a mental model is essential to expertise, to transfer and application, and to extending that expertise. Meeting any standard, like inferencing, analyzing, or understanding how authors achieve meanings and effects, or using evidentiary reasoning to make an argument, requires a rich mental model of how this task is pursued.

Experts capture threshold knowledge (i.e., knowledge that takes one through a gateway to a new and more expert way of knowing and doing) through a mental model or map that guides future problem solving, and that encourages the extension, revision, transfer, and sharpening of knowledge over time. Without evolving mental models, we would all have to start from square one every time we wanted to solve a problem. Scientists would argue about how to conduct fair experiments every time they wanted to test something instead of applying the scientific method. First responders would lose precious seconds during emergencies instead of performing life-saving assessment and action protocols. And the list could go on and on. With any teaching event, we need to plan for how we will induct students into competence and expertise, helping them to master mental models used by experts. In other words, we are apprenticing our students down the correspondence continuum toward mastery, deep knowledge, and high-road transfer. Cognitive scientists call this process cognitive apprenticeship (Collins, Brown, & Newman, 1992), and this is the basis of our form of guided inquiry.

Expertise is socially held in what is known as a *community of practice*, defined by Lave and Wenger (1991) as groups of people who share a concern or a passion for something they do and learn how to do it better as they regularly interact. When we inquire about a common topic and help each other to understand, we form a community of practice. When we engage in guided inquiry, we are apprenticed into an expert community of practice.

We want to make this point clear: *Guided inquiry as cognitive apprenticeship can be used with any kind of curriculum, material, or text and will deepen the teaching and learning.*

In Vygotskian terms (1978), cognitive apprenticeship moves students from their zone of actual development (ZAD) with a strategy or task and through their zone of proximal development (ZPD). This means that learners are taken from where they currently are and what they can currently do independently and without help (ZAD), and are assisted and supported to do what they *cannot yet* do alone and without support (moving through the ZPD). This helps one move toward the expertise held by the community of practice made up of experts in the discipline. Vygotsky considered the help we give learners to do what they cannot yet do alone—but can do with support—*the very act of teaching.* Let's put it this way: School is where you go to learn what you don't *yet* know how to do. Otherwise, what's the point? One of the great motivations and joys of being human is transformation: outgrowing ourselves and developing new competencies (Seligman, 2002).

Further, no one was ever motivated to read by the *cr-* blend or by learning to infer, but kids will learn such things with joy in the context of learning something they care about! Unfortunately, learners—and boys in particular—tend to see school learning as separate from real-life applications, and it is precisely because typically they are taught new concepts or strategies not in a context of use but rather through decontextualized readings and worksheets (Smith & Wilhelm, 2002). It's important to remember that

- The linchpin of motivation is developing usable competence

- In order to be engaged, kids (1) need to see the value/usefulness of what they are learning and (2) need to feel assured they'll get the support needed to be successful

- Engagement is necessary to the development of competence, and competence is necessary to staking your identity, which is the central task of human development

- Teachers need a growth mindset about their students and to develop this mindset in their learners (Dweck, 2006)

GUIDED INQUIRY: WHY THE BIG SHIFT IS NECESSARY

Guided inquiry as cognitive apprenticeship is the rigorous mentoring of students into the disciplinary expertise required to become more expert and to address real-world problems. Guided inquiry involves framing what is to be learned—the objective of the apprenticeship—as a problem to be addressed and perhaps solved. For example, instead of teaching *Romeo and Juliet*, you reframe instruction as an exploration of problems like *What makes and breaks relationships?* Instead of teaching the civil rights era as history, you reframe it as *How can we best protect and promote civil rights in our school and community?* Instead of teaching the water cycle, you reframe it as *What are the water problems in our community, and how can we help to address these?*

It's important to note that guided inquiry is *not student-centered discovery* learning where students find their own way. Instead, we explicitly invite learners into a community of expert practice, provide them with models of expertise, give assistance, and offer guided deliberate practice over time to master the know-how of experts. We support students in applying what they have learned in order to solve real-world problems in the ways experts do, and in naming and reflecting on and honing expert processes. Over time, learners come to practice and use what they have learned on their own as they explore and extend the uses of their newly developed expertise. In this phase, learning may look like discovery, but learners are making use of newly developed capacities achieved through apprenticeship.

Though there are many large-scale studies demonstrating the unique power of guided inquiry and apprenticeship approaches, our favorites include the Fred M. Newmann restructuring schools and authentic intellectual work studies (Newmann & Associates, 1996; Newmann et al., 2016; Newmann & Wehlage, 1995) because these studies show how our approach engages students, helps them deeply understand and develop expertise with value beyond school, and helps them retain gains over time. Literacy researcher George Hillocks made a career out of showing that guided inquiry is the way to most effectively teach writing (1986a, 1986b) and language use/grammar (2001) and to promote engagement and conceptual learning generally (1999). He found that for deep learning, students need to be *positioned* as inquirers and assisted to explore how texts and language work for meaning and effect.

John Hattie's (2008) influential review conflates inquiry as student-centered discovery learning with guided inquiry approaches such as inquiry as cognitive apprenticeship, and this alone accounts for the diminished effect size he reports. When data are collected about guided inquiry as cognitive apprenticeship, this approach is shown to be far and away the superior approach to teaching for engagement, understanding, and application.

Further, although this is not why we teach, we must acknowledge the elephant in the room: next-generation standards and assessments. Rest assured, the model we propose is the most effective teaching model for the goals of higher scores and meeting standards as evidenced by disaggregation of standardized test data like the National Assessment of Educational Progress (NAEP), Trends in International Mathematics and Science Study (TIMSS), and Programme for International Student Assessment (PISA) based on the effect of teaching treatment (e.g., McTighe, Seif, & Wiggins, 2004).

Perhaps most crucially, meeting the demands and solving the problems facing our local and global communities will require new kinds of knowledge and new ways of making knowledge—in other words, traditional methods and rote learning of established information is woefully insufficient to our current and future needs.

THE EMPOWER MODEL: A FRAMEWORK FOR PLANNING AND TEACHING THROUGH GUIDED INQUIRY

We've been arguing that (1) we need to teach toward real-world expertise, which is captured by mental models, and (2) guided inquiry is the way to motivate and apprentice learners into expertise. Now we want to show you a framework—the EMPOWER model—as a highly effective model for planning/teaching through guided inquiry. Figure 1.2 shows the steps of EMPOWER at a glance.

■ **FIGURE 1.2: THE EMPOWER MODEL**

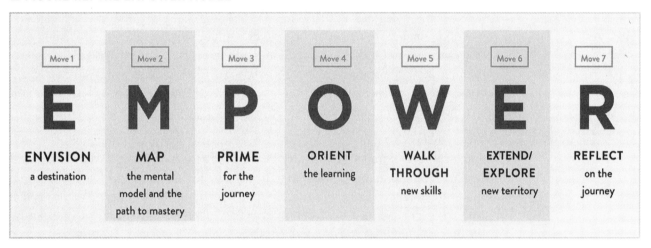

EMPOWER is *not* a formula; it *is* a mental model or map—a representation of how an expert teacher performs the complex tasks of teaching. *The possession of a complex mental model or map for complex task completion is considered to be the hallmark of expertise* (Ericsson & Poole, 2016). Thus, possessing EMPOWER helps you on your journey toward expert teaching. According to Ericsson and Poole's (2016) seminal research, *deliberate practice* through the apprenticeship process is the way anyone becomes expert at anything. Deliberate practice always has the following elements, which also correspond to EMPOWER:

- Clear and specific goals (E-M)
- Preparation for success (P-O)
- Focused practice (W-E)
- Pushing beyond one's comfort zone (W-E)
- Receiving high-quality feedback (R)
- Developing a mental model of the expert task (R)

EMPOWER provides a map for teachers to follow as you plan and then apprentice learners through navigating and completing a complex task using particular kinds of expert stances, concepts, and strategies. As we will explain, EMPOWER provides a process for planning and implementing instruction, and for learning itself, that reflects the expert knowledge and research in a wide variety of areas. Here's how the stages of EMPOWER unfold:

E-M: Offstage, before students enter the classroom, expert educators first *envision* (E) a destination for learners and then *map* (M) out each step of the journey necessary to achieving that destination, including how to develop the knowledge, tools, and mental models (the process experts use for this task) required for achievement of mastery. This is often known as *backwards planning*, mapping out instruction with the end goals and deliverables in mind.

P-O: Once in front of students, educators build motivation and personal connection as they *prime* (P) learners by activating and building their background knowledge and preexisting interests so these can be used as resources for the new learning, and *orient* (O) learners toward the new destination, and the purpose and payoffs of reaching it. Orienting identifies learning outcomes in terms of what students will be able to do and compose/make *independently* by the close of the unit, and how they will use their new capacities now and in the future.

W-E: Students now require explicit instruction and active apprenticeship in developing new ways of understanding and performing knowledge that is required to meet the goals. Educators model the use of new strategies and concepts for learners, and support them in deliberately practicing their use. This *walk-through* (W), or explicit instructional modeling and deliberate practice, develops and extends the expertise of learners through a variety of guided and collaborative tasks. These tasks increase in challenge/complexity and decrease in scaffolding/support over time, embodying a gradual release of responsibility to achieve independence. This is the time for modeling, coaching, and feedback as students rehearse, practice, and "scrimmage" as they approximate ever more closely the robust understandings and practices of experts. These activities are purposeful, contextualized, low-stakes learning experiences that prepare students for success on higher-stakes tasks.

With their skills and knowledge built, it is then time for students to put their learning to the ultimate test. Educators challenge students to *extend* their learning and to *explore* (E) new territory to apply their learning more independently, transferring what has been learned into novel situations that present the possibility of failure and the necessity of consolidating, revising, and improving on what has already been learned. This is very much like the "call to action" found in the hero's journey, the build-up to the "big game" in sports, or an opening-night performance in the arts. At this point, the mentor has moved mostly onto the sidelines. The teacher's job now is to step back and let students create new meanings and navigate trouble together so that they become ever more independent. Teachers intervene only as necessary to keep the learning moving forward. This is where high-road transfer is put into play.

R: Throughout this entire process, at each step, but especially near the end, with the big game, opening-night performance, culminating project, and general dragon slaying behind us, we—as teachers and learners—collectively *reflect* (R). What is being learned/was learned, and how? Why is it important, and how does it connect to our current and future goals? How can we use it now and in the future? What are our individual and collective strengths and struggles? How did we navigate trouble? What will we change and do next time we meet this kind of challenge? What opportunities do we foresee for using and further developing this knowledge now and in the future? What are our next steps?

When you teach via EMPOWER, students do and make things every day (*daily deliverables*) that engage them, promote learning, involve deliberate practice, and provide the learner and teacher with opportunities to reflect, and to name what's been learned and possibilities for moving forward. This kind of reflection is formative assessment *as* and *for* learning.

It's important to note that every step in EMPOWER (Figure 1.3) is essential. Figure 3.8 (at the end of Part 1) demonstrates what might happen if a step is skipped or removed from your planning and instruction.

■ **FIGURE 1.3: SIX ELEMENTS OF DELIBERATE PRACTICE**

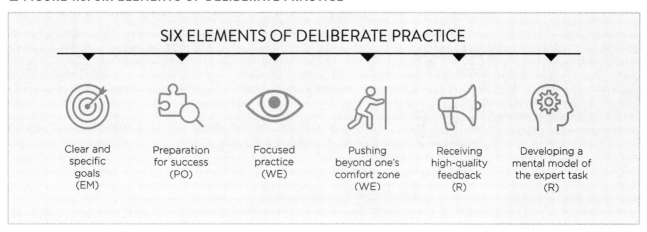

THE PRIMACY OF PLANNING

Planning instruction for your specific students in your particular context at this moment in time (something that you are the world's only expert on), at the unit and lesson level, *is the central challenge of teaching.*

Professions are defined by knowledge creation, and planning instructional practice is a special province of teacher professional knowledge. At first glance, planning might seem like a fairly simple and even mundane task. But it is neither. Planning is the foundational and prerequisite process of teacher expertise and creativity. The EMPOWER model helps us get after the big questions of *why* we teach, and *why* we teach *what* we teach and in *the ways* that we do. *What* should be our major goals, and *why* are these goals worth achieving? *How* can we most effectively assist learners into motivation and even joy, and then into deep understanding and application of their learning as they work toward these goals? *When, where,* and under *what* conditions is teaching and learning most engaging, joyful, and effective? All of these questions are in service of becoming more expert teachers, and making our students more expert as readers, composers, and disciplinary knowledge makers. With time, teachers become agile planners who can intuitively replan and reorient their teaching in the middle of a lesson because they know what they are trying to accomplish and the various ways to do so, and they see opportunities for goal accomplishment arise. This capacity is developed through deliberate practice over time.

TEACHING FOR TRANSFER

EMPOWER captures the "must-make moves" of planning and implementing guided inquiry. It cultivates a spirit of high-road transfer, which is the crux of inquiry as cognitive apprenticeship.

A focus on transfer may seem obvious, but research shows that transfer rarely occurs in school (Haskell, 2000; Perkins & Salomon, 1988). And when it does, the transfer is usually *low-road transfer*, when two tasks so closely resemble each other that you automatically use the same strategies. For example, if you get a rental car, you transfer what you do to drive your own car to driving the rental. *High-road transfer*, on the other hand, requires "mindful abstraction of skill or knowledge from one context to another" (Perkins & Salomon, 1988, p. 25). For example, if you suddenly had to drive a forklift or a truck with multiple clutches, you'd have to ask yourself, "Okay, what do I do first?" This mindful abstraction constitutes what Haskell (2000) calls "theoretical understanding"; that is, to transfer knowledge from one context to a dissimilar context requires you to possess *conscious competence* with *principles of practice*. You need to know just what it is you do, why you do it and do it that way, how you do it, how you know it works, in what kinds of situations you might use the knowledge, and how to self-correct and think through problems if things don't work.

Again, research shows that high-road transfer rarely occurs in school. For example, students don't automatically apply strategies required by one reading to subsequent readings. The good news is that learners can and do transfer new strategies if particular conditions are met. Haskell (2000) presents 11 of those conditions, which we have collapsed to 4:

1. Learners must deeply understand the knowledge that is to be transferred and the purposes served by using this knowledge; the conceptual principles and the payoffs of using that knowledge must be clear.

2. Learners must understand the principles and processes of practice to be transferred; students must have a mental model and map for applying the principles.

3. The classroom culture must cultivate a spirit of transfer; students must be continually considering and rehearsing how the knowledge can be used in a variety of potential contexts, both immediately and in the future.

4. Learners must deliberately and repeatedly practice applying the meaning-making and problem-solving principles to new situations.

In our work as thinking partners with thousands of teachers over the years, we have found that EMPOWER helps teachers know *how* to teach students *how* to develop and use expert strategies as readers, writers, and problem solvers in ways that promote high-road transfer.

DEVELOPING CONSCIOUS COMPETENCE
(AS TEACHERS AND IN LEARNERS)

Here's a big itchy problem: Teachers, even those who have a repertoire for transformational teaching, often revert to traditional practices of the pedagogy of poverty (Haberman, 2010; see Chapter 2), often due to the pressures of curriculum, school structures and schedules, parental/student/colleague expectations, standardized assessments, and so on. EMPOWER is a powerful solution because it helps you to be vigilant, wide awake, and mindful in the face of the salience of the traditional.

This kind of conscious competence occurs when you achieve a level of mindful awareness and the necessary tools to successfully navigate, monitor progress, productively struggle through challenges, and reflect to consolidate and justify learning and to move forward.

When we proceed with conscious competence as teachers, we can assist students to conscious competence as readers, composers, and problem solvers. With the achievement of conscious competence in students, a room full of teachers and thinking partners is created. The hallmark of expertise, and the goal of all teaching and learning, is the achievement of conscious competence through the possession of a transferable mental model. Conscious competence does not mean that solving any problem at hand will run smoothly. What it does mean is that the teacher or learner has a sense of when things go awry, can explain why that might be, and has paths of action for what to do about it. Teachers and learners have the capacity to monitor, to reframe, to develop, and to draw on a repertoire for moving forward. This kind of expertise can eventually be internalized and might look like unconscious competence, but experts can dig deep to go back to their map and make it conscious again when needed. Figure 1.4 details the progression from unconscious incompetence to conscious competence.

■ **FIGURE 1.4: CONSCIOUS COMPETENCE MATRIX: DELIBERATE PRACTICE IS THE WAY TO MOVE FROM STAGE 2 OR 3 TO STAGE 4**

	UNCONSCIOUS	CONSCIOUS
INCOMPETENCE	1. **Unconscious incompetence** • The learner is not aware of the existence or relevance of the conceptual/skill area or his or her deficiency in it.	2. **Conscious incompetence** • The learner becomes aware of the existence, significance, and relevance of the skill area/knowledge—and his or her deficiency and struggles to master and apply competence; this is where new learning can begin.
COMPETENCE	3. **Unconscious competence** • The learner is able to make use of the skill/concept area, but the learner does not know why or how this is made to happen, so he or she cannot mindfully repeat it, impart it, reflect on it, transform it, or extend it. The skill/concept is not yet conscious, nor does it constitute "knowledge."	4. **Conscious competence** • The learner has developed a rich map and mental representation of the task and can mindfully perform it—talk through it, reflect on it, self-monitor and correct it, share it with others, procedurally provide feedback about it, and revise and extend it reliably and at will.

Note: We align ourselves with researchers who see an advanced form of unconscious competence as a potential stage 5, when the competence is so internalized and automatized that it has become second nature. In this case, the competence can be retrieved, extended, or revised as needed as problems arise.

POWERFUL PLANNING WITH SO MUCH AT STAKE

There is a lot at stake when we consider how to most effectively teach.

For teachers, this is about achieving higher purposes as a teacher; achieving a higher level of professionalism; developing *conscious competence*, the capacity to develop knowledge about teaching and our subject(s); and experiencing joy as a teacher. It's about working to actualize the fullest potential for each and every student, especially those who may be reluctant, who may struggle, or who are marginalized in any way. *For students*, it's about engagement and joy through learning; achieving understanding and conscious competence; an agentive identity as a reader, learner, scientist, mathematician, and so on; and a sense of evolving possibilities for these identities. Most of all, it's about achieving competence and then transfer of

learning into the next task and into the future. *For teachers and students*, it's about creating a collaborative and supportive classroom community that is a disciplinary *community of practice*, and that meets the deepest needs and expresses the deepest hopes, aspirations, values, and commitments of all its members. EMPOWER assists all of these stakes and goals.

Bottom line: What is at stake is whether we truly *teach* and learners really *learn*.

Really, teaching means that learners and their understandings are transformed, and that learners achieve new transferable ways of doing and being and a conscious competence that justifies what they know, how they know it, and how they will use it. So yes, there is very much at stake.

Chapter 2

MAKING THE SHIFT FROM INFORMATIONAL TO TRANSFORMATIONAL TEACHING

> **ESSENTIAL QUESTION**
> How can we make the shift to transformational teaching?

Of course, we all want our teaching to matter right now and to make the biggest difference possible through the future. This requires a momentous shift away from traditional teaching practices: moving from providing information to teaching for transformation; moving away from lecturing, reading textbooks, and teacher-led discussions and toward collaborative inquiry and apprenticeship into expert practice.

There is a gap between what is known about transformational teaching and what teachers typically do, despite the best of intentions. Part of the problem is the old Donald Rumsfeld dilemma: We don't know what we don't know. Often, teachers are not aware of the consensus understandings from cognitive science, educational research, human development, and other fields, so they don't know how to put these insights into practice. Another part of the problem is that even when we do know the research and best practices, we often suffer from the knowing–doing gap. Research shows that teachers tend to default back to traditional informational forms of teaching. Traditional teaching is invited by many traditional school structures and expectations. So even when we do know what to do, we often don't do it as individuals or as systems (see, e.g., Bryk, Gomez, Grunow, & LeMahieu, 2017; Zeichner & Tabachik, 1981). Teachers who think they are making the necessary shifts may not be doing so or may be doing so inconsistently. This second problem is a bit like knowing you should floss your teeth every day, or that you should start off your day with some guided meditation. We know we should do it, but we often don't for various reasons. In these pages, we name the elements of the shift to transformational teaching, in an effort to develop awareness and conscious competence about the shifts we need to make, so that we can monitor how well we are making these shifts and continue making progress.

Our educational practices are not yet meeting the demands of the present moment or the future. Many of the problems our students must deal with are still evolving, and many of our most pressing current problems do not yet have solutions. For example, kids are hyperaware of climate change and anxious about finding solutions. Social agreements about knowledge are constantly changing. Did you notice that Pluto is no longer a planet? And the job market is rapidly changing, too. The World Economic Forum (2016) estimates that over two-thirds of today's kindergartners will enter fields that do not yet exist. Likewise, studies by Autor, Levy, and Murnane (2003) and Autor and Price (2013) explore the changing demand for skills in the U.S. workplace. The *only* jobs that are growing—and they are growing exponentially—are *nonroutine* analytical and *nonroutine* interactive. As an example, managing people and projects involves nonroutine analysis of ever-changing factors and nonroutine interactions with different groups of workers and clients. Teaching is a classic job of this type. Routine jobs (e.g., in mining, agriculture, and manufacturing) that do not require creative communication, analysis, and on-the-spot problem solving are all but disappearing. In other words, our learners need to *learn how to learn*, how to relate, and how to collaborate to solve new problems and create new knowledge. What good is traditional information-download-style instruction in a world like this?

Here's the gist: The way American schools traditionally—and typically still—teach kids does not suffice to meet the demands of next-generation standards and assessments, nor does it meet the demands for real-world expertise, for learning how to continuously learn and improve, and for learning how to meet new challenges. Yet, as various studies show (e.g., Newmann, Carmichael, & King, 2016; TNTP, 2018), authoritative and informational teaching practices still dominate American teaching. This kind of teaching hurts all learners, but those learners who are minorities, living in poverty, or marginalized in any way are especially at risk. (We discuss this more later in this chapter; it's what Martin Haberman [2010] refers to as "the pedagogy of poverty.")

Guided inquiry through EMPOWER directly addresses the most significant problems with traditional schooling. For example, nearly 50 percent of high school dropouts reveal that they left school because it was not interesting or authentic, and 70 percent disclose that they were neither motivated nor assisted to work hard by typical school assignments and structures (Bridgeland, DiIulio, & Morrison, 2006). In contrast, we have found that nearly all learners, especially students who often struggle or are considered at risk, enthusiastically embrace guided inquiry approaches (Smith & Wilhelm, 2002, 2006). Schooling suddenly makes sense; is purposeful, usable, and culturally relevant; and promotes competence and personal power, and students get the help they need at the point of need.

The Knowing–Doing Divide: A Real-World Story

Thirteen years ago, Jeff's wife, Peggy, collapsed from what was thought to be brain cancer but turned out to be a massive cerebral hemorrhage. Jeff was told that Peggy was terminal on four different occasions over the course of the next six years. In year 5, Peggy spent two months in a coma. The doctors could not explain her fluctuating blood counts. Because they did not know the *why* behind her condition, they did not know what to do. Their lack of a mental model meant they could not articulate and pursue a theory of action. For the first few years, there was no diagnosis and no viable treatment plan.

How did Jeff and Peggy succeed in meeting Peggy's medical challenge? Of course, Peggy is a woman of immense grit and grace. But there is also this: The two were thinking partners and teachers for each other throughout this health journey. They never gave up in the face of dire diagnoses. They tirelessly researched medical options and kept open minds toward all perspectives and possibilities. They had friends and family to support them (including everyone on this author team).

The turning point came when Jeff and Peggy were referred to the Mayo Clinic, a research hospital, and from there to the National Institutes of Health Undiagnosed Diseases Program, a research program, and from there to the Hai-Shan Eastern Medicine Research Clinic. Up until that point, the doctors were caring, but they thought with information and algorithms. This kind of informational and one-size-fits-all shortcut thinking suffices if you have a condition that is already understood. It did not suffice for Peggy. It was not until she entered a research hospital that the doctors thought with mental models and maps, working together on the unsolved problem using the strategies of inquiry, and apprenticing each other through multiple perspectives into deeper understanding.

Jeff can assure you of this: When someone you love is dying of an undiagnosed disease, you will get on your knees and thank the animating spirit of the universe when you find a doctor who knows how to inquire and work with a community of practice. This kind of ill-formed and unsolved problem is what Autor and colleagues (Autor et al., 2003; Autor & Price, 2013) call a nonroutine analytic and interactive task—and these are the jobs that are coming to dominate the American workplace. So we ask: What kind of learner do you want your teaching to produce? We know our answer.

BRIDGING THE KNOWING-DOING DIVIDE IN SCHOOL

The real challenge of improving teaching and learning is not a lack of knowledge. *We know what works* to engage learners and to develop learner capacity. We know it from robust research bases into motivation and engagement, optimal experience, human development, educational psychology, cognitive science, development of expertise, social–emotional learning, and many other fields. The challenge is translating what we know into practice, and achieving sustained focus on implementing this knowledge (Bryk et al., 2017; Newmann et al., 2016). The EMPOWER model is powerful because it captures the central insights from all of these research areas *and* puts them into practice. EMPOWER helps us plan instruction, do the teaching, study/reflect on learning, and revise our instruction in a focused process of continuous improvement.

EMPOWER is also powerful because it naturally integrates many diverse goals into our instruction. We then get many things done—and done more effectively—through the one thing of our instructional practice. EMPOWER allows us to do things together that actually go together, like reading about topics that we will write about. Learning how to navigate complex tasks through guided inquiry requires executive functioning and the use of mental models. As another example, EMPOWER is about learning through relationships, dialogue, sharing, and procedural feedback. Engaging in all of these activities requires us to develop social–emotional learning.

We use EMPOWER to improve teaching because it bridges the knowing–doing divide. It provides a context and focus for *all that we do* in schools, from professional development to lesson planning and instruction.

THE SHIFT FROM A PEDAGOGY OF POVERTY TO ONE OF EMPOWERMENT

The shifts necessary to move from teaching information to teaching for transformation, deep understanding, and knowledge performance are captured by the lifetime research of Martin Haberman (e.g., 2010), who argues that purely informational teaching, or "the pedagogy of poverty," does not work to build engagement or expertise and is particularly harmful to children in poverty or otherwise marginalized. Haberman (2010) has shown that this approach keeps students in poverty because it does not engage them or develop expertise. It likewise undermines teacher expertise and growth. This kind of traditional teaching is curriculum-centered, with the teacher controlling everything, whereas transformational teaching centers on the learning, with the learners taking more and more ownership over their learning. Haberman shows that the traditional approach to teaching is deeply embedded in American schooling. His work also demonstrates that this traditional approach is extremely challenging to change without conscious and deliberate efforts over time.

The recent "opportunity myth" study (TNTP, 2018) demonstrates that American schools continue to fail at promoting deep learner engagement and capacity. This study found that the vast majority of work required of learners is unengaging and below grade level, involves passive reception instead of active participation, and does not reflect expert practice. Even if learners do the work, it does not create a continuing impulse to learn, nor does it lead to deep, usable learning; future growth; or opportunity.

Haberman (2010) contrasts the pedagogy of poverty with what he calls "good" or "effective" teaching. We call this the pedagogy of EMPOWERment because research shows that this kind of transformational teaching is highly effective, internally persuasive to learners, inductive/restorative, pegged to expert practice, and empowering for both teachers and learners. Learning-centered instruction, when planned using the EMPOWER model, is both culturally relevant and in service of social justice; all students have more control over their learning, use their personal and cultural resources, and are apprenticed toward learning that can actually solve real-world problems. Figure 2.1 compares these two styles of teaching.

PEDAGOGY OF POVERTY	PEDAGOGY OF EMPOWERMENT
CURRICULUM- AND TEACHER-CENTERED (AUTHORITATIVE INSTRUCTION)	LEARNER- AND LEARNING-CENTERED (INTERNALLY PERSUASIVE INSTRUCTION)
<ul><li>Curriculum determines content and timing of learning.</li><li>Teacher/textbook purveys established authoritative information.</li><li>Teacher gives directions.</li><li>Teacher makes assignments requiring repetition and mirroring of purveyed information.</li><li>Teacher asks factual questions.</li><li>Teacher gives tests and grades.</li><li>Teacher monitors individual seatwork.</li><li>Teacher reviews and assesses assignments.</li><li>Learners are compliant.</li></ul>	<ul><li>Curriculum is responsive to student interests and capacities, asking learners to stretch interests and understanding about issues they see as vital concerns.</li><li>Learners are involved with exploring and applying ideals such as fairness, equity, justice, and best applications, putting what is learned into practice.</li><li>Learners are actively inducted into expertise by being supported in doing what experts do.</li><li>Learners craft explanations of phenomena, processes, human differences, and perspectives.</li><li>Learners master major concepts and expert strategies of learning (i.e., threshold knowledge) through meaningful use and deliberate practice.</li><li>Learners help with planning and are actively involved in learning each day, creating deliverables and proof positives of progress or productive struggle.</li><li>Learners actively collaborate in heterogeneous groups and are helped to learn how to collaborate.</li><li>Learners reflect on their lives and how they have come to think, believe, and feel as they do, and actively question commonsense assumptions and practices.</li><li>Learners justify what, how, and why they know according to disciplinary standards (i.e., they develop conscious competence).</li><li>Learners help set critical standards and are involved in all feedback and assessment.</li><li>Learners take over and personalize the work—including peer assistance and assessment.</li><li>Ways of thinking and being are transformed, and learners move into the future with new ways of being and performing.</li><li>Learners become independent as they explore and extend their own work.</li></ul>

MAKING THE SHIFT FROM INFORMATION TO TRANSFORMATION

When we consciously adopt a pedagogy of EMPOWERment, we leave the pedagogy of poverty and the salience of the traditional far behind. Through decades of work with teachers, we have found that *any unit in any subject at any grade can be reframed into transformational teaching, if* the teacher is willing to share some of the classroom power with the learners, to decenter him- or herself as the only authority, and to become a collaborative meaning-making participant with learners.

The contrasts between informational teaching, or the pedagogy of poverty, and transformational teaching, or the pedagogy of EMPOWERment, mirror the differences cognitive science describes between information, which is inert, and knowledge, which is dynamic, generative, usable, revisable, and extensible (see Figure 2.2). The achievement of this kind of knowledge is called 3D learning: The focus is not on knowing information, but on *knowing* conceptually, *doing* by putting the concepts into use to get work done, and *thinking* through naming what was learned, justifying the learning like an expert, reflecting, and metacognating on the learning, rehearsing future uses, and achieving high-road transfer for the learning.

■ FIGURE 2.2: TRADITIONAL INFORMATIONAL VS. TRANSFORMATIONAL KNOWLEDGE-BASED LEARNING

TRADITIONAL INFORMATIONAL TEACHING AND LEARNING: NONSITUATED	AUTHENTIC AND TRANSFORMATIONAL TEACHING AND LEARNING: SITUATED IN ACTUAL USE
Learners learn something because it is in the curriculum or on the test; knowing is focused on the *what*.	**E-M:** There are clear and authentic real-world purposes, goals, and payoffs for the learning. **P-O:** Learners understand the purpose and payoff of learning, both immediately and in the future. They work to understand how experts develop and use knowledge. Knowing involves the *why*, *how*, and *what*, in that order of priority. Knowing considers the *when* and *where* of application. Human purposes for using knowledge are foregrounded.
Learning is primarily rote skills, algorithms, and information. Learning is about knowing information.	**M:** Learning involves creating a new (to the learner) and generative mental model/map for understanding and making use of a concept, or for pursuing a problem-solving and knowledge-making process. Teaching and learning are 3D: about knowing, doing, *and* thinking—reflecting/metacognating/rehearsing for transfer.
Learning is linear and sometimes fragmented.	**M:** Teaching episodes are carefully sequenced to build on each other. Learning is structured, systematic, and weblike—concepts and processes are interconnected, and there is a clear relationship and interplay between structure, details, meaning, and use. Knowledge is perceived as a network.
Learning is often decontextualized (taught separately from use). Although concepts or problems may have classroom applications, they rarely extend beyond this. (We call this "school-ish"—as the learning only counts in school contexts.)	**P-O:** Learning is authentic and contextualized: learned and applied in a situation (or simulated context) in which the knowledge is required to respond to real-world questions and needs. (We call this "tool-ish"—as the learning extends human abilities to perform tasks in the world outside of school.)
Knowledge and practice are static: *presented* as established and unquestioned facts and ways of doing things; learners have no role except to accept and repeat.	**W-E:** Knowledge and practice are dynamic: *understood* to be context-dependent, evolving, extensible, and revisable. Knowledge is socially constructed, negotiated, and justified based on disciplinary standards, so competing viewpoints are honored and considered; learners play an integral role in knowledge creation.
Learning is received from outside sources and typically constrained (it cannot be extended by the learner); it is *authoritatively* imposed and requires learner acceptance and compliance.	**W-E:** Learning is constructivist and unconstrained because it can be built upon throughout a lifetime. Learning must involve personal effort, contributions, and connection making to be internalized by an individual—the learning is *internally persuasive* because it is convincing to the learner and it is understood why and how the process or concept works. Learning demands to be used and extended.
Learning is *receptive* and isolated; finding out new information is often the end of learning.	**W-E:** Learning is *active* and generative and occurs while doing real disciplinary work with proper guidance; finding out new information is typically the beginning of learning as one considers how to use, perform, explore, and extend knowledge.

TRADITIONAL INFORMATIONAL TEACHING AND LEARNING: NONSITUATED	AUTHENTIC AND TRANSFORMATIONAL TEACHING AND LEARNING: SITUATED IN ACTUAL USE
Teaching is considered to be the donation of information to the learners: Learners *listen* to a teacher or read a textbook.	**W-E:** Teaching helps learners to *transform their capacity to participate* in learning and problem solving by gaining knowledge, constructing deep understandings, and developing strategies that promote independence: Learners *do* the discipline in a context to develop knowledge and solve and address real-world questions.
Learners *hear* about disciplines and communities of practice.	**W-E:** Learners *participate* in a community of practice that is doing disciplinary work.
Work is typically discarded once completed and submitted for a grade (e.g., term papers, tests, homework).	**E:** Learning creations are "knowledge artifacts" that are archival and extendable over time, by creator and others, and can be continually referred to, revised, and built upon by the self and by others, now and in the future, as well as adapted and transferred to new situations.
Learning is recapitulated.	**E:** Learning is transformed, transmediated, re-represented, explored, extended, and used in new and multimodal ways.
The end of learning is telling back; learners rarely reflect on and justify their learning.	**R:** Learners are presented with ongoing daily opportunities and support to reflect on learning, self-assess, and consider immediate and future applications to transfer threshold knowledge, which continues to develop and evolve throughout life as it is applied in new situations.

Source: Adapted from Barab & Hay, 2001; Moore, 2016; Wilhelm, 2013b.

You are certainly already affected in some way by this shift from informational to transformational teaching. It is represented by the Common Core State Standards (CCSS) and the Next Generation Science Standards (NGSS), or by its correlates in states like ours, where the free and independent republic of Idaho has adopted the Idaho Content Standards for English Language Arts/Literacy, Mathematics, and Science. Take a look at the new standards. You will see that they are expressed through higher-order thinking verbs such as *analyze, interpret, create,* and *revise.* The standards are now about *doing:* about *how* to read, compose, problem solve, do science and math, and so on, and about dynamic ways of making meaning, as opposed to the banking of established information in learners' minds.

Using the EMPOWER framework does not require you to teach new texts or content. EMPOWER can *reframe any lesson, unit, text, or topic in any subject* so the teaching and learning are more motivating and powerful. The next-generation standards worldwide provide the *what* (the descriptions of the processes and cross-cutting concepts to be learned), but they do not provide the *how* for implementation. In this way, the standards are empowering, as they honor teacher professionalism and expertise to determine the best way to teach, and guided inquiry through apprenticeship is that highly adaptable best way.

When it comes to challenges of teaching and learning, many of the solutions are hidden in plain sight: in powerful examples of real-world teaching and learning. Whether it's a child being taught how to ride a bike, a hobbyist being taught to fly fish, or an intern being taught how to perform surgery, we can see guided inquiry and mental mapping at work. It's not the materials or the standards that are the real challenge. The challenge is apprenticing learners toward meeting the standards of real-world expertise, in helping them to learn how to do what experts do, and into developing the habits of mind and mental maps necessary to achieving competence and then expertise. Figure 2.3 shows what the shifts in teaching practice look like in an actual unit.

■ FIGURE 2.3: A TRADITIONAL UNIT VS. AN INQUIRY AS COGNITIVE APPRENTICESHIP EMPOWER UNIT

	TRADITIONAL, INFORMATIONAL, AUTHORITATIVE INSTRUCTION	GUIDED INQUIRY/APPRENTICESHIP TEACHING THROUGH EMPOWER: ACHIEVING TRANSFORMATIONAL AND INTERNALLY PERSUASIVE UNDERSTANDINGS AND DISCIPLINARY KNOWLEDGE
Topic	Civil War	**E-M-P-O:** Framed as an essential question or a problem to solve (e.g., Why did the Union win the Civil War? What determines who wins or gets their way in any conflict?).
Goals	Some retention of factual knowledge about the Civil War	**E-M:** *Understanding* and *transfer*! Apprenticeship into historical enthusiasms and thinking and therefore induction into the community of practice of doing history; development of grounded theory and threshold knowledge about causes, effects, and results of conflict and warfare; ability to analyze historical data and theorize from it as a novice historian; making predictions about current and future conflicts; excitement about history.
Frontloading	None or pretest	**P-O:** Brainstorm causes of conflict (e.g., rank those most likely to cause a war); brainstorm advantages to be sought in any conflict and especially in war (e.g., rank those most likely to determine outcome).
Organization	Teacher leads; everyone does the same thing	**W-E:** Teacher-guided explorations of various topics. Small groups and then individuals eventually divide up and take ownership of various aspects of the inquiry; distributed expertise and personalized learning is achieved and shared.
Instructional Activities	Textbooks, worksheets, lectures, teacher-led discussion	**W-E:** Historical simulations. Drama/action strategies that put learners in the position of combatants, politicians, citizens, or enslaved people to develop perspective and social imagination. Jigsawed small group inquiry discussions based on readings or direct experiences. Report out to class on small group learning progress. Analyze data, create interpretations, make visual representations of learning, present findings and arguments to others, and share and discuss.
Questions	Factually oriented; asked by teacher	**W-E:** Interpretive, evaluative, and applicative. Teachers ask questions of all types to model generation of higher-order question types for learners. Learners learn to generate questions and how to find or generate the data to answer them.
Discussion Format	I-R-E: Teacher *initiates*; learners *respond*; teacher *evaluates*	**W-E:** Learners bring questions to class, pursued in small group discussions and a variety of formats like Socratic Seminar. Roundtable reports on small group inquiries through Gallery Walks and presentations that elicit feedback and uptake from class. Whole group identifies connections among small group inquiries.

	TRADITIONAL, INFORMATIONAL, AUTHORITATIVE INSTRUCTION	GUIDED INQUIRY/APPRENTICESHIP TEACHING THROUGH EMPOWER: ACHIEVING TRANSFORMATIONAL AND INTERNALLY PERSUASIVE UNDERSTANDINGS AND DISCIPLINARY KNOWLEDGE
Reading Materials	Textbooks, worksheets	**W-E:** Textbook as possible reference. Primary documents regarding industrial base, trade and trading partners, weaponry, raw materials, foreign relations, organization of armed forces, leadership and generals, transportation, and economic base. Diaries (e.g., *In the Eye of the Storm*). Battle accounts, maps, drawings. Internet sites. Informant interview (e.g., with local history buff, reenactor, or Civil War roundtable group). Young adult novels; YA nonfiction; children's books (e.g., *Across Five Aprils*, *Pink and Say*).
Assessment, Proof of Learning	Quizzes and exams; primarily of factual information	**E-R:** Daily deliverables, formative assessments, and procedural feedback. Written argument about why the Union won the war, or what could have helped the South win. Living history museum exhibits exploring findings. Application of findings to a different war. Multimedia presentation of findings. Ongoing reflection and procedural feedback focused on threshold knowledge and expert moves of doing history.

As we've stated, EMPOWER is a highly functional tool for planning and implementing inquiry-oriented units and lessons. Beyond this, however, EMPOWER inspires us because it helps us meet other related and deeply held commitments. There are six areas of research pertaining to learner needs that provide a foundation for the necessity of as well as the way to make the shifts from informational to transformational teaching (see Figure 2.4).

■ FIGURE 2.4: STUDENT NEEDS CAPTURED BY THE EMPOWER MODEL

1. *Provides motivation* (the continuing impulse to learn) and *supports engagement* (behavioral and cognitive strategies) by meeting the conditions of flow experience.

2. *Creates personal connection* and *cultural relevance* by starting with each learner's needs, concerns, lived-through experiences, and cultural funds of knowledge.

3. *Provides access to all, working for equity and social justice* by differentiating so that all learners get the assistance they need to grow from their point of need. This constitutes inductive and restorative practice.

4. *Creates a community of caring* by meeting the social contract to care, by developing social–emotional learning, through collaboration, and by fostering social connection and support to develop expertise managing complex tasks, relationships, and emotions.

5. *Bridges the knowing–doing divide* by teaching in a context of use, creating classroom communities of practice, and working for real-world application.

6. *Promotes the growth mindset* for teachers and learners (Dweck, 2006) by supporting the development of learners' identity as agents who can always learn how to get new things done if they get the proper support and the opportunity to deliberately practice.

EMPOWER INCLUDES THE USE OF DIFFERENTIATION STRATEGIES

One of the many great advantages of guided inquiry through EMPOWER is its flexibility. Teachers can differentiate elements of instruction improvisationally at the point of need and use peers and groups to help teach, all while learners are engaged in the common classroom inquiry project. In fact, EMPOWER incorporates the features of universal design for learning (UDL) through its basic processes and also through how it accommodates differentiation. Differentiation is necessary to inductive and restorative practice because it provides access to all. It is a way to personalize learning and leverage different forms of relational learning for the benefit of all (see Figure 2.5).

■ FIGURE 2.5: WAYS TO DIFFERENTIATE INSTRUCTION IN THE CONTEXT OF GUIDED INQUIRY

- *Materials, Levels of Text, or Task Complexity:* Learners read different materials written at different levels or read the same materials written at different levels (Newsela is a great source for this).

- *Time/Pacing:* Learning is scaffolded, consolidated, or extended based on learner needs to promote deep understanding; this means spending more time on some strategies with some learners.

- *Methods and Modalities:* Various means of representation, expression, and engagement (in line with UDL) are used to support the unique learners and learning needs in the classroom; learners should be provided opportunities to use their own strengths but also be challenged to learn in new ways to develop new strengths.

- *Groupings:* Learners engage in partnerships, triads, small groups, and whole group at different times for different purposes (by using learning centers, literature circles, inquiry teams, etc.).

- *Levels of Independence in Task Navigation:* Different levels of teacher or peer assistance (e.g., thinking partnerships, peer conferencing, and teacher conferring) are employed.

- *Levels of Assistance:* Different scaffolds are used to support learners in moving from their current level of understanding to a higher level of understanding and independence. (*Note:* Scaffolds should be gradually removed as students increase their level of independence.)

- *Ways of Demonstrating Competence* (including culminating projects and assessments): Different kinds of assessment opportunities are provided throughout the unit (self-assessments, formative assessments, portfolios and conferences, etc.), and learners are provided a choice in how they share their learning (options for culminating project format).

- *Levels of Accomplishment Criteria:* Rubrics, semantic scales, or progressions are used to show learners' level of achievement and also to demonstrate growth toward goals.

POWERFUL PLANNING: EMBRACING THE TRANSFORMATIVE POSSIBILITIES

These may seem like a lot of shifts. In our work, we promote the mantra "Eat your elephant one bite at a time." In other words, you can start with what feels accessible and keep making changes bit by bit. Making one shift naturally brings other related changes.

Informational teaching is like being a cook who warms up pre-prepared food. Transformational teaching is like being a chef who can create a meal specific to the guests and the occasion based on the available materials. A chef has conscious competence that can be creatively deployed to invent what is needed to meet the needs of the moment.

When we embrace transformational teaching, we necessarily meet the conditions of flow (our basic motivational needs), the social contract to care, and needs for social connection (our basic human need to be recognized and belong); the conditions of SEL and inductive/restorative practice; and the process of becoming more expert with complex tasks (our need to be assisted into expertise). All of those shifts are closely related, and focusing on one will make it easier to leverage the others.

Transformational teaching and learning are achieved through guided inquiry by using the mental map of EMPOWER.

Only if we understand and articulate our theoretical orientation—our beliefs and philosophies about teaching and learning—can we consciously implement and reflect on a theory of action—our practices—to move forward and monitor ourselves from reverting to less productive ways of teaching.

And it is to practices of planning and teaching that we now turn our attention.

Chapter 3

INTRODUCTION TO THE EMPOWER CANVAS

> **ESSENTIAL QUESTION**
> How can we capture the seven "must-make moves" of teaching at the unit, module/instructional sequence, or lesson level?

Just as artists practice their craft and continually create anew on canvas, educators also need a space that assists them to practice their craft and continually design the highest-quality instructional experiences possible. Instructional planning at its core is an act of imaginative design: You are creating something from nothing (or translating an existing plan that could use improvement) and doing so within certain rules so it will "land" with learners.

An educator's "canvas" in most cases is a unit or lesson plan. The question we always ask when we see a teacher's template is whether it mirrors and accords with *mental models* that accurately represent how expert educators and researchers approach the task of planning to promote deep engagement and learning. Typically, the answer is a hard no.

Although we respect the history teacher who embraces a project-based pedagogy, the English language arts teacher who subscribes to the "workshop" approach, or the constructivist math teacher who facilitates open-ended problem solving—and, in fact, all these approaches can be consistent with and supercharged by EMPOWER—it is a challenge to foster collegial conversations around curriculum when everyone has a different understanding and a different language for instructional designs. Naturally, teachers' templates reflect these differences, making this dialogue even tougher.

Here is our simple solution: Because all these pedagogies aim at a common destination— empowering learners to be independent and interdependent in using expert disciplinary strategies and mental models for pursuing complex tasks—all the pedagogies should contain the elements of EMPOWER, as it represents a research-based "meta"-design for *all* teaching and learning. For the sake of consistency, clarity, and ease, we advocate that teachers use what we call an EMPOWER canvas, a one-page form, to formally capture or at least spot-check all the necessary elements of an effective teaching and learning design. This way, everyone is on the same page, literally and figuratively speaking.

INTRODUCING THE EMPOWER CANVAS

The EMPOWER canvas is meant to serve as a convenient tool to reinforce the seven must-make moves that expert educators enact in designing effective instruction. The framework naturally organizes into two categories: behind-the-scenes "big-picture" planning and student-facing instructional planning, as demonstrated in Figure 3.1.

▪ FIGURE 3.1: TWO CATEGORIES OF THE EMPOWER FRAMEWORK

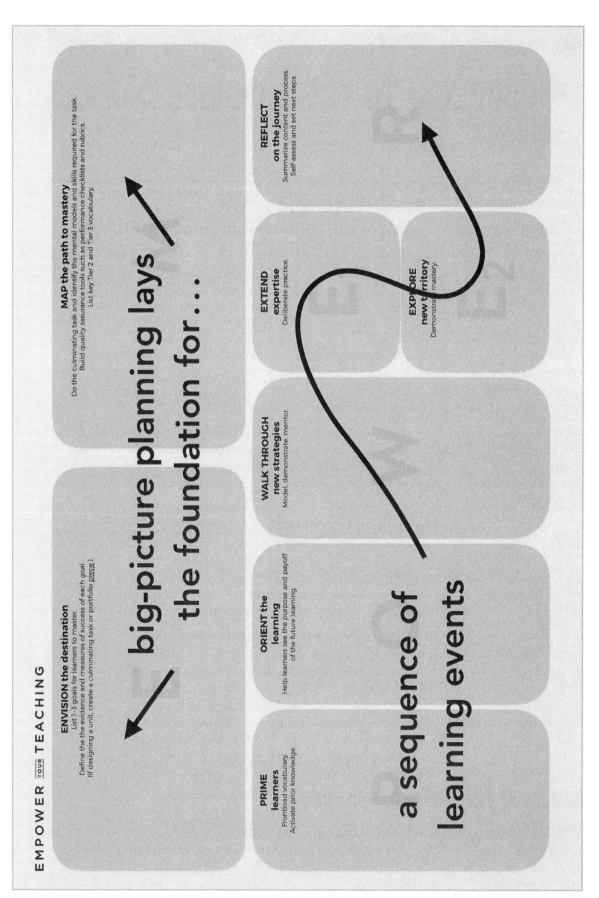

EMPOWER YOUR TEACHING

ENVISION the destination
List 1–3 goals for learners to master.
Define the the evidence and measures of success of each goal.
(If designing a unit, create a culminating task or portfolio piece.)

MAP the path to mastery
Do the culminating task and identify the mental models and skills required for the task.
Build quality assurance tools such as performance checklists and rubrics.
List key Tier 2 and Tier 3 vocabulary.

big-picture planning lays the foundation for....

PRIME learners
Frontload vocabulary.
Activate prior knowledge.

ORIENT the learning
Help learners see the purpose and payoff of the future learning.

WALK THROUGH new strategies
Model. demonstrate. mentor.

EXTEND expertise
Deliberate practice.

EXPLORE new territory
Demonstrate. mastery.

REFLECT on the journey
Summarize content and process.
Self-assess and set next steps.

a sequence of learning events

And digging one level deeper, Figure 3.2 breaks down what we have briefly explained about each phase of the framework in previous chapters.

■ FIGURE 3.2: PHASES OF THE EMPOWER FRAMEWORK

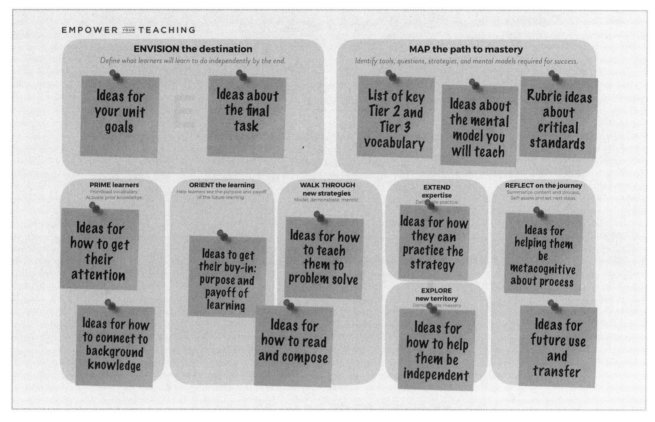

We call this tool a canvas instead of a template in order to emphasize its flexibility. First of all, most educators bounce between *envisioning* and *mapping* because these two big-picture planning pursuits complement one another. Some educators prefer that *priming* come after students experience *orienting*. Learners can bounce back and forth between *walking through* new strategies and *extending* those strategies (such as in the case of a modular unit) before moving toward *exploration* (performance task). Once students have performed one of the ongoing *reflections* (after a lesson of a module, for example), they can move back into *walk-throughs* and so on (see Figure 3.3). (Chapters 4 through 15 provide plenty of strategies and suggestions for each of these phases of EMPOWER, too, because we want you to have plenty in this book to get you started and feel successful.)

Educators who wish to build a new canvas work through each stage of the framework, populating it with ideas that can be captured via sticky notes or writing on a physical canvas or digitally.

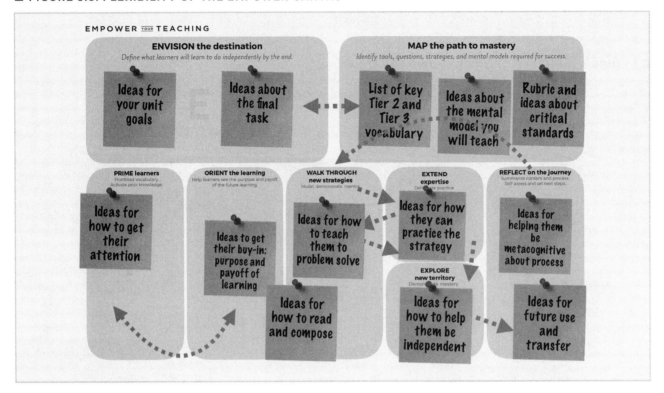

UNDERSTANDING OUR THROUGHLINE UNIT: THE EMPOWER CANVAS IN ACTION

Throughout this book, we refer to our "throughline unit," which is centered on exploring notions of civil rights alongside reading Lois Lowry's classic *Number the Stars* (though any text about civil rights issues could serve as the central text). Figure 3.4 shows our EMPOWER canvas for this unit.

Each sticky note on the canvas serves as a "placeholder" and represents what will become a more evolved instructional activity or plan. For example, the "civil rights survey" sticky note refers to a survey activity that is expanded in Chapter 8, which explores strategies for frontloading.

EMPOWERING YOUR CURRICULUM AT EVERY LEVEL

While most designs for learning only allow you to design at one level—either the lesson or the unit—EMPOWER works at every level of the instructional design process (see Figure 3.5). Educators who EMPOWER their curriculum infuse design thinking that operates consistently to inform each level of their planning: Macro-level unit canvases inform modules/instructional sequences, which inform lessons.

■ FIGURE 3.4: EMPOWER CANVAS FOR THE THROUGHLINE UNIT ON CIVIL RIGHTS

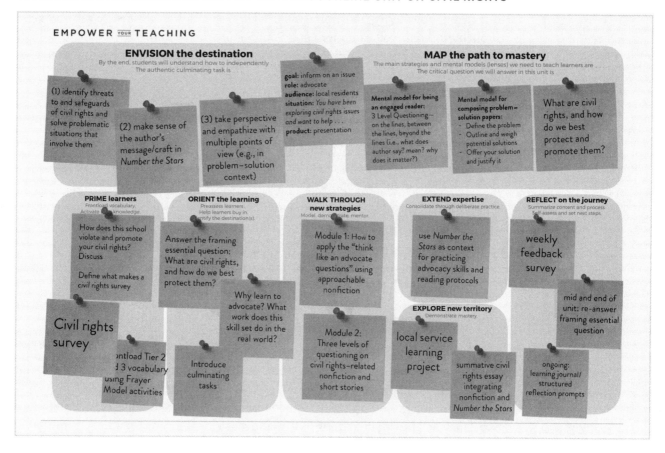

■ FIGURE 3.5: EMPOWER AFFECTS EVERY LEVEL OF INSTRUCTIONAL DESIGN

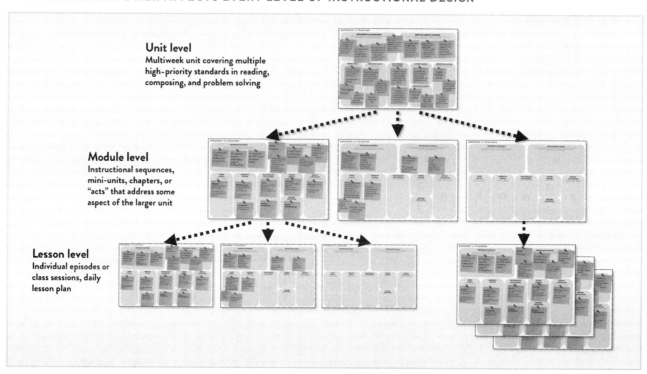

Each upcoming chapter will provide you with ideas to move from general concept to concrete operations, and from initial idea to actualized lessons. As you progress through this book, you can internalize your big-picture thinking around the unit-level design (what's captured on sticky notes) before circling back to explore each strategy (and lesson-level canvases).

Using our throughline unit on civil rights as an example, we first *envision* the most significant outcomes for learners:

- Identify threats to and safeguards of civil rights, problem solve challenges to civil rights, produce an extended definition of civil rights, and write multiple problem–solution papers.

- Make sense of Lois Lowry's thematic messages in *Number the Stars* (literature connected to the unit theme of civil rights).

- Take various perspectives and empathize with multiple points of view, developing social imagination and social–emotional learning (i.e., in a problem–solution context). Develop strategies for social imagination and responsibility, as well as stances and strategies for advocating for oneself and others in regard to civil rights issues.

As part of this stage, we create an authentic culminating task that puts students in a real-world role and has them compose or design knowledge artifacts or services that address real-world problems for a real-world audience. In this case, in addition to several short problem–solution papers students will write throughout reading *Number the Stars*, they will use their learning to act as advocates, informing their local community of a civil rights–related issue and potential ways to address it (what they work toward in *explore*). They may even engage in service learning that addresses the issues they've identified in the school or community.

Next, we *map* out the way to these outcomes in terms of the conceptual understandings, strategies, and mental models required for expertly fulfilling them. In this case, students need to be highly skilled at

- Reading and composing in a problem–solution structure (which is a specific kind of argument; Smith, Wilhelm, & Fredricksen, 2013).

- Inferring and "reading between the lines"—in other words, going beyond what's literal in the text by bringing to bear not only background knowledge but also discourse knowledge of how authors encode meaning into literature through character choices, literary devices, structure, and word choice, and informational writing through various structures and conventions. We teach a way of reading that asks students to focus *on* the lines (literal comprehension), *between* the lines (inferences), and *beyond* the lines (evaluation and application).

- Perspective taking to understand, empathize with, and even live through the experiences of those distant from them in time, place, or situation.

To frame the inquiry, we craft an essential question, also known as a frame question: *What are civil rights, and how do we best protect and promote them?* (Note well: We always have a tentative essential question. The final version, however, is often crafted in collaboration with students, particularly as we move through the year. This can often be done after initial priming and orienting activities.)

With the "behind the scenes" planning complete, we turn our attention to how we will *prime* learners, or get their attention, activate prior knowledge and interests, and engage through novelty and relevance triggers:

- To trigger relevance, we ask students to list all the ways that their school violates their own and others' civil rights. Students get excited by this prompt and end up listing multiple aspects of school that they dislike (e.g., cafeteria food). After the initial brainstorm, we classify the responses as actual civil rights issues or just preferences. (Note that we are already on our way to defining civil rights by differentiating what civil rights are versus what they are not.)

- To trigger novelty, we frontload new conceptual Tier 2 and Tier 3 vocabulary that students will use throughout the unit, such as *advocate, stakeholder, obligation,* and *consequences,* as well as Tier 2 literary words from *Number the Stars,* such as *stern, obstinate, lanky, sabotage, belligerently,* and others, using a Frayer Model or a similar defining protocol (see Figure 3.6).

- To trigger prior knowledge, we administer a civil rights survey that has questions to probe current feelings and attitudes on the topic.

■ FIGURE 3.6: FRONTLOADING TIER 2 AND 3 VOCABULARY

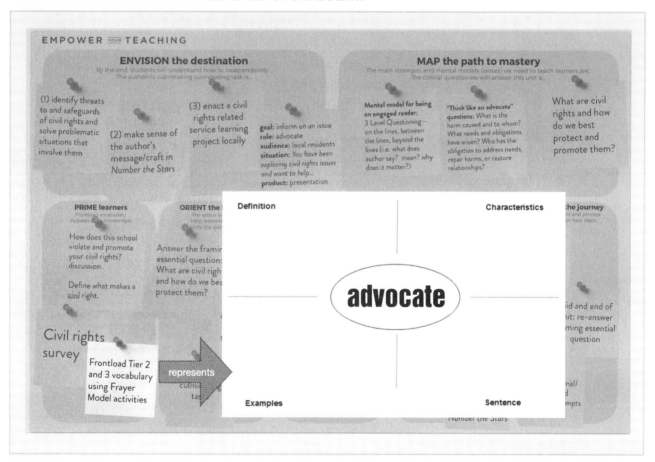

Next, we *orient* learners toward the big-picture objectives: using inferencing and other reading strategies to identify main ideas and themes in literary and informational texts; identifying the causes and effects of problems and ways to address these; exercising social imagination, responsibility, and empathy; thinking and acting like an advocate; and applying our learning to make an impact in our own lives and the community. In this phase, we help learners understand what these outcomes mean and begin moving them toward them by

- Preassessing by having learners answer the frame question (a task they'll repeat at the mid- and endpoints of the unit, providing a detailed account of how their thoughts have developed over time).
- Using questioning tools to help students develop and pursue their own related inquiries.

The next episodes of the unit covering *walk-through*, *extension*, and *exploration* play out through instructional sequences or modules:

- *Walk-through* (Module 1): Facilitate students' uptake of civil rights advocacy questions *and* the strategies of reading on, between, and beyond the lines with accessible civil rights–themed text.

- *Extension* (Module 2): Apply civil rights lens and reading strategies learned in Module 1 to *Number the Stars*.
- *Exploration* (Module 3): Transfer all experience and strategy from Modules 1 and 2 into a community service project that works to promote civil rights awareness in the community, as well as a formal and publicly shared problem–solution composition summarizing the three modules of learning.

Even though *reflection* is the last box on the canvas, and there is certainly a place for formal reflection in the way of weekly, midpoint, and end-of-unit introspection, the truth is that we are *continuously* asking students to generalize what they have learned, to think about ways they could transfer new knowledge or skills into new contexts, or to self-assess their level of effort and understanding. Unlike a traditional "exit ticket" that asks students to perform one more repetition of the target strategy or demonstrate mastery via a quiz, ongoing daily reflection opportunities are designed to promote *metacognition*, thinking about the thinking, and independence with the target strategy and its future uses/importance to learners.

GETTING TO YOUR FIRST DRAFT

Like a painter who consciously considers every brushstroke of a new painting, educators engaged in the nitty-gritty work of curriculum design can find it takes time to truly nail down their learning plans. But in an environment where we often need our curricular solutions done yesterday, our processes have to be ultra-efficient. Therefore, we recommend the following tips:

1. **Sketch a canvas in one sitting.** While a unit plan can take considerable time and iterations (often over several years of teaching the unit) to approach completion, your initial canvas should be sketched quickly—potentially in an hour or less. Yes, you read that right. *Set a timer and get your first draft down in the space of one prep period.* (See one example in Figure 3.7.) You are going to come back to the document anyway, and as the saying goes, something is better than nothing. Having most of

the canvas boxes completed with 50 percent detail beats one complete, thoroughly detailed box any day. You don't have to work alone; if you have a thinking partner at school, jointly planning your units together is very productive and can be fun. As Vygotsky (1978) would say: We are always smarter together than we are alone!

■ **FIGURE 3.7: AN EARLY DRAFT OF AN EMPOWER CANVAS**

2. **It's okay to leave sections blank . . .** Rather than trying to research or debate the "right" answers, put something down quickly or leave it blank and come back to it later. Some elements, like your unit's mental models, take time to figure out. The canvas is meant to be an organic document that evolves over time. It's okay to say "I don't know" right now.

3. **. . . but not the first two sections.** Remember: If you're adopting a learning-centered transformational approach, your learning designs will focus less on what you will teach and more on what students will learn to do to become more expert and independent. (We have found that the more expert a teacher, the more he or she focuses on students and what they do in response to teaching versus what he or she does as a teacher.) If you skip *envisioning* and *mapping*, you have no chance of successfully POWERing the rest of your unit. We advocate flexibility, but starting with *E* and *M* is a must.

POWERFUL PLANNING:
UNDERSTANDING THE BIG PICTURE OF PLANNING

We are all subject to the laws of gravity whether we "believe" in gravity or not. We feel similarly about EMPOWER, which is based on the research from sciences of human development, cognition, motivation, and development of expertise, as well as other fields. Whether or not educators acknowledge that the EMPOWER pattern underlies all of the most effective teaching–learning situations, we (and, by extension, our learners) are still subject to its effects.

Imagine a teacher who does not *envision* his or her students' learning outcomes in sufficient enough detail and the resulting aimlessness that teacher's students are likely to feel. After all, if the educator does not know the direction of the unit, how can students? Similarly, if an educator fails to *map* out the unit into digestible pieces, it can lead to learners feeling overwhelmed at the depth or breadth of the content; and if that same educator chooses not to *prime* or *orient* students at the beginning of the unit, then those students may feel too uninterested or unmotivated to pursue the energy-intensive act of learning. (See Figure 3.8.)

But consider: If you do *envision*, then the teaching will be highly focused and coherent. If you *map* out the steps, then you and your students can learn complex strategies together step by step, in ways that promote vital personal connections, energetic motivation, the development of expert strategies used for navigating challenges, and then: independence. In future chapters, we explain exactly how to enact pedagogical moves aligned to each of these principles, ensuring a successful learning journey for each of your students.

We cannot defy gravity any more than we can defy the "laws" embodied in a principled paradigm like EMPOWER. In fact, once we started using EMPOWER, we began noticing missed opportunities in even our most successful lessons and units, and steps we were tempted to skip in the instructional design process that would have come back to haunt us later.

With the must-make moves embedded into our teaching tool kit, we are focused on including essential elements of sound pedagogy in every teaching and learning situation. Next, we dive deeper into the core design strategies that drive planning, *envisioning*, and *mapping*, and determine how to move from initial teaching ideas to concrete clarity and actualization as we pursue our planning canvas.

■ FIGURE 3.8: EFFECTS OF MISSED STEPS IN EMPOWER

When an educator does not _____, then it usually causes learners to feel or be _____ .

M P O W E R = **AIMLESS**

E P O W E R = **OVERWHELMED**

E M O W E R = **DISCONNECTED**

E M P W E R = **UNMOTIVATED**

E M P O E R = **UNSKILLED**

E M P O W R = **UNCHALLENGED**

E M P O W E = **DEPENDENT**

PART 2: ENVISIONING AND MAPPING

ENVISION   MAP   PRIME   ORIENT   WALK THROUGH   EXTEND/EXPLORE   REFLECT

Chapter 4

ENVISIONING THE DESTINATION THROUGH PRINCIPLED PLANNING PROTOCOLS

ESSENTIAL QUESTION
How do we lay the groundwork for a unit of instruction?

Thinking like a designer instead of a presenter is the first step toward transformational teaching and enacting a pedagogy of EMPOWERment. However, it also represents one of the hardest shifts for educators to make. There can be a temptation to start with what we're teaching rather than to design backwards from what our students need to learn to do independently. We understand this urge. With limited time, you want to focus on the experiences learners will actually have rather than "big-picture" planning that seems far off as opposed to immediate. You must fight this feeling!

Let's focus on some principled planning protocols that will help you set meaningful learning goals that you can clearly communicate to your students, colleagues, parents, and other stakeholders. Maybe more than any other section of the framework, *envisioning* and *mapping* will push your intellectual boundaries, testing and expanding the limits of your pedagogical expertise. Once you've done these exercises over and over, this patterned way of thinking will become your new normal. And then you will be an instructional powerhouse: a teacher with conscious competence, a mental map of expertise, and a craft informed by the soundest of principles.

MUST-MAKE ENVISIONING MOVES

We capture our ideas about the unit goal and about our final task via two protocols: GEMS for clarifying ideas for our unit goals and GRASP for fleshing out the final product or products for the unit, which must require and reward the meeting of our threshold learning goals. Although we realize there are already a number of acronyms in education, we've developed what we intend to be the last two you'll need when it comes to productive goal setting.

In our work with teachers, we have found success starting with GEMS (Figure 4.1) to crystallize learning outcomes:

- **Goal:** Defining some significant new way of thinking or doing that learners cannot do *yet* but will learn to do independently and will use throughout their lives (threshold knowledge); this goal is often an abstract process.

- **Evidence:** Capturing the abstract goal in a concrete task (or tasks) that "proves" learners actually achieved the goal; this must be observable and concrete.

- **Measures of success:** Describing the sought-after qualities and characteristics that "strong work" exhibits and then using those traits to measure progress toward mastery.

- **Stakes:** Why this unit and its goals matter *right now*, and why students should buy in, use it in the future, and so on.

■ FIGURE 4.1: IDEAS FOR YOUR UNIT GOALS: GEMS

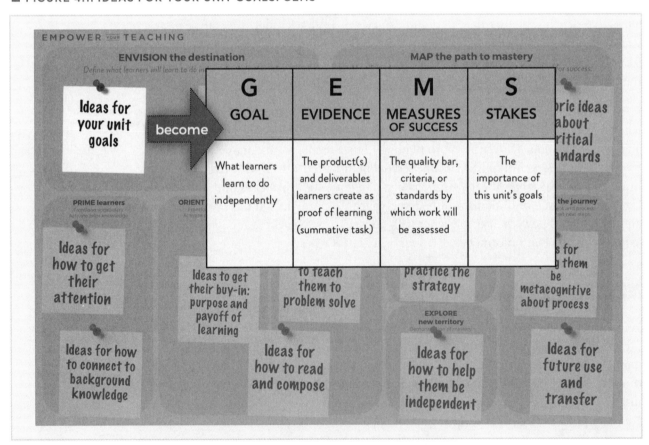

The primary measure of success in constructing GEMS (Figure 4.2) is *alignment*. In the best examples, GEMS captures the relationship between something abstract (a goal such as conducting research), the concretization of that abstract goal or process (e.g., a portfolio, report, podcast, performance, or presentation), and what "quality" means when practitioners in this discipline evaluate products in this genre (qualities such as *informative*, *evidence-based*, *clear*, and *organized* might describe a strong informational text).

■ FIGURE 4.2: GEMS SCAFFOLDED ORGANIZER

G GOAL	E EVIDENCE	M MEASURES OF SUCCESS	S STAKES
☐ Explain/prove/define/ determine causes and effects/sequence ☐ Interpret/evaluate/ describe/rate/judge ☐ Apply/create/solve ☐ Analyze/compare ☐ Empathize/role-play ☐ Self-assess/reflect	☐ **Oral:** conversation, podcast, interview, teach a lesson, rap ☐ **Written:** letter, blog, essay, newscast, proposal, story, article, position paper, poem ☐ **Visual:** diagram, comic, Thinking Map®, video, model, storyboard, design, advertisement ☐ **Service:** provide service or social action related to the inquiry topic/problem under study	*Create a scale or checklist for the critical standards:* ☐ **For arguments:** persuasive, logical, evidence-based, coherent ☐ **For narratives:** engaging, detail-rich, clear, polished ☐ **For informational:** informative, thorough, accurate, balanced ☐ **General criteria:** level of independence, clarity, accuracy, frequency, planning, originality, etc.	*Show how the skill is used in the real world:* ☐ Explore personal uses for the skill/content ☐ Find an audience to share the learning with ☐ Create personal stakes ("carrots and sticks") for sticking to the task ☐ Contribute to solving a real-world social problem and be of help to others ☐ Provide a service to the class, school or larger community

The scaffolded organizer in Figure 4.3, plus your relevant national or local standards and district expectations, should spark your thinking about the first three elements.

■ FIGURE 4.3: A SCAFFOLDED GEMS ORGANIZER

G GOAL	E EVIDENCE	M MEASURES OF SUCCESS	S STAKES
Research and critically analyze information related to local and social justice issues	Research portfolio	☐ Pulls from credible sources ☐ Information organized with appropriate mind map (step-by-step boxes for sequences, columns for categories, etc.)	Two words: fake news! Students face it every day and need practice navigating online and researching. Students will be engaged in distinguishing credible from noncredible sources *especially* if it pertains to personal situations. Research skills help them in all their other classes.
Make a defensible argument on a researched topic	Op-ed-style editorial	☐ Informative: *The point of view should be thoroughly expressed and explained.* ☐ Engaging: *The writing should capture and keep attention.* ☐ Widely researched and evidence-based: *The op-ed should draw from multiple worthy sources.* ☐ Conventionally sound: *The op-ed adheres to norms of this genre in published forums.*	

A high school language arts teacher reported in a recent workshop that she felt her unit was "all over the place" and struggled to articulate her intentions for her learners. While she was intending to teach research skills, her evidence was usually just a series of reading comprehension questions from a publisher's curriculum. This, we agreed, was not exactly proof of learners' ability to conduct real-world research.

(Continued)

(Continued)

So, we began the GEMS pattern of questioning: What will learners learn to do independently? (Goal) What products would "prove" they actually learned what you sought to teach? (Evidence) By what standards or qualities will you and students collectively assess the products of their learning labor? (Measures of success) What is important about this goal? (Stakes)

Based on her knowledge of her students, this teacher wanted to focus her unit on the following anchor standards:

Research to Build and Present Knowledge:

CCSS.ELA-LITERACY.CCRA.W.7

Conduct short as well as more sustained research projects based on focused questions, demonstrating understanding of the subject under investigation.

CCSS.ELA-LITERACY.CCRA.W.8

Gather relevant information from multiple print and digital sources, assess the credibility and accuracy of each source, and integrate the information while avoiding plagiarism.

CCSS.ELA-LITERACY.CCRA.W.9

Draw evidence from literary or informational texts to support analysis, reflection, and research.

Within a few minutes of playing with a scaffolded GEMS organizer, she managed to capture the unit outcomes clearly and succinctly (see Figure 4.4).

■ FIGURE 4.4: ENVISIONING THE DESTINATION WITH GEM

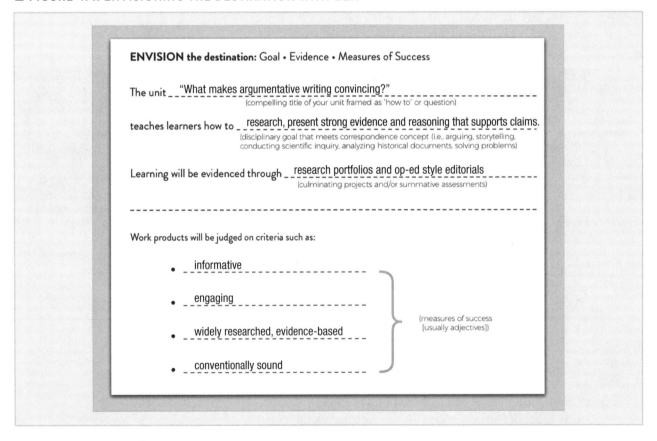

Notice the following features:

1. **Goals are interrelated and interdependent.** Critical reading and writing complement one another. In this example, the learners would engage in the process of researching a topic to develop understanding in it before making an argument about it. Students would also need to learn how to critically evaluate and consume examples of the target argumentative genre in order to compose in it. With authentic goals like these, you are often weaving together and addressing multiple standards at once. Knowledge is a network, not a linear checklist (Perkins, 1986).

2. **Product ≠ process.** The mental model we're teaching students to master, apply, and transfer is different from the task used as evidence of its completion. "Compose an op-ed" is the product; the process is learning how to argue (i.e., weave claims, evidence, and reasoning together to persuade, convince, or explain). You may need multiple evidentiary artifacts to substantiate and corroborate the learning of complex processes such as researching, arguing, or conducting scientific inquiry.

3. **Quality matters.** Merely completing the final task is not the same as completing the task with excellence and an eye on quality. Applying measures of success means that students' work products will be assessed against critical standards of expertise and held to a high bar. (We will show you a student-friendly way to share your GEMS in a student-friendly format later in the chapter.)

WHAT'S THE POINT? WHAT'S AT STAKE?

In a good marketing message, a copywriter will often include the "promise" of buying the advertised product and the "peril" of not. Articulating the potential success or pain customers might experience as a result of their choice can create a sense of urgency within their minds. We will borrow from this discipline in thinking through the final element of our GEMS, the stakes.

When we think through the stakes, we try and take a step back: What's the point of this learning? Who would learners be *without* this learning? Who could they be *with* it?

Said another way, perhaps with more urgency, this generation of learners will not accept "it's on the test" as justification for learning subject matter. And neither should we. This kind of "stakes" is an example of authoritative informational teaching, not internally persuasive and transformational teaching and learning.

Here are some prompts to help you fill your *stakes* box:

- How would students answer "Why are we learning this?" if asked halfway through the unit? What about at the end?

- What would happen if learners did *not* learn this subject matter and/or strategy? What transformational possibilities could happen if they did?

(Continued)

(Continued)

- In what ways will this learning be transferable to learners' current and future lives?

- What's the "emotional spark" of this subject matter?

- How can we justify spending extended time on working toward these specific goals given other competing priorities?

- What value will learners perceive in learning this?

These answers should come more or less naturally to you. If you find yourself struggling to answer many of these questions, it might be time to reconsider outcomes for your unit, or at least to modify them to address these compelling questions.

POLISHING YOUR GEMS

Here are some common roadblocks to look out for as you're thinking through your GEMS:

THE GOAL DOES NOT MEET THE CORRESPONDENCE CONCEPT.

This usually happens when a goal is too narrow to be sufficiently authentic. Students are often asked to perform *part* of a process instead of the whole thing. So, while distinguishing essential from inessential information, asking questions at different levels, and making predictions are all checkpoints along the path toward the destination of interpreting the author's message, they should not serve as the central idea of your unit because those tasks do not constitute actual expertise. Once readers have distinguished essential from inessential information, generated and asked their own questions, and made predictions, *then* they can construct a summary, write their review, compare it to other works, and complete other tasks wherein the skills are not divorced from the "big picture."

This is not to say that we don't need principled practice in a skill or facet of the bigger task. In many cases, it makes great sense to do this. For example, to get skilled at dribbling, basketball players run drills; students learning to write descriptively practice penning scenes off of prepared prompts. But just as the players would know the context in which dribbling counts and then transfer their learning into the game, we must challenge our learners to deploy their descriptive writing skills into a fictional story or historical narrative so they can apply what they learned in its fullest context.

THE GOAL IS FRAMED AS A DISCRETE APPLICATION INSTEAD OF A TRANSFERABLE STRATEGY OR SKILL SET.

Consider the difference between (1) reading *Fahrenheit 451* and making sense of the message and (2) making sense of dystopian/utopian art *as a genre* and then using that "mental model" to tackle other graphic novels, films, short stories, and eventually novels in this genre. In this example, putting *Fahrenheit 451* into conversation with multiple dystopian works deepens students' concept of what the category means and what it's for. The point is developing a strategic mental model, not simply reading any one specific book. This mental model will guide reading and composing of other dystopian texts. It also helps students to think about genre as much more than form. Genre is a set of structural elements about particular kinds of content to accomplish particular kinds of understandings and social actions.

THE GOAL DOES NOT REPRESENT WHAT STUDENTS ARE EXPECTED TO DO INDEPENDENTLY AT THE END.

At the unit level, the goals you list under G represent what learners will do without you by the end. If you know that learners will still require serious assistance for whatever you deem as their final product, consider scaling back what you are teaching and define something learners will truly be empowered to do independently, which is the entire focus of the pedagogy of EMPOWERment. In other words, find a task that is in the learner's zone of proximal development.

THE EVIDENCE DOES NOT MEASURE THE GOAL.

Building and labeling a model of the heart in science class does not prove that students can explain the function of each part (a matching exercise would prove this better, as would asking "What if there were no chambers in the heart? What effect would this have on its functioning?"). A student could easily build a model and look up how it's labeled without true understanding of the part-to-function relationship.

Similarly, completing a worksheet of comprehension questions does not prove students can read, research, or argue. You must ask yourself whether students could complete the task without truly understanding the goal. Remember: The evidence must substantiate achievement, not just be the last thing students do.

MEASURES OF SUCCESS ARE A LIST OF INDICATORS INSTEAD OF A BAND OF QUALITIES.

"Vanity metrics" are indicators that make someone feel good but don't actually provide insight into overall quality. For example, when buying a car, you might notice one has a shiny coat of paint and a gorgeous interior. These are vanity metrics. But what's going on underneath the hood? Whether the car runs, not whether it has cushy leather seats, is the bottom line and what really matters most. Similarly, we must pay attention to more than just the "surface features" when judging students' work.

In looking at student assessment, vanity metrics include specific numbers of paragraphs (traditionally, three or five), as well as neatness or spelling, when these are certainly not the most pressing qualities of, say, a written story or argument. When we read a real-world essay in a journal or newspaper, we judge it by its content and style, not by the number of paragraphs it has. Teachers' efforts to inculcate responsibility in their learners are laudable, but taking 10 points off for lateness is not the way to do so, nor is it an authentic measure of success of an essay. Differentiate between troubleshooting work habits and discussing the quality of the finished product.

(Continued)

(Continued)

Measures of success should refer to *general* characteristics of quality rather than its specific indicators—as a guideline, think adjectives and adjective phrases. So, instead of listing out that the writing piece *has* an intro, body, and conclusion, think about the *impact* of having those pieces—a written text being *organized* or *structured*. Instead of explaining that there need to be citations from five different sources on a subject woven throughout the essay, think of how you would describe such a piece—*widely researched* or *evidence-based*. That's not something you can count. Instead of explaining that there should be a claim, reasons, and evidence, think about the *impact* of those claims, reasons, and evidence—*convincing*. Again, this is a subjective quality. Save those specific characteristics for the upcoming exercises in which you will convert your measures of success into a full-fledged quality assurance rubric and delineate multiple levels. For now, it's more about the *impression* of the work in big-picture terms.

ENVISIONING MOVE 2: GRASP

By now, you have created a GEMS protocol that succinctly and successively captures the intended outcomes for your unit. While colleagues, instructional coaches, and supervisors will appreciate your clearly formulated goal, your learners may have trouble accessing it. In the next step, you will translate your GEMS into a student-facing GRASP task.

But first, let's examine why this step is important. Consider the differences between the following two columns of tasks:

DOING SCHOOL	DOING LEARNING
Write five paragraphs on a topic using previously conducted research that someone else did	Conduct original research using primary and secondary sources and present it to an audience
Name the subject, predicate, and verbs of sentences	Compose a story for a real-world audience: local senior citizens
Complete a lab based off a list of procedures and prove an already-understood principle	Investigate a local phenomenon, report about findings, and make recommendations
Answer problems 1–20 (odds) in the textbook	Model an open-ended problem situation using mathematics and attempt to solve it
Recall the answers to factual questions from the end of the history textbook chapter	Role-play as one of many stakeholders in a complicated international crisis and negotiate with fellow "stakeholders" to find a resolution
Copy notes off of the SMART board, whiteboard, or chalkboard	Given specific purposes for learning, determine essential and inessential information in varied texts and visual media and represent it using mind maps

How would you rename the first category? The second? What's different?

The left-hand column represents "doing school," or *inauthentic* learning tasks, while the right-hand column represents "doing learning," or *authentic* intellectual work. Authentic tasks like the ones in the right-hand column promote long-term retention, extension, and use; create opportunities for collaboration within the classroom and with the community beyond the classroom; and are more likely to generate buy-in from your learners than school-ish kinds of work like traditional tests.

Authentic tasks represent "aims worth aiming for" in school because they approximate the kind of challenges, problems, and opportunities that students will face throughout a lifetime: messy, real-world problems that require some kind of technical expertise or strategic thinking and mindful doing to complete. These tasks represent the real work of fields of study, disciplines, professions, and lifelong pursuits (Newmann, Carmichael, & King, 2016).

When students are given authentic intellectual tasks, they have the opportunity to learn something of obvious current and future use, and to rise to an occasion and show what they have learned. Provided they experience proper instructional preparation beforehand, most students relish these opportunities as star actors relish opening night. Everyone is motivated by staking identity through developing competence (Smith & Wilhelm, 2002, 2006).

Moreover, without authentic tasks, students will not have the opportunity to practice transferring what they know into new situations. And without the chance to deliberately practice in the classroom, there is little to no chance that they will be able to transfer threshold knowledge to when they are out "in the wild," either.

The major litmus test to keep in mind is this: Does this task have application and transfer value to the world beyond school? Does it *correspond* to real-world work?

Whether we imagine lawyers arguing in front of a jury through prepared statements and witness examination, a team of architects discussing plans in a charrette and then constructing blueprints that satisfy the needs of their clients, performers entertaining theatergoers, or journalists interviewing, investigating, and reporting to the public, these real-world tasks are complex, require expert knowledge of concept and strategy, and ultimately have value to one or more discourse communities.

The GRASP protocol, drawn from *Understanding by Design* (Wiggins & McTighe, 1998), will help you envision and plan your unit's culminating task. Figure 4.5 shows the components of GRASP: goal, real-world role, audience, story/situation, and product/performance.

(Continued)

(Continued)

■ FIGURE 4.5: THE GRASP PROTOCOL

GOAL	REAL-WORLD ROLE	AUDIENCE	STORY/ SITUATION	PRODUCT/ PERFORMANCE
Convince	Storyteller	Client/customer	You have been asked to . . .	Discussion/debate
Analyze	Historian	Fellow students	The context/challenge is . . .	Presentation
Inform	Politician	Expert panel		Article/essay
Explain	Engineer	Community	The issue you must address is . . .	Podcast
Design	Scientist	School official		Webpage
Test	Artist	Pen pal	The problem is . . .	Speech
	CEO	Reader	You have an opportunity to . . .	Story

You can convert your GEMS into a GRASP by simply expanding on the details of your evidence and stakes, as the goal and measures of success move neatly into slots around the task (see Figure 4.6).

■ FIGURE 4.6: CONVERTING GEMS TO GRASP

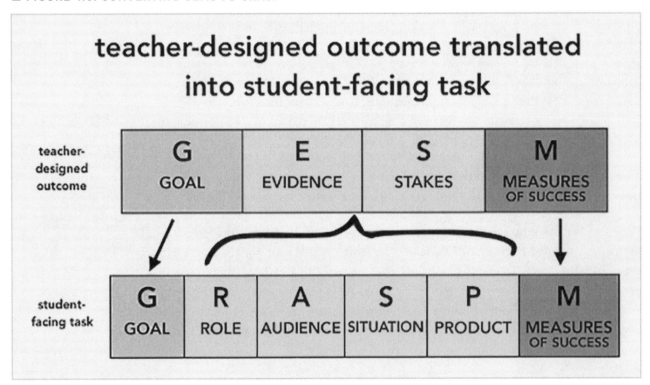

For example, the English teacher mentioned in the GEMS segment converted her research assignment into the GRASP task shown in Figure 4.7.

Your **goal** is to research a key issue facing young adults in your area in the coming years and write an op-ed that lays out the issue—and your stance on it—in an easy-to-understand way.

Your **role** is an investigative reporter and local expert.

Your **audience** is composed of young adults aged 16–22 in your area.

Your **situation** is as follows: Your newspaper has been losing readership among its younger demographic, aged 16–22, as short-form media like Twitter, Instagram, and Snapchat gain traction. Your editors have turned to you to compose a headline story that will get the attention and continued readership of this critical demographic. Up for the challenge?

Product: Compose an op-ed that galvanizes and informs the target demographic of teens around a core issue facing the community. In addition to the piece, you will need to produce a portfolio of annotated background research in case anyone needs to fact-check your work.

You will have to submit your written piece to one additional outlet, such as a blog, magazine, or local venue, that might appreciate your insight and publish your work. (All part of getting your name out there, young journalist!)

Last, in a separate document, you will need to explain your process, including (1) why this particular issue was selected and (2) the techniques you used to capture this particular audience's attention.

Measures of success: Your piece should be both informative and engaging for the 16–22 demographic, evidence-based, and aligned with conventions of a traditional op-ed. Your explanation of your strategy should be clear. Your portfolio of research must be *organized*, *thorough*, and *summarized*.

The "Timely Topics" task outshines answering comprehension questions and composing an essay only the teacher will read by a significant margin. It's rigorous, and it's relevant to students' lives. This educator even provided *additional* stakes in the task by requiring students to find a local or online outlet for their work.

By asking yourself what experts in your subject area actually *do* and how they *use* the content, you will find yourself on the track toward authenticity.

POWERFUL PLANNING: GETTING CRYSTAL CLEAR ON YOUR OUTCOMES

The Latin roots of the word *decide* translate to "cut off." In other words, a decision literally "cuts off" other possibilities and allows you to move forward with focus on your chosen path.

When you say yes to teaching a great goal, it means focusing like a laser on that goal. This can be hard because it bucks against traditional "more, more, more" thinking in school and the informational coverage approach in general. But knowing that in any unit students will only remember a few major concepts

or develop a few generative skills at a truly deep and independent level, where can you focus to have the maximum benefit for the greatest number of your students? Which wildly important goals will you fully *envision* and apprentice students into understanding?

Really, we're just looking for a few major focal outcomes—outcomes that take learners over a threshold to new ways of being, learning, thinking, and doing; outcomes that make learners into experts, that promote personal power, and that meet the standard of social significance.

Transferring Our Learning: What to Remember When Envisioning the Destination

- Confirm your unit goal and culminating task (evidence) correspond to performance standards found in disciplines, trades, and other authentic domains.

- Assess the extent to which the evidence you selected represents a *reliable* way to test learners' new abilities.

- Distinguish between the high-impact qualities (often subjective) of strong performance, not just surface features (often objective). For example, for an argument, focus on persuasiveness, support, and clarity rather than whether the piece has "three details."

- Build sufficient context into your final task for your learners.

Chapter 5

MAPPING THE PATH TO MASTERY THROUGH TASK DECONSTRUCTION

ESSENTIAL QUESTION
How can we best prepare for planning
student-facing instruction?

There is a simple way to determine chefs' abilities without tasting a morsel of their food: watch what happens *before* they cook.

Before a meal service in any professional kitchen, trained chefs practice an ancient culinary art called *mise en place*. Meaning roughly "putting [everything] in its place," the ritual consists of thinking through and deconstructing all the day's tasks—then gathering the tools, prepping and chopping ingredients, visualizing and rehearsing steps of the service, and reasoning through potential trouble spots—*in advance* of the meal service.

Imagine how chaotic cooking for yourself or your family can be. Now, multiply that by a few dozen, and you get a typical, popular restaurant on any given night of the week. Chefs want (1) to complete tasks ahead of time and (2) to surface issues like being short on ingredients or having broken equipment *before* hungry guests' orders pile up. The analytical act of *mise en place* helps chefs anticipate and navigate problems preemptively, preventing them from "getting in the weeds" during a busy service.

Lest we imply otherwise, chefs cannot anticipate *every* issue in the kitchen—troubleshooting along the way comes with cooking—nor can they guarantee a delicious outcome every time; after all, chefs still need to execute. However, there is a big difference between an amateur who must troubleshoot everything on the spot and an expert who plans ahead and can focus on the real task at hand: cooking the meal. *Mise en place* sets up chefs for success.

Now, let's extend the analogy to your classroom:

- Do you set goals and jump right to lesson planning?

- Do you take the time to process what goals actually mean for learners and to strategize about the steps you need to take to achieve the goals?

- Do you react to roadblocks with surprise when they arise? Or can you respond with perspective because you looked down the road and rehearsed various ways to differentiate and problem solve?

We know how frustrating it can be to get halfway into a unit before realizing students are missing a big piece of the puzzle. This is exactly why we intentionally *map the path to mastery.*

MUST-MAKE MAPPING MOVES

In the previous chapter, we captured ideas about our learning outcomes and culminating task and turned them into easy-to-communicate, tangible products: GEMS and GRASP. In this chapter, you'll learn how to perform *"mise en place* for your unit," a careful consideration and analysis of your unit goals to make teaching toward them go as smoothly as possible.

Expert chefs break down meal prep before delivering a meal; we will break down a learning goal before delivering our lessons. The process consists of four disciplines related to your end-of-unit tasks, content, and standards (see Figure 5.1).

■ FIGURE 5.1: THE PROCESS OF BREAKING DOWN A LEARNING GOAL

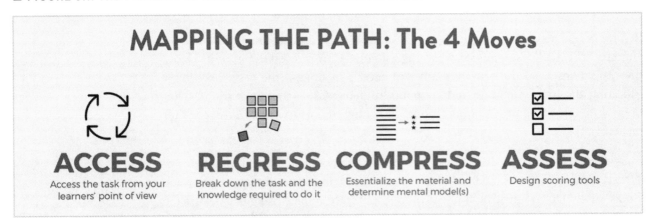

Each move yields specific insights into your unit and its culminating tasks:

- *Accessing* the task gives you empathy and insight into its cognitive, social, and emotional demands as it requires you to do (ideally)—or imaginatively rehearse doing (at the very least)—the culminating task on your own, and to reflect on the process.
- *Regressing* the task helps you break the task down into manageable, teachable pieces.
- *Compressing* means refining your content into an easy-to-communicate mental model or instructional anchor charts you can refer to again and again in your unit.
- *Assessing* the task refers to developing quality assurance tools (aligned to your measures of success) to help manage and message progress toward the overarching goal.

While we recommend progressing through the steps in this order, the best order is the one in which all the steps get completed, so feel free to skip around if it feels better.

Before we begin, we again offer fair warning that—like the principled protocols of *envisioning the destination*—the disciplines of *mapping* are simplistic, not simple. At first, they might feel unnatural. Over repeated attempts, you will get better at them; the more reps you get under your belt, the easier it will get until this way of thinking is internalized and becomes natural for you.

Learning *mise en place* is not easy for chefs, either. Once they learn it, though, it changes their practice forever. Such is the case with the *mapping* moves. These exercises will initially prove challenging, and you might occasionally feel lost, or "in the weeds." But we'll provide navigational tools for finding your way out, and the lesson you'll be able to "serve" at the end will be well worth it.

MAPPING MOVE 1: ACCESS TO UNDERSTAND THE TASK'S DEMANDS

One profoundly difficult aspect of teaching is the act of empathizing with learners' level of understanding. As educators, we possess levels of disciplinary expertise and content mastery, not to mention years' (if not decades') more lived experience that fills out our background knowledge. *Accessing* asks us to acknowledge the blind spots our expertise causes and to assume a "beginner's mind" with respect to navigating and achieving our culminating tasks. To achieve this, we advocate you

- **Do the task you plan to assign to students.** Write a short narrative of your own; craft a literary argument around the reading you will assign; identify the causes and effects of an intractable problem found in society today and research a solution for some outlet. *Whatever you want your learners to do, do it—at least a miniature version (e.g., write a scene instead of a narrative)—yourself.*

- **Reflect on the process through a learner's lens.** To be metacognitive is to literally "think about our thinking." Reflecting on our composing (e.g., of an argument, narrative, or informational piece), we must ask:
  - What is challenging about this type of composing or problem solving? What do you have to know to get started and to navigate this kind of task?
  - What aspects of the material are counterintuitive or complex?
  - Where might learners typically stumble? Why?
  - What preconceptions and/or misconceptions will learners likely have, and how might these help or provide obstacles to achieving expertise?

WARNING: Skipping this simple (not simplistic) step will render the rest of the exercises in this chapter less effective. Remember that in inquiry as cognitive apprenticeship, teachers are collaborative participants in learning and in knowledge creation. Do not skip accessing the task!

MAPPING MOVE 2: REGRESS TO UNDERSTAND THE COMPONENTS OF THE CULMINATING TASK

Regression is the heart of the *mise en place* practice we described at the start of the chapter: breaking a complex task into "micro skills" or progressions. Regressing tasks and standards often means seeing "between the lines" and extending the line of thought authors of national or local standards intended. The insight you gain during your accessing of the task will prove invaluable here, as it will surface many of the implicit aspects of your chosen learning goals.

When a task is cognitive or literacy-based, its component parts tend to fall into eight fundamental categories of thought patterns:

1. *Describing*: assigning qualities, traits, and attributes; describing processes
2. *Defining*: identifying features, characteristics, associations
3. *Classifying*: identifying kinds, groups, sorting, classifying
4. *Comparing*: finding similarities, differences, commonalities, distinctions
5. *Identifying relationships*: explaining analogies, matching sets, guess the rule
6. *Whole-to-part reasoning*: seeing the structure of things, anatomy, components
7. *Sequencing*: naming steps, ordering, processes
8. *Seeing causes and/or effects of events*: identifying reasons, motives, why, *and* impacts, consequences; seeing the reasons for a problem and possibilities for addressing these in a solution

For example, composing a literary character analysis might require us to

- Define a context in which literary analysis is a privileged discourse form (What is its value? What work does such analysis do for us and others in the real world?)
- Internalize rules of notice for the genre (For example, this involves knowledge of expectations composers and readers bring to the composing and reading of those genre conventions for content, structure, and purpose/social actions.)
- Explain causes and effects of characters' decisions
- Describe a character at the beginning, middle, and end of the story
- Compare a character at one point in the story to that same character at another point; compare a character to characters in other stories
- Explain causes (and sometimes effects) of a character's transformations
- Identify the relationship between authorial choices and their impact on our reading
- Reason how parts of the setting influenced the story's development (e.g., by inviting or constraining character action)

Then, putting that thinking (substance) into a genre (form) might require us to

- Compare effective and ineffective models of the target genre
- Define the features and characteristics of effective literary analysis, and identify how the parts work as a whole
- Understand the genre as a type of text organizing specific kinds of content in particular ways *to do specific kinds of work and engage in targeted social actions*
- Describe the qualities, or *measures of success*, of effective examples in the genre (e.g., evidence-based, focused on textual content about a particular literary element of the interactions of elements, provides generalizations that can be applied to other texts and to our lives)

We often marvel at the complexity hidden within tasks when we approach them with this analytical lens. In a live workshop on *mapping the path*, Adam and a group of high school educators regressed "taking notes" and found the two words in the phrase belie the sophisticated thought processes beneath the surface (see Figure 5.2).

■ **FIGURE 5.2: REGRESSION ON "TAKING NOTES"**

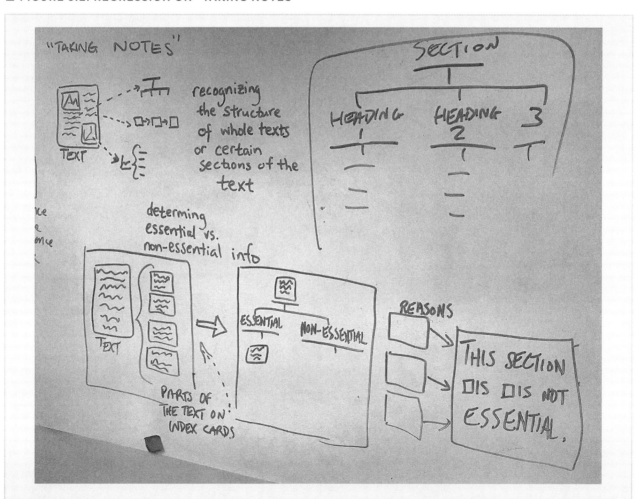

(Continued)

(Continued)

"Taking notes," or more appropriately *making* them, from an informational text could mean recognizing miniature instances of thought patterns (e.g., embedded text structures) within an informational text (e.g., a section where the author compares and contrasts, a section where the author explains a process, a section where the author uses an analogy) and organizing that information using an appropriate visual tool (such as the classification tree in the top right-hand corner of Figure 5.2 that organizes headings underneath a section).

Beyond what ends up in their visual maps, in summarizing any information, students will also have to distinguish essential from nonessential information and justify their decisions (shown in the bottom half of Figure 5.2).

Consider the previous chapter's GEMS example describing a research/argument unit culminating in an op-ed-style writing piece and research portfolio (see Chapter 4, Figure 4.4, page 54). While not exhaustive, the beginning of this portfolio regression revealed students will have to (1) identify and use reliable websites, (2) define key concepts in advocacy, and (3) summarize important information from the articles (see Figure 5.3).

■ **FIGURE 5.3: REGRESSION OF RESEARCH PORTFOLIO**

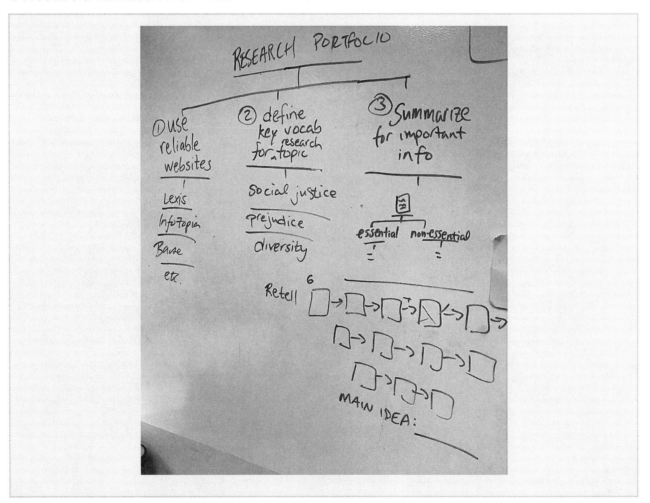

In another live session with a middle school science department "regressing" the Next Generation Science Standards, we inferred the phrase "Gather and make sense of information to describe that synthetic materials come from natural resources and impact society" to mean the following:

- Exploring the process by which fossil fuels become plastic

- Describing plastic's qualities, especially what makes it attractive to companies (it's cheap, pliable, and durable) and disastrous to the environment (it's nonbiodegradable)

- Defining uses for plastic

- Seeing the simple causes and then complex first-, second-, and third-order effects of plastic's widespread use

You can see how this was all visualized in Figure 5.4.

■ FIGURE 5.4: REGRESSION OF NEXT GENERATION SCIENCE STANDARDS

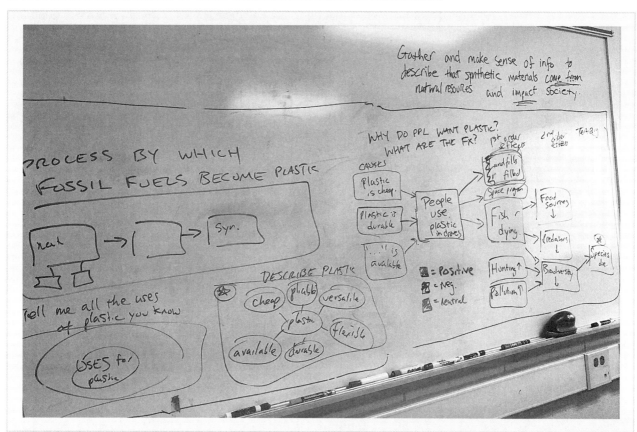

MAPPING MOVE 3: COMPRESS INTO MENTAL MODELS THAT CAPTURE THRESHOLD KNOWLEDGE

Unpacking your expertise and repackaging it for someone else is hard work. How do you get what's inside your head into someone else's? This is essentially what we're doing when we move from regressing to compressing. And the key is identifying *mental models*: a deep and visualized understanding of the interrelated aspects of a concept or a map for understanding the process of how to complete a task. Mental models can be understood and expressed through helpful representations, powerful analogies, illustrations, examples, and explanations that make your content comprehensible.

HELPFUL ANALOGIES AND ILLUSTRATIONS

As our beloved mentor George Hillocks used to say, "All learning proceeds from what is currently known to the new." Teaching through analogies leverages this wisdom.

Consider the analogy at the beginning of this chapter explaining how the *mise en place* of a chef compares to the preplanning of a teacher. To us, the image of a chef deconstructing a physical meal provides a helpful analog for imagining the somewhat less tangible image of a teacher deconstructing an abstract thinking goal. By linking the two, we identified a simple conceptual hook: *Mapping the path* is the *mise en place* of teaching.

Students might not know what chloroplasts, which are invisible to the naked eye, do on the surface of a leaf. However, they might already understand the function of solar panels on the roof of a house. If we can engineer a prompt that has them explain how a roof needs solar panels to collect sunlight for the use of the house, it creates a bridge because it's the same way that chloroplasts collect sunlight for the use of the plant. Therefore, chloroplasts represent the "solar panels" of the house.

Looking in and outside of your discipline, what analogs exist for the concept or the strategic capacity you wish to teach? What might serve as a good "this for that" replacement that might make a concept easier to grasp for your learners?

MNEMONICS AND FRAMEWORKS

Consolidating a process or set of strategies into a mnemonic is another way of thinking about this. For example, we have simplified the tenets of transformative teaching into an easy-to-remember framework in EMPOWER.

In thinking through student-facing examples, consider the cornerstone of academic argumentation, a skill set we approach with much urgency. A quick Google search for "logical argumentation" will bring you to the work of Stephen Toulmin (see, e.g., Toulmin, 1958), a British philosopher and academic famous for establishing a model of informal reasoning, the Toulmin Method. While we've taken a few liberties in our simplification of the Toulmin Method to make the "CREW" acronym memorable (your framework does not have to spell a word or phrase, but it doesn't hurt!), the basics of the model follow (see also Figure 5.5):

Claim: The conclusion we seek to establish through argument. Claims require support; without evidence and reasoning, a claim cannot hold because an audience cannot evaluate its grounding or logic.

Reasons: Subclaims that support a larger claim like pillars supporting a roof.

Evidence: The facts, data, rulings, statistics, testimony, etc., on which a claim sits.

Warrant: The explicitly explained connection between evidence and a claim (i.e., the reasoning and explanation of how specific evidence supports this claim). Even when an argument has a compelling claim and strong data to back it up, the most vulnerable part of an argument is often the explanation connecting the two, and in most arguments, novices neglect this component.

■ FIGURE 5.5: CREW MODEL FOR LOGICAL ARGUMENTATION

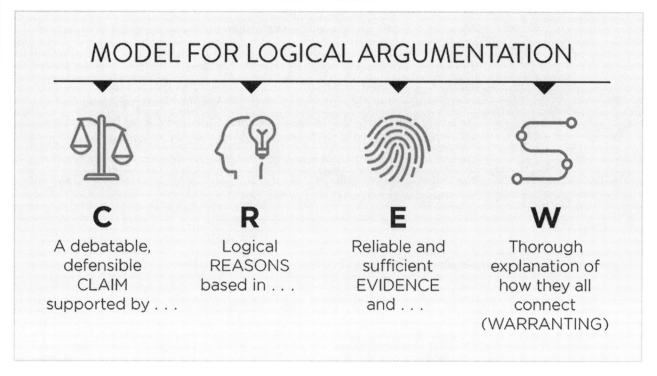

By teaching deeply into the Toulmin Method as a mental model and map—focusing on the individual elements, their connections, and ways to fortify each—we can help students build transferable understanding for creating arguments in any situation throughout their lives.

TEMPLATES

Another way to mentally model is to "template" a task. Far from simply turning something complex into a simplistic worksheet, to template means elucidating a pattern for shaping a piece of work. In crafting imaginative narratives, for example, students often neglect story structure. The following template can be used analytically to summarize stories or generatively to create them:

(Continued)

(Continued)

> Once upon a time *something happened to someone*, and s/he decided that s/he would pursue (a) *goal*. So, with the help of a *guide*, s/he *devised a plan of action*, and even though s/he faced *obstacles*, s/he *kept going* in light of the *stakes of succeeding or failing*. And just as s/he *hit rock bottom*, s/he *learned a lesson or got clarity*, and when offered *the goal*, s/he *made a tough decision*, resulting in *success or failure* and *resolving past issues*.

Take the plot of the Pixar classic *Finding Nemo*, the 10th-highest-grossing animated film of all time and owner of an impressive 99 percent score on the movie review website Rotten Tomatoes. *Warning: spoilers ahead!*

> Once upon a time *an overprotective father fish named Marlin lost his son, Nemo,* and he decided that he would pursue *finding Nemo*. So, with the help of *Dory*, he *searched the ocean blue*, and even though he faced *sharks, turtles, and being swallowed by a whale*, he *"just kept swimming"* in light of the *prospect of finding his only son*. And just as he *thought Nemo was dead and saw Dory caught in a net*, he learned *"If you love something, set it free,"* and when offered *Nemo being alive and safe*, he *made the tough decision to let him help free Dory, who was stuck in a net*, resulting in *everyone successfully returning home safely* and *resolving Marlin's overprotective parenting tendencies caused by Nemo's mother being eaten in the first scene.*

Finding Nemo not only won critical accolades from its audience but also received a nomination for Best *Original* Screenplay despite it fitting the template beat by beat. The template also explains the hero quest archetype, superhero flicks, romantic comedies, and even *Romeo & Juliet* with minor tweaking. If your favorite film is a Hollywood classic, there is 90-plus-percent likelihood that it falls into the structure of the passage above. So, what gives? Isn't the popular wisdom to "think outside of the box" when telling a story?

Template mental models address *exactly* this kind of predictable misconception. It is mostly novices who resist "inside the box" thinking and rail against confining themselves to a predictable story pattern. As it turns out, the brain *loves* predictable patterns! When authors try to be clever and stray too far from tried-and-true structures, readers often get confused and lose the thread. Effective storytelling becomes less about reinventing the wheel than about leveraging the known elements to maximal effect.

Students first learning how to compose narratives need scaffolds to create the familiar ebb and flow, the tension and release, of an engaging narrative. And by "standing on the shoulders" of Pixar, Aristotle, and storytellers who have come before them via a template, students in Adam's eighth-grade class were able to craft dramatic story structures that would make Pixar proud (see, e.g., Figure 5.6).

NAME: **Briana Pinales**   STEP 2: I can structure my story dramatically.

Once upon a time, **(something happened to someone)**

Marie Underwood, 86, a master jewel thief arrived in NY only a few days before the red-eyed ruby from Africa arrived at the Museum of Natural History. Harry, age classified, an agent of the CIA, is assigned to the case. His mission: stop Marie.

and (s)he decided that (s)he would pursue **(a goal)**.

Stop the elderly criminal before she got the gem; stop her once and for all...

So (s)he devised a **(plan of action)**,

Harry would first down Marie's hiding spot. Then he would figure out when she is going to strike the museum. After that, he would catch her. Also, he switched out the gem for a fake, so she would not steal the real one.

and even though there were **(complications/forces trying to stop her/obstacles)**,

Harry soon found that it wasn't Underwood who was trying to steal the ruby but someone else: Le Thief LeClare.

(s)he **(responded to the conflict and moved forward with a plan)**

Harry interrogated Underwood and used CIA information to research LeClare.

because there was **(a lot at stake)**.

If Harry doesn't stop LeCLare, he would get away with the ruby worth millions. If this happens, Harry would lose his job and probably be stuck in the mailroom.

And just as things seemed as **(bad as they could get)**,

Harry is at a dead end and cannot figure *anything* out. The unveiling of the red-eyed ruby is that night...

(s)he learned, realized, or finally understood **(an important lesson)**,

Patience is a virtue; patience is everything; if you rush things, you miss clues...

and when **(offered the "prize")** (s)he had wanted so badly,

A note finds his way to Harry's hotel room: it is an anonymous tip saying where LeClare is going to be. But he acts patiently and sees that it might be a trap.

(s)he had to **(make a big decision about whether or not to take it)**

He avoids taking this "easy way out" and goes with his gut to find LeClare. At the unveiling, Harry finds LeClare who turns out to be Underwood's 10-year-old grandson on vacation from France. He was trying to impress his grandmother by going into the family business. Plus, who would ever suspect a 10-year-old of being a master thief?

and in making that decision (s)he **(*changed or grew in a way connected to past events/personality*.)**

In the past, Harry jumped to hasty conclusions, never acted patiently, and was never promoted because of these characteristics. Now, he has grown to be more patient, more professional, and more thoughtful. He gets his big promotion!

THE END

(Continued)

Later on, Briana may choose to strategically bend rules and make bolder creative choices to advance her agency as an author, but by familiarizing herself first with the template pattern, she has a strong foundation in classic structure. With this expert understanding, she can now extend, explore, and revise the basic structure to work for meaning and effect.

MAPPING MOVE 4: ASSESS TO UNDERSTAND DIMENSIONS OF AN EXPERT PERFORMANCE

In drafting your GEMS in the previous chapter, you identified "measures of success," the traits of exemplary work in the genre or process your learners will master. In the final move of *mapping the path*, you will flesh out each measure of success and articulate different levels of performance in specific detail.

In order to produce the most real-world rubric you can, we recommend you generate it from real-world models via the following process.

1. Gather and sort a range of student work in a particular genre or writing form. Grab a stack of arguments, narratives, or presentations from previous years or the internet.

2. Ask yourself: What makes the strong ones strong? What makes the weak ones weak? Name characteristics and qualities of these work samples. (See also "Bringing It All Together Move 1: Ranking Models to Articulate Critical Standards" in Chapter 15, page 247.) On one color of sticky notes, write phrases that characterize the work, such as "cites evidence from multiple sources" or "jumps around from topic to topic." On another color of sticky notes, name traits that capture characteristics (adjectives such as *convincing, logically organized, clear,* etc.).

3. Cluster the sticky notes (or your written ideas) into traits or important dimensions of performance. This is your rudimentary rubric (see, e.g., Figure 5.7).

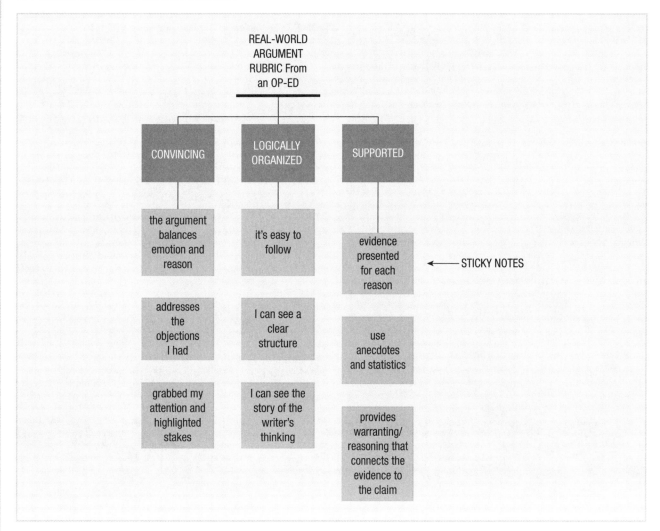

4. Repeat this process with students during *orientation* (discussed in Chapters 6 and 7) and continuously refine it based on real-world examples.

POWERFUL PLANNING:
DIGGING DEEP AND DECONSTRUCTING THE LEARNING JOURNEY AHEAD

It cannot be said enough that each of these mapping exercises represents an acquired expert skill set that you will develop not only throughout your reading of this text but also throughout your *career*. What we discussed in this chapter represents critical, often overlooked aspects of instructional design.

If you're feeling overwhelmed, we encourage you to "knock over the first domino": do the culminating task that you want students to be able to do. Additional advantages of doing the culminating assignment yourself are that you will now have a model of the completed task to share with students, you have a model of the process you took and knowledge of how to navigate obstacles, and you have demonstrated that you are a collaborative inquirer and learner within the classroom community. This makes clear that you are a person who values the work you assign, who is still learning, who is reflective, and who is willing to keep getting better. Once you do your task, you will automatically begin the process of task breakdown. Once you're breaking down your task, you might start seeking out the mental models or resources that will anchor your instruction. Once you've done the task and maybe compared your process with a colleague, you will likely have a good sense of how to set up some meaningful milestones or checkpoints. Once you've read a few models from past students and experts, building a rubric that communicates the characteristics of quality will get easier.

But it all begins with the first domino: Do your task, eat your own cooking, and commit yourself to the inquiry, and you will be transformed toward "conscious competence" and expertise because of it!

Transferring Our Learning: What to Remember When Mapping the Path to Mastery Through Task Deconstruction

- Access and understand your culminating task through doing it or imagining doing it.

- Define the underlying skills and knowledge required to complete the culminating task successfully.

- Articulate or locate a *mental model* that captures how experts actually approach this task, not a "school-ish" formula that reduces complex thinking into rote learning.

- Flesh out your measures of success into three to five levels of performance in the form of a rubric.

PART 3: PRIMING AND ORIENTING

ENVISION   MAP   PRIME   ORIENT   WALK THROUGH   EXTEND/EXPLORE   REFLECT

Chapter 6

PRIMING LEARNERS THROUGH CARING COMMUNITY AND COLLABORATIVE CLASSROOM CULTURE

A Prerequisite "Must-Make Move" for ICA

ESSENTIAL QUESTION

How do we create the prerequisites of guided inquiry through inquiry as cognitive apprenticeship (ICA): the conditions for a community of transformational learning?

Jeff was once kayaking the Kennebec River in Maine with several of his favorite students. Just above the mile-long gorge drop, the toughest section of the river descending between two steep canyon walls, the group stopped to drain their boats. Teacher extraordinaire Ryan Mahan fumbled his drain plug into the river and watched it float away down the gorge. There was general disbelief and not a little cursing. What was to be done? A kayak can't make it down that kind of whitewater stretch with a hole in the boat! Jeff's been in many groups where Ryan might have been told "too bad, so sad—hike your boat up the canyon walls because we're taking off without you." But luckily this group had a sense of community and the ethic that "no kayaker will be left behind." Jeff instructed the group to empty their pockets to see what resources they possessed. Jeff had a Bit-O-Honey bar, and Ryan had a strip of duct tape around his water bottle. Jeff chewed up the bar and stuck it in the hole. Ryan put the duct tape over the patch so the bar wouldn't turn to mush. It worked! The group successfully navigated the gorge and the rest of an amazing whitewater run!

See *Lesson Plan Canvas* on page 95

Developing a communal sense that "we are all in this together" and the tools to successfully relate, combine resources, navigate differences, and help each other are crucial prerequisites to guided inquiry/ICA approaches. As Vygotsky (1978) pointed out, all teaching and learning is relational and occurs in relationship. This means that we have to develop strong caring relationships with learners, and kids have to develop healthy ways of being together and of responding to and helping each other. Numerous studies bear this out: Feeling safe, secure, and part of a caring community helps students focus their energy on learning. Researchers (Cook, Fiat, & Larson, 2018) found that when teachers make one simple move to deliberately foster a sense of belonging by greeting individual students as they enter the classroom, there are "significant improvements in academic engaged time and reductions in disruptive behavior" (p. 149).

Although it's different from priming and orienting to learn particular content and processes (the subject of the next two chapters), community building is a foundational element of guided inquiry and the EMPOWER approach: Without it, the rest of the strategies presented in this book won't be nearly as successful. In this chapter, priming and orienting is about making sure all learners are comfortable, part of the community, and being apprenticed to know, care about, and collaborate with each other. Priming and orienting the learning of specific content and strategies they have not yet mastered comes in Chapters 7 and 8.

Priming and orienting is all about *preparing learners for success* with upcoming challenges. This is in direct and powerful contrast to the traditional move of assigning and then trying to correct and remediate shortfalls. Priming and orienting involves activating, accessing, and building on prior knowledge and resources so these can be consciously applied to the common learning project. A culture of caring and reciprocity is an essential part of inquiry as cognitive apprenticeship, so these ways of being together must be *primed from the start of the year and cultivated throughout the year.* When people learn together in a caring and collaborative community, everyone is smarter, everything runs smoother, challenges are more powerfully navigated, and learning can be pursued with deep camaraderie and joy.

Every teacher wants students who think and act as a community: working together, building on each other's ideas, explaining and justifying learning to each other, extending understanding, and helping out those who don't get it yet. The thought of enabling such a caring community is one of the main reasons many teachers teach. Unfortunately, proclaiming a classroom to be a safe and supportive place does not magically make it so. Such a space must be worked for: It must be seeded, cultivated, apprenticed, and deliberately practiced from day one. This chapter explores how to create expectations for respecting and caring for one another and helping each other learn, and how to consciously practice the moves and strategies that will help all to do so.

From the start of the year, as we begin any instructional journey, we focus on building community and the collaborative culture essential to an EMPOWERed classroom. We focus on setting, meeting, and monitoring classroom norms that support everyone on our collaborative learning journey. Throughout every unit, we use various techniques to get to know each other and to elicit and use our personal and cultural funds of knowledge (Moll, Amani, Neff, & Gonzalez, 1992) to create a learning community of continuous and reciprocal improvement. We deliberately practice providing procedural feedback to authors, to disciplinary experts like historians or scientists, to ourselves, and to our peers, which helps move learning forward.

The positive effect of community building is multiplied when it's not been siloed as a separate endeavor from our teaching. As you'll see in our civil rights unit, we do considerable work on building community that applies directly to the issue of civil rights. (We've found that community and collaboration can complement major conceptual and strategic goals in any unit, giving us a powerful twofer.) We prime learning with a survey about civil rights issues (see Chapter 7). Students write micro-arguments justifying their responses, so they are sharing their different perspectives. Next, they provide procedural feedback to each other: describing what their peers have done in the argument, and how those moves have created meaning and effect. They then provide "feedforward" with ideas for possible revisions. Throughout the unit, learners work together as community members toward a common purpose and for mutual benefit. They learn to advocate for themselves, for peers, and for others outside the classroom. (The lesson plan canvas for each chapter is presented in the context of our throughline unit on how to promote and protect civil rights, but each strategy can be adapted for use in any unit, performance, or learning situation.)

HOW CARING COMMUNITY FITS INTO EMPOWER

Tackling a complex problem, like how to work toward civil rights in the classroom, school, community, and wider culture, requires a division of labor, many different perspectives, and careful listening. Our students need to envision themselves as democratic citizens and workers who willingly solicit and carefully listen to the views of others. In this chapter, we provide a few of the more powerful ways we *prime* and *orient* learners to meet these kinds of goals, which will lead into the ongoing *walk-through* for apprenticing them into the skills of creating caring and responsive community, extending and exploring new ways to do this, and reflecting on how to continue to do so throughout their lives. The last 50-plus years of cognitive science have taught us that teaching and learning for understanding and application occur best within communities of collaborative relationships.

We know that

- Learners need to be recognized as individuals (Smith & Wilhelm, 2002)

- Learners need to have their challenges and efforts acknowledged (Joiner, 2005)

- Deep teaching and learning are relational and occur in relationships like apprenticeship (Smith & Wilhelm, 2002; Vygotsky, 1978)

- Students have a social contract to care with their teachers (Smith & Wilhelm, 2002)

- Deep learning requires social assistance in the context of doing real disciplinary work (Brown, Collins, & Duguid, 1989; Vygotsky, 1978)

- We are smarter and more resilient together than we are alone (Vygotsky, 1978)

- The social is essential to engagement, flow, and peak experience (Csikszentmihalyi, 1990; Heath & Heath, 2017)

- The recognition and use of personal and cultural funds of knowledge are essential to learning (Bransford & Johnson, 1972; Moll et al., 1992)

- Becoming an expert requires induction into a community of practice (Lave & Wenger, 1991)

- Human beings are intensely social and crave deep relationships and connections (Heath & Heath, 2017; Lieberman, 2013)

- 100 hours of time sharing significant experiences or doing significant work together builds enduring and respectful relationships (so shouldn't every classroom achieve this?) (Fehr, 2008; Hall, 2018)

Here is the major takeaway: *The unique power of a classroom learning environment is its social power.*

All teachers know the costs for learners of exclusion and isolation. We must engage students in collaborative activity each and every day that requires and rewards working together because *this is necessary to human well-being* and *this is how disciplines and democratic communities do their work together.* If we do not foster community, then we fail to leverage this unique social power, and we leave ourselves open to being replaced by virtual academies that excel at purveying inert information without social interaction and that cannot teach us how to establish and maintain community.

What does this mean for us as teachers, when we consider priming and orienting learners for success? Students do not necessarily know how to create community, to respond respectfully and helpfully, to care for each other, and so on. If they cannot do these things *yet*, then they need structures, invitations, scaffolds, and feedback to grow in these directions.

In this chapter, we explore some must-make priming and orienting routines for

- Creating, cultivating, and leveraging collaborative community

- Getting to know each other, and moving toward caring community

- Preparing to engage in responsive *joint productive activity* (Tharp & Gallimore, 1988)

- Providing opportunities for learners to see themselves and others as valuable members in the classroom community who have something to offer

- Providing pathways of access into the discipline and for staking and evolving personal and group identities as people who do the discipline

All of these moves will prime and orient students to engage in the inquiries that will lead to transformed understanding and ways of being and doing. (Chapters 11 and 12 follow up on these ideas through ways to use collaborative group structures and promote dialogue.)

The "must-make move" activities that follow are for *priming* students for success by activating and cultivating a sharing community, by accessing resources and creating environments of responsive social support. As is the case in each chapter, we offer a few of the powerful strategies we use to enact the featured must-make move. We provide these as exemplar strategies for you to adapt and use, but even more so as a model for adapting, or for finding and creating your own moves of each type for whatever units you teach. Please note that we've tagged the principles of each must-make move to the elements of EMPOWER to show that even though a move may be for priming in the context of a unit (or walking through or reflecting, etc.), we still use all the steps of EMPOWER to plan the lesson.

Principles of an Effective Collaborative Classroom Culture Activity

- Has a clear purpose for creating and learning together in community (E-M)

- Highlights that teaching and learning are relational and occur in relationship (E-M)

- Sets personally compelling and culturally relevant purposes for learning (P-O)

- Motivates students to engage together with the topic of the current inquiry (P-O)

- Helps students see personal and community connections to the learning (P-O)

- Identifies clear deliverables valuable for sharing with others in the community (P-O)

- Invites students to embrace community purposes and applications, inviting them to actively work together toward these purposes and applications (P-O)

- Shows that knowledge is socially constructed (W-E)

- Promotes reciprocal commitment to each other's learning and well-being (W-E)

- Is dialogic in that everyone's ideas are elicited, all are listened to, and all perspectives are respectfully considered (W-E)

- Promotes bricolage: low-risk playing with ideas and just trying things out (W-E)

- Promotes reflection on building healthy and collaborative community, and on ways to move forward in promoting it, positively addressing challenges, and so on (R)

COLLABORATIVE CLASSROOM CULTURE MOVE 1: PROCEDURAL FEEDBACK

Our first must-make move for community building is learning to provide and receive procedural feedback—also known as descriptive or causal feedback. This move primes learners to *recognize* and *pay careful attention* to the work of others (and oneself), to notice significant ideas and moves in that work, and to describe these and the resulting meaning and effect. Procedural feedback also involves offering new ways forward to deepen the work and causally justifying these suggestions. These moves of procedural feedback prime and promote mutual responsibility and community, and help the community to learn together. Providing procedural feedback positions learners as thinking partners and primes them to build supportive relationships.

Procedural feedback generally starts with a description of what the writer (or reader/performer/problem solver) has done, and then the consequence that follows from this activity. Procedural feedback recognizes effort and names expert strategy use. This kind of recognition of effort, performance, and developing competence is essential to human development, identity building, and agency (e.g., Carlone & Johnson, 2007). This recognition is therefore an inductive and restorative instructional practice. The ultimate purpose of the technique is to prime and assist students to notice expert ways of making meaning (we call these "power moves"), as well as to identify concrete ways forward to continue honing expert practice ("potential moves"). (See Chapter 14 for more on peer and self-assessment.)

One could provide procedural feedback to a student narrative by saying: "*The way you* used descriptive language in your story *had the effect* of helping me visualize the setting and how this setting affected the characters *because* the setting offered particular constraints and invitations that were both functional and psychological." This names a power move for meeting a particular purpose that students should continue to use.

Frames for providing this kind of feedback include stems like these:

- The way you . . . led me to . . . because . . .
- When you . . . , it had the effect of . . . because . . .
- The move you made to . . . resulted in . . . /should lead to . . . /exhibited the principle of . . . because . . .
- This quote/expert move . . . made me think/consider/rethink . . . because . . .

Anything that explores how to name moves and describe *cause and effect* in the writing, reading, problem solving, and so on would constitute procedural feedback that promotes deep understanding of how various processes and strategies work.

Procedural feedback is meant to be nonevaluative and leaves the authority and decision making to the author/problem solver, but it is specific in describing the effort and moves made as well as the meaning and effect achieved. (Note well: When we start with "I *like* the way . . . ," we are positioning ourselves as judges who need to be pleased, and the feedback becomes evaluative. We know this is a well-intentioned default move for many teachers and learners. We consciously work to avoid it so that the feedback is descriptive and not evaluative.)

Procedural *feedforward* works by suggesting a potential move to use in moving forward, to revise, improve, or deepen the work. Responders are responsible for providing concrete ways forward and describing causally why they think this move might work for particular purposes. Composers or problem solvers are responsible for accepting, adapting, or rejecting the suggestion, and being able to justify that decision. Procedural feedforward might use language such as this:

> *I wonder what would happen if . . . (you made this specific move/tried this strategy) because . . . (describe the meaning and effect that you think might accrue from this move, and include cause).*

Figure 6.1 is a protocol for group procedural feedback. Working to provide feedback in a group under the teacher's direction is a kind of deliberate practice that leads directly into providing feedback in smaller groups or pairs. Note that this process should become a conversation in which the author or presenter can ask questions or for clarifications, in which respondents uptake each other's ideas, and so on.

■ FIGURE 6.1: STEPS FOR GIVING PROCEDURAL FEEDBACK IN A GROUP

1. Thank authors or peers for sharing their work (express appreciation for the gift they've given us by sharing to fulfill the purpose of helping us all learn).

2. Ask the authors or peers (if present) to provide procedural feedback and feedforward to themselves—name some moves they made and the meaning and effect, then name some other possibilities to be used in revision or the future.

3. Ask the roundtable forum (e.g., the rest of the class or learning group) to think individually and then in pairs about how to phrase additional procedural feedback and procedural feedforward to the authors or presenters.

4. Ask the authors or presenters for permission to be their thinking partner and offer some procedural feedback and feedforward.

5. Offer feedback:

   - Name and describe a specific move made (e.g., *When you . . .*) and then the meaning and effect (*the effect on me as the reader was . . . because . . .*).

   - Be descriptive, causal, and nonevaluative (e.g., try to refrain from saying "I liked . . . ," etc., since this positions the respondent as an authority to be pleased instead of a thinking partner).

   - Name and describe a potential move forward for revision or a future use of the lesson or problem-solving endeavor and phrase as a possibility for growth (e.g., *I wonder what would happen if you . . . because . . .* [describe possible meanings and effects or extensions that might be achieved]).

As Vivian Paley (1993) has maintained, we can't sing happy songs or discuss civilly or perform scenes from Shakespeare if we fear ridicule and derision. While Paley worked with kindergarten students, the same spirit applies in middle school and high school: Students are not going to take risks or contribute actively and enthusiastically if they feel threatened or anxious. Procedural feedback is a powerful way to respectfully recognize effort, agency, expert moves, and the meaning these create, as well as ways forward, in ways that prime social support and community building.

COLLABORATIVE CLASSROOM CULTURE MOVE 2: CREATING CLASSROOM AND GROUP NORMS

One of the major goals of education must be the articulation and cultivation of critical standards, and then practicing together as a community to refine and meet these standards. We therefore involve students in articulating and applying critical standards in informal and formal ways throughout our work, since we need to apprentice students into this vital skill set.

One place to prime this kind of work is at the beginning of the school year (or any learning cycle) by setting general classroom norms (see Figure 6.2). Likewise, norming and standard setting can be revisited throughout the year and adapted to specific goals like group work or working well with people who are different, or for any specific activity (see also Chapters 14 and 15).

■ **FIGURE 6.2: PROCESS FOR CREATING CLASSROOM NORMS**

1. Start by asking students the following questions: *What does a good community (learning group/pair work, etc.) look like? Sound like? Feel like?*

2. Ask individual students to answer on their own. Research on brainstorming (e.g., Kahnemann, 2011) shows that if brainstorming is first private and individual, then the later sharing of ideas is richer, more diverse, and more likely to be shared.

3. Ask pairs and triads to share with each other. Challenge the small groups to come to consensus.

4. Model how to come up with an analogy or metaphor for their thinking. For example, an effective group is like a sports team because everyone must work together and use each other's strengths to win.

5. Ask the small groups to come up with a metaphor or analogy that captures their thinking. Ask them to be able to explain how the metaphor works to communicate something about effective groups.

6. Groups share with the whole class by posting their answers, doing a Gallery Walk, then discussing points of agreement.

7. An anchor chart is created with the norms that the reports share, and students are asked to refer to it and challenged to refine it over time.

8. Whenever there is a group activity, ask students to consider beforehand and reflect afterward how well they met their norms/critical standards and what they could do to move forward. These reflections can be phrased as procedural feedback.

9. Teachers can use reflections and observations to consider how to apprentice and support students in moving forward toward meeting the norms more fully.

10. Students can create memes to reinforce the central ideas about creating successful community, productive groups, and so on.

This kind of activity primes a focus on the importance of community, how to create it, and the agentive role of all students in creating, monitoring, and refining a productive, compassionate, and supportive community. Figure 6.3 shows a sample group norms poster from a classroom.

COLLABORATIVE CLASSROOM CULTURE MOVE 3: DAILY GUT CHECKS

Teachers know that learners come into class each day with different kinds of energy, and we must deal with that energy, harness or sometimes reframe and refocus it, and help the learners to learn to do the same as well. (For example, if there has been a fight at lunch, then there has to be a sharing or debrief of that fight before learning can proceed without distraction.) Daily Gut Checks (see Figure 6.4) are a quick formative assessment strategy that provides important information about what and how students are noticing and feeling regarding their own learning (also see Chapter 14 for more on formative assessment *for* and *as* learning).

(Continued)

(Continued)

■ **FIGURE 6.4: ORGANIZING THE GUT CHECK**

1. Make the first two to three minutes of class a time to reflect and privately report out on one's status and needs, in general and in terms of the current inquiry and learning.

2. Remind learners of what was done yesterday, and the learning goals/culminating projects being worked toward (we usually put a quick summary on the board or screen).

3. Ask students to compose a notecard or sticky note or even an email to the teacher. On one side (or in one column) they can write what is going well (we call these "marvy," for *marvelously*) for them personally and in terms of the learning. On the other side they can record any questions, challenges, or needs that they have both personally (Are they hungry? Is their mom sick?) and in terms of the learning in class (we call these "muddies").

4. Students can respond confidentially, or by name if they want the teacher to follow up or celebrate success.

5. The teacher collects the responses and gets students started on a lesson activity. Early in the class, the teacher can quickly flip through the notes to (1) see if he or she needs to check in with a learner and (2) get a sense of individual needs and group trends in terms of success and struggle. These findings should inform planning for both immediate and longer-term interventions and supports.

6. Options include having a follow-up classroom discussion or having students reframe the marvys and muddies into procedural feedback to themselves or to someone else, including the teacher, about what is going well, what is challenging, what might be helpful ways forward, and why they think so.

To prime a focus on learning goals, students could list the most important thing they learned yesterday or so far in the unit, and the biggest challenge they have yet to meet—and what kind of assistance might help them. This provides the teacher with rich formative assessment data and gives the students deliberate practice in self-monitoring, decomposing, and monitoring completion of a complex task, feeding back, and feeding forward.

Asking what's going well or what's challenging is powerful because the question communicates that someone cares how you are doing and about what is making sense or not making sense to you. It also communicates that you are not alone, and that by asking for help, you can get help. The technique gives students practice in self-monitoring and describing their successes and challenges, in asking for the help they need, and in devising action plans for moving forward. We like Gut Checking as a way to model elements like self-care, attention, kindness, compassion, and connection that leads to reciprocity and mutual assistance. Learners are being primed and apprenticed into success as lifelong learners and in how to be caring adults.

Gut Checks are meant to be quick and to happen immediately at the start or end of class. If they become a ritual structure/standard routine, then students will begin doing their Gut Check even before the bell rings. We have two major purposes of the daily Gut Check (though you can adapt the prompts to cover other ground as well):

1. To see how learners are doing in general—emotionally and physically—so that we can address these needs and follow up and support them as needed. This creates a compassionate and supportive space in the classroom, but also

guides us to be attentive and responsive to larger student needs, and works to make sure learners are ready to learn.

2. To check in on successes and productive struggles with the learning goals of the class. Even if students do not choose to share particular insights, they are being invited to, and a culture of caring and sharing is being primed that makes it more likely they will share in the future, or if something significant comes up for them.

Maslow's (1943) hierarchy demonstrates that people need to have basic needs met before they can learn. They need to be fed, and to feel loved and safe. They need to feel recognized and attended to, and that they have a way for their concerns and needs to be shared and heard. The Gut Check elicits questions and needs, and primes finding an opportunity to address general or individual needs. Gut Checking also helps us identify what practice is needed by groups and individuals to navigate the work at hand. It is about monitoring how we are doing, what we are doing, how we are doing it, what challenges we are facing, and how we are going to proceed. It primes and promotes self-regulation and a future orientation toward growth.

Recognition of challenges and successes is part of inductive/restorative instruction, culturally responsive teaching, identity formation, growth mindset cultivation (Dweck, 2006), and much else. All feelings are about needs that are met and unmet. Positive emotion promotes learning, and negative emotion can be an obstacle that must be addressed. For example, research on trauma demonstrates that learners need acknowledgement of what they have gone through or are going through before they can move forward productively (Zacarain, Alvarez-Ortiz, & Haynes, 2017).

As a classroom community, we need a shared reality and communal space, and Gut Checking provides both. Problems do not go away simply because we are not aware of them or because we ignore them. If our students have particular needs or problems, it is our job to recognize and name these and then apprentice students as individuals and as a group to address these issues so we can move forward. (The companion website at http://resources.corwin.com/EMPOWER-secondary contains a downloadable list of guidelines for empathic listening.)

COLLABORATIVE CLASSROOM CULTURE MOVE 4: WHO'S DONE IT?/WHO KNOWS ABOUT IT?

Here learners are primed at the start of a school year or unit to see how personal experiences (or values, commitments, etc.) connect to the learning that is to come. In the activity shown in Figure 6.5, we share a list of experiences that provide background for a year of eighth-grade science topics so that learners can see that a wide variety of their experiences, interests, and knowledge connect to the inquiries that will be pursued. A list of

(Continued)

(Continued)

connected experiences, personal connections, attitudes, values, commitments, and so on can be adapted for any course or unit. Note well that we work hard to make sure all learners' experiences are privileged and highlighted by providing a wide variety of connections.

■ **FIGURE 6.5: WHO'S DONE IT?**

In this activity, we will get to know other students who have had some wild experiences. *First*, read through the experiences below to see which ones *you* have had. *Next*, we'll all engage in a mixer as you walk around the classroom to find out who else in the class has experienced any of the following. *Then* write the person's first name in the place provided. So that you can talk to more thinking partners, please write each person's name only once. *Last*, ask the people you meet about their experience and carefully listen to their answer. *Fill in* the answer to the question and record any other interesting details you learned about the person. Use the back if you need more room. Don't worry about filling in all of the answers. Instead be a good listener and accurate recorder. By the way, all of these experiences are going to be important to our future inquiries!

Experience	Student's Name	Follow-Up Questions and Other Details
has broken a bone _____		which one(s)? _____
had/has a pet _____		type? _____
felt an earthquake _____		how bad? _____
experienced high winds _____		place? _____
saw a wild animal in nature _____		type? _____
found a fossil _____		where? _____
plays a musical instrument _____		which? _____
was close to lightning strike _____		damage? _____
speaks a foreign language _____		which? _____
has lived outside of Idaho _____		where? _____
went to ocean _____		description? _____
has gone river running _____		what was it like? _____
caught a fish _____		type? _____
looked through a telescope _____		saw what? _____
visited a volcano _____		where? _____
been in bad storm _____		type? _____
saw an eclipse, comet, etc. _____		what? _____
climbed to top of a mountain _____		which? _____
gone below sea level on land _____		where? _____
has been in a salty lake _____		name? _____
went to tropics _____		where? _____
hiked through desert _____		where? _____
likes to cook _____		details: _____
can repair a bike _____		details: _____
can work on a car motor _____		details: _____

Once they get going, you can ask students to come up with other experiences to add to the list that connect to classroom topics. The idea is to have items that focus on diversity and diverse experiences that will lead the other students (and you!) to learn things you wouldn't have otherwise known about each other. Later on you can tie some of the questions to the topic of the class and units of study so you will know who has experiences that can be drawn on when that unit of study comes around. This can also be made into a "Who Knows About It?" activity to identify what students know or want to know about particular concepts or ideas, such as knowledge of literary or historical characters that will be useful to our understanding of inquiry topics: *Who is your favorite president? What questions would we want to ask former presidents? What are the important experiences, habits, qualifications, values, typical moves, and problem-solving processes of effective presidents?*

COLLABORATIVE CLASSROOM CULTURE MOVE 5: GETTING TO KNOW EACH OTHER AS PEOPLE AND LEARNERS

Here are a few other quick ways to prime students to recognize and name themselves and each other with positivity and possibility, and to get to know each other better in a supportive learning context. We're aware, painfully sometimes, how little substantive and personally compelling sharing might occur in a classroom. We're also aware how much students develop over the course of a school year. Often, they don't take time on their own to stop and reflect about their deepest growth, evolving values, commitments, interests, capacity, and potential. We prime students to learn actively, and to listen and attend by teaching empathic listening, nonviolent communication, and other strategies. And we can create multiple opportunities to prime students to share and reflect about their thinking, their deepest commitments and values, and their personal evolution and identity in a positive context.

There are many ways, most quite quick, to encourage students to identify themselves and know each other, identify personal resources and cultural funds of knowledge, move toward caring and compassion, learn how to work together, and advocate for each other. Anything that helps you know your students, or helps students know each other, can do this kind of work. Actions that help you recognize students for anything from accomplishments to haircuts, that help you integrate their interests into the classroom, and that express care for students as people and learners are all useful. Among the many short techniques we use are sharing responses to reflective prompts like these:

- *The most important thing/three most important things about me is/are . . . because . . .*

- *My most important passions/interests/commitments are . . .*

- *The most important connection I can make to our new topic of study is . . .*

- *I wish my teacher/my classmates knew . . .*

Do not share, of course, unless you have permission—it's typically much more powerful to help the learner figure out how to share important information and insights. (There's a popular TED Talk on this topic titled "What Kids Wish Their Teachers Knew" by Kyle Schwartz from TEDxKyoto.)

(Continued)

Techniques quite useful early in the year or prior to a new unit include the following:

- *Interest inventories and teacher notecatchers of student interest* that can be referred to while conferencing or planning instruction. (See the companion website at http://resources.corwin.com/EMPOWER-secondary for a downloadable interest ranking activity.)

- *Autobiographies or personality profiles.* Begin units with short writing about students' experiences with the unit topic. Or have students write personality profiles or introductory speeches to introduce each other's experiences (Wilhelm, 1995).

- *Autobiographical timelines or museum exhibits.* Students create and share timelines about their life or reading history. These can accommodate personal connections to unit topics by asking learners to include references (e.g., to civil rights issues/events from their lives, or to issues and events from the wider culture that occurred during their lifetimes). Students often enjoy creating visual timelines with photographs or museum exhibits of their lives, or of their connections to an inquiry (Wilhelm, 2013a).

- *How is this topic—or how can this topic be—connected to your interests?* This is a useful question to ask when new units are introduced to help students connect to the learning.

- *"What's on your mind?" meetings.* To begin a unit or a week, or to end a week, students write about what is on their mind, both generally and in terms of the inquiry unit, including enthusiasms or worries, personal connections, and successes or challenges. These can be shared privately with the teacher and/or discussed with the whole class.

- *Nerding out.* Teacher and students report out on enthusiasms, explorations, and extensions being developed; ways they can see using what they have learned; and so on.

Standard routines we use at the start of a week include these:

- *Happy news.* This activity can be done in five minutes. It's important for students' psychic health to recognize blessings and develop gratitude.

- *What I'm looking forward to.* Likewise, we ask students to name and share what they are looking forward to that day, and perhaps in the unit at hand.

- *Hosts/jobs.* Assign students jobs to run the classroom, such as taking attendance, taking care of absent students, taking care of newcomers, providing an opening moment, being a note-taker or historian—anything that needs to be done. Reassign jobs each week. This primes community and reciprocal responsibility and caring.

- *Rituals of appreciation and recognition.* Recognition—particularly of contributions to the community, of caring, and of conceptual understanding or performances that show evolving expertise—is essential to identity formation and to community. So we try to ritualize appreciations in which we thank learners for contributions, provide procedural feedback, clap for each other, write notes of appreciation to each other, and so on.

- *Quad seating/discussion groups/writing groups/project teams.* Have students sit in desk or table groups of four. You can get quick collaboration by asking students to talk to their elbow, face, or crisscross buddy, then as a whole table. This structure expresses that we are going to learn together and that we must talk and listen to each other. Also consider using writing groups and project teams throughout units. Groups can be assigned by the teacher, or students can apply to be in groups that the teacher can approve or rearrange as necessary for collaborative learning and success (see Chapter 12 for more on collaborative group structures).

- *Naming/name gaming/team naming.* Students give themselves a nickname that reveals something they are proud of or indicates a personal strength. Sometimes we ask that students provide an adjective or moniker before their name that starts with the same letter. So, for example, Jeff could be "Jump Shot Jeff" to show his love of basketball, or "Jazz-Loving Jeff" to show his passion for jazz music. Another naming activity is for learning groups who sit together or literature circle or project groups to give themselves a name that reveals interests, passions, purposes, goals, or strengths.

Two essential tenets of guided inquiry/apprenticeship are that (1) we learn socially in community and (2) we learn through challenge and productive struggle, including disagreements. In guided inquiry, we necessarily consider all perspectives before making judgments. So, in community, we must learn how to respect and hear people with different points of view, even those we might find offensive. It's our belief that conversing with people who are different from us is essential to inquiry, to growth, and to democracy and that this effort must be strategically supported. (For more on this, see Chapters 12 and 13.) One way we do this is through the believing game.

- *Believing game.* This technique is based on the notion of charitable interpretation from wisdom philosophy. Basically, we assume the best intentions of any speaker. If we truly find something offensive, then we use procedural feedback stems like "I'm guessing that you did not mean to be offensive, but some people might/could interpret your comment as aggressive or as marginalizing them because . . ." or "I wonder what would happen if you rephrased as . . .".

POWERFUL PLANNING: CREATING COMMUNITY KNOWLEDGE TOGETHER

Nothing creates community like working together and helping others do significant and meaningful work. In the context of communal activity and the induction into a community of practice, learners are apprenticed into expertise. This induction, though communal, can be personalized in many ways. Learners are positioned as contributing members to a community's knowledge building.

In our civil rights unit, our learners are primed to become novice historians reading about civil rights issues and then interviewing community members, and documentarians telling and then archiving stories about civil rights struggles and accomplishments. They are primed to consider social actions that can be taken in our own classrooms, schools, and lives that will promote civil rights, like adopting a class grandparent from the nearby senior citizens' home and creating ongoing programs to support refugee families and students to enter our school and community. These advocacies and accomplishments are made possible because community and community building are primed and then deliberately practiced and extended in the ways we describe here.

In our teaching and in our National Writing Project work on teacher development, we are always promoting what we call "thinking partnership"—the idea that we are all responsible for our own learning, our own energy, and our own experience, but that we are also responsible to promote the learning, the positive energy, and the experiences of all others in our community. We work to ensure that every single day we are doing something with our learners that leverages community and the social nature of the classroom, that we are doing something together that learners could not be doing on their own, and that requires all of us to be together. We also work each day to prime and promote community, and to proactively address issues that come up. Only through such mindful vigilance can we create the best community of caring and learning for all of us.

Transferring Our Learning: What to Remember When Designing Activities to Prime Community

- Clarify the purpose, potential payoffs, and satisfactions of community and collaborative work.

- Explicitly teach the importance of listening, responding, expressing appreciation for, and assisting each other.

- Help students learn how to *decompose complex tasks*, and how to assign distributed areas of responsibility so that they experience how the whole community benefits from individual contributions.

- Be proactive in anticipating and rehearsing how to deal with the inevitable challenges that will occur.

Lesson: Using Procedural Feedback (PF) to Promote Learning and Create Collaborative Community

Unit: How do we protect and promote civil rights?

ENVISION the destination
(Where are learners going, and why?)

| GOAL

What kind of thinking is targeted? | EVIDENCE

What product(s) will serve as proof of learning? | MEASURES OF SUCCESS

What's the standard and quality-assurance tool? | STAKES

Why will learners buy in?

What's the "why" behind the learning? |
|---|---|---|---|
| ✓ Application of skill/strategy
✓ Perspective taking
✓ Empathizing
✓ Self-assessing/reflecting | ✓ Performance assessment: Open-ended essay/writing, products (e.g., role-audience-format-topic [RAFT]), concept map
✓ Structured/unstructured observation | ✓ **SIMPLE:** √−, √, √+ on discrete capacities | Use ESSENCE as a guide for buy-in. Your lesson should have one or more of the following:
✓ E-S: Emotional spark/salience (i.e., relevance)
✓ S-E: Social engagement (i.e., collaboration)
✓ N: Novelty (i.e., new concepts and skills)
✓ C-E: Critical/creative exploration opportunities |
| **Provide** empathic and responsive PF to the work of others (peers, authors, observed problem solvers in the world, etc.) and eventually oneself that specifically notices and describes powerful and must-make strategic moves of the task, and then describes the meanings and effects that follow from the efforts using these moves. Generate feedforward of wonderings about potential moves and strategies to use in moving the work forward and doing similar work in the future (rehearsing for high-road transfer). | 1. Teacher and students use PF as default instead of saying "good job" or "I don't like it."
2. Students generate empathic PF to others that describes power moves both of successful task completion and of the meanings and effects that follow from the mindful and effortful use of the strategies.
3. Students provide feedforward in terms of wonderings about specifically described potential moves that could be used next to move the work forward.
4. Students consider feedback and feedforward they receive and mindfully choose to use it (or not) with justification. | To what degree does the learner notice and describe power moves of task completion, and to what degree can the learner describe the meanings and effects achieved by those moves? How well does the learner demonstrate a repertoire of strategies for using the appropriate expert mental model to complete this particular task? Can the student explain what makes each move worthy of attention and use? Can the learner identify potential moves for moving the performance forward and explain why they might work? Is conscious competence displayed?
√− = Notices power moves only
√ = Notices and describes meanings and effects of moves
√+ = Can also describe and justify potential ways forward for achieving more meaning/effect | **E-S:** Learners pay attention to authors/problem solvers and to each other, speaking to the achievements and needs of others and responding empathically as thinking partners and helpmates.
S-E: PF is entirely about responding to others in an effort to help them do their own and the community's work and achieve goals and high-road transfer.
N: The strategy or its extensions will probably be new to students. Giving and getting careful response is powerful as it acknowledges challenge, effort, and strategy use.
C-E: Learners apply PF to their own reading and life experiences, to any text of interaction or problem-solving situation that comes up for them. They can begin to internalize the strategy and give PF to others to learn from their work and themselves to self-monitor and problem solve challenges. |

MAP out the path to expertise/mastery
(How would an expert deconstruct and approach this task, step by step?)

| TWITTER SUMMARY

(3 bullets max)	MENTAL MODELS, PROCESS GUIDES, MAPS	A MODEL OF GOOD WORK LOOKS LIKE . . .	DIFFERENTIATION AND LAYERING
Experts at feeding back and feeding forward about a particular task know how to notice and describe power moves made by an author or problem solver, the meaning and effect of each move, and potential moves for progressing even further forward.	• Notice must-make power moves
• Describe must-make moves
• Identify meaning and effect that result from each power move for task completion
• Identify potential moves for moving forward in revising or improving performance, and transferring what is learned into the future | *"The way you expressed your claim as debatable, defensible, and significant means that you have chosen a topic worth arguing about with high stakes, and that you used an appropriate strategy such as PMI (Plus-Minus-Interesting) to get this done."* | Levels of assistance: Work with models and then stems, create anchor chart of stems
Different pairings and triads, with observer noting how the mental model was used
More modeling as needed, from peers and teacher
More deliberate practice mirroring mental model
Name features of naturally occurring examples of PF |

(Continued)

POWER through your lesson

(What is the sequence of initial major must-make instructional moves?)

PRIME	ORIENT	WALK THROUGH (and check for understanding)	EXTEND AND EXPLORE	REFLECT
ASK students to reflect on times that they have received useful feedback and unhelpful feedback. Examples will be used to articulate criteria for useful feedback as well as moves to avoid. Students create anchor charts of principles and examples of useful and unhelpful feedback. Create tips for giving useful feedback and tips for things to avoid to create acknowledgments of effort and strategy use, openness to feedback, reciprocity and relationality in giving and receiving feedback, etc.	FRAME today's lesson: "Procedural feedback develops deep understanding and conscious competence about a task and the mental model for completing it. Today, we'll learn how to engage in the process of procedural feedback . . . First, I want you to self-assess your current skills around naming expert moves of a task and providing feedback to work samples of this task." Students self-score their current aptitude on a semantic scale of procedural feedback moves: 1. I rarely provide feedback to myself or others. 2. I can regularly notice power moves in a performance. 3. I can regularly describe the meaning and effect achieved by the use of power moves. 4. I can regularly identify potential moves for moving a performance forward. 5. I naturally provide procedural feedback and feedforward to others and myself as a default.	EXPLAIN: PF involves 1. Noticing and naming power moves of expert performance on a specific task 2. Describing the meanings and effects of each move 3. Suggesting potential moves to use in moving forward 4. Explaining why you think those moves may work to improve performance 5. Rehearsing for high-road transfer of the mental model for task completion MODEL: Teacher provides a think-aloud of how he or she generates procedural feedback to an author, models how to use PF to analyze a different text or student work, etc. CHECK FOR UNDERSTANDING: Ask students, *What did you see me doing? What strategies helped me generate PF? Highlight rules of notice for the moves of featured task or text type.* GUIDED PRACTICE: Role-play learners providing unhelpful feedback and then reframe and revise it into PF. On the next section of text, have students generate PF to authors in triads or pairs. DIFFERENTIATE: If some students are struggling, work with them to assist, or have other successful individuals or groups assist. DEBRIEF: Share, revise, and evaluate PF students came up with. Name power moves and mental model of PF.	DELIBERATE PRACTICE/ ARTICULATE CONSCIOUS AWARENESS: Teacher reminds students of stems and how these enact the mental model and explains how he or she uses these in many learning and life situations. Learners provide their own think-aloud as they plan and generate procedural feedback to a text, then to the work of a peer, then to their own work. Students then use PF to analyze a different text, visual text, a classroom episode, student work, a sequence from a sporting event, etc. Learners think about a performance or activity they care deeply about. How can PF be used to improve their own or others' performance? How can PF help relationships? Provide options to getting angry or pushing back? Help you articulate what is going well and what might be bothering you? Develop social–emotional learning? Help to induct or restore learners into expertise and the classroom community of practice?	Summarize what you learned. Why is it important? Self-score yourself on PF now. What did you learn through your practice this week or today that affected your capacity to use PF to help others and yourself? What do you want to work on next? What is your action plan for doing this work? How can you use PF in other classes, at home, in your favorite activities, etc.? HOMEWORK EXTENSION: Generate PF to a favorite book or movie. Practice using PF with friends when you are engaged in a mutual activity. Play the PF game and provide PF to everything that you can! Then reflect seriously on what you learned from providing or hearing the PF.

online resources ▶ A blank version of this canvas is available for download at **http://resources.corwin.com/EMPOWER-secondary**

Chapter 7

FRAMING THE FUTURE CHALLENGE

Priming and Orienting Learning Through Essential Questions

> **ESSENTIAL QUESTION**
> How can we frame instruction to provide focus, foster engagement, create coherence, and highlight purpose and payoffs?

Jeff has taught a unit on civil rights many times at several grade levels over the last 36 years. Early on, when he would announce the unit topic to his students, which he thought to be tremendously exciting, his students would often react with the equivalent of mental yawns.

See *Lesson Plan Canvas* on page 113

Then one year he framed his unit with an essential question: *What are civil rights, and how do we best promote and protect them?* But he went even further, introducing the unit with a subquestion he thought would both prime and orient his students: *In what ways does this school violate students' civil rights (and what can we do about it)?* Have you ever met a seventh grader who does not think his civil rights are continually violated? It took the class less than five minutes to enthusiastically fill up the board with ideas. It was a short step to the essential question about civil rights in the wider world beyond school.

Crafting an essential question that requires and rewards inquiry coupled with the support provided through guided inquiry and cognitive apprenticeship invites deep engagement and future learning. But many such questions fail to meet the criteria of essential questions and can work against our purposes.

For instance, compare these questions that students might be asked to address:

1. What are the three reasons for the Civil Rights Act?

2. From the perspective of an immigrant living in the 21st century, what are some of the most compelling and urgent benefits of the Civil Rights Act?

Which one of these questions is a real-world practitioner or an expert, like a social scientist or historian, more likely to find engaging and to pursue? Which of these questions is most timely today, most culturally relevant, humanistic, significant, transformative, inductive, and restorative to a community of practice, and compelling to learners?

Essential questions fit the mental map of EMPOWER because they envision and frame the learning to come, prime learners' personal connection and background in regard to the question and problems it highlights, and orient learners to the purposes and payoffs of addressing the question. Essential questions provide a meaningful context for learning and using the requisite strategies and concepts for addressing the issue at hand. Essential questions also provide focus and curricular coherence, connecting what is learned today to what was learned yesterday and will be learned tomorrow. All learning clearly contributes to completing the culminating project that will address the essential question by the unit's end. Such coherence has been found to be a highly supportive factor for all learners, but particularly significant for those who struggle or are marginalized, making curricular coherence a necessary element of inductive and restorative instructional practice (Applebee, Burroughs, & Cruz, 2000; Applebee, Burroughs, & Stevens, 2000).

Essential questions will lead to learners

- Making evidence-based and justified judgments, decisions, and actions

- Developing a knowledge artifact/culminating project that archives usable knowledge, or that does work to address or even solve part of the problem

- Developing a service learning project or social action

- Creating a plan or course of action for moving forward with learning and problem solving, giving learners the tools to explore, extend, and transfer learning as they move into the future

QUESTIONS FRAME LEARNING

Questions matter because of how they position us, what connections they elicit, and what they help us to notice and do and learn in our evolving expertise as readers, composers, problem solvers, and disciplinary thinkers. Questioning strategies, properly deployed, can do a tremendous amount of work to move us toward understanding and getting tasks more expertly done in the world. Poorly used questions can work against all of these goals.

The first question in our preceding civil rights example expresses a "school-ish" fixed mindset and asks for predetermined, circumscribed, informational answers. It implies that knowledge is static and possessed by someone else who is an authority. It asks learners to guess "what the teacher already thinks." The second question, however, is a "tool-ish" question that positions the answerer as a knowledge maker with a growth mindset (Dweck, 2006) who can be apprenticed into solving problems and asking questions and creating knowledge of one's own. That's because the second question invites many other questions that are extensions of the original question—for example, what would have been the importance of the Civil Rights Act to females or African Americans (or any other group) living in the 18th or 19th century (or another era)? What will happen to particular people if civil rights legislation is weakened? The second question is an example of an essential question—one that can frame an inquiry and provide a guide to deep and transferable learning (see Figure 7.1).

■ **FIGURE 7.1: WHAT IS AN ESSENTIAL QUESTION? A MENTAL MODEL**

An essential question

- Frames learning and guides inquiry as a problem to be solved
- Gives an inquiry a personally and socially compelling frame, a focus, and an immediate and future context of use
- Is clear and concise
- Has no single "right" answer but does have justifiable answers
- Alerts us as questioners—and our fellow learners/audience—to what problems and issues our specific inquiry and the projects that come from it will address

The apprenticeship and instruction that take place during a unit's learning process are for the purpose of helping learners to develop new expert concepts and strategies (threshold knowledge) for addressing the essential question, for progressing toward expert use of new knowledge, for more fully entering an expert community of practice, and for completing culminating projects that learners do not know enough to complete at the start of the unit (see Chapter 15). The unit, guided by the essential question, becomes a context that supports and encourages students to develop usable real-world knowledge with value beyond school.

THE MENTAL MODELS AT PLAY

Generating essential questions (EQs) begins by identifying potential issues in the topic to be studied, activating and mining one's own experience and personal connections to these issues, intuiting possible socially significant applications, sharing, and discussing. Noticing throughlines, repetitions, emotional charges, and especially *contact zones* where different perspectives meet and contend assists in focusing the EQ. These noticings are used to frame a generative, open-ended question about the topic/issue that leads to deeper expert understanding and application. EQs and subquestions (SQs) are of course refined and continue to be generated as the inquiry progresses through reading, reviews of important texts and data, collection of data, and so forth. The basic mental model for generating EQs is to ask a contended open-ended question that is personally engaging, is socially significant, and will require the learning of threshold knowledge about the topic and lead to applications in one's personal life and the world.

It's also important for learners to begin seeing how EQs fit in the mental model of inquiry—that inquiry is framed by a problem or issue to be explored, which will imply applications and social actions, and that understanding will be pursued through priming (frontloading) one's background, orienting to higher purposes and payoffs for oneself and others, and then sequencing activities to build expert understanding necessary for completing the projects to address the problem or issue. Take a look at Figure 7.2 for an example of a mental model. Although this particular mental model is about scientific inquiry, it nicely fits our own notion of inquiry across disciplines. Note that generating and refining EQs fits in the Exploration and Discovery phase.

■ FIGURE 7.2: MENTAL MODEL FOR SCIENTIFIC INQUIRY

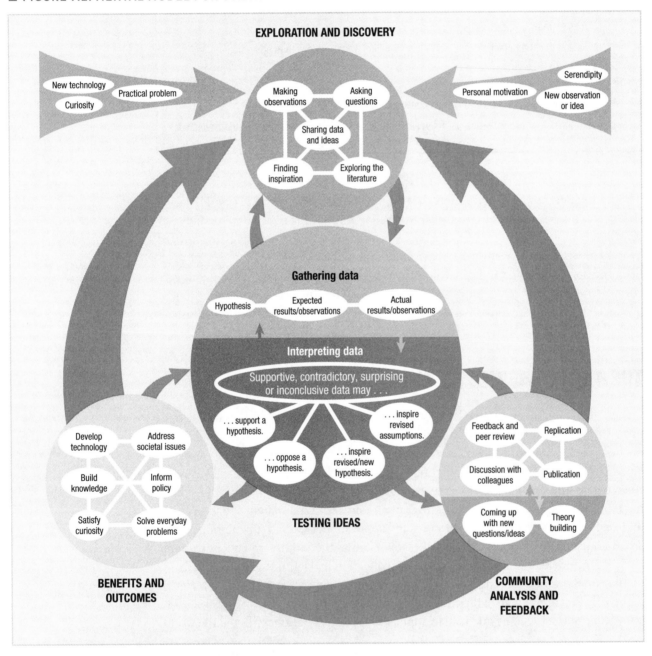

Source: The University of California Museum of Paleontology at UC Berkeley. Used with permission.

HOW ESSENTIAL QUESTIONS FIT INTO EMPOWER

EQs express and focus the *envisioning* of the learning process/unit. They direct attention onto the threshold learning goals and the application of learning. In this way, the EQ is also a tool of *mapping* in that it shows the framing, the reasons, and the starting point of the learning process, and indicates where the learning will go. Most significantly, EQs powerfully *prime* learning by activating personal connections and social significance, and *orient* learning by indicating the direction learning will take; the purposes, payoffs, immediate applications of the learning; and much more.

The EQ coherently connects to threshold knowledge goals, to the instructional sequence, and to the culminating projects. Therefore, changing the EQ will change the instructional sequence and the culminating projects and actions. Just as one example, the question *What makes a good relationship?* requires an argument of definition. If we revise the question to *What can we do to promote healthy relationships?* an argument of policy or problem–solution paper is required. Asking *What are the major threats (or supports) to good and healthy relationships?* will focus on cause and effect and require an argument of causation. In this way, teachers and students can frame EQs that will require, support, and reward certain kinds of learning goals and projects without any changes to required texts and materials.

Likewise, in our civil rights unit, we could ask *How can we best protect and promote civil rights?* This question requires an argument of judgment or policy to address. Or we can reframe to *What are the greatest obstacles to achieving civil rights (in our school, community, or country)?* This will focus on cause and effect and can be addressed at the immediate micro level, meso level, or macro level of classroom, community, or country. Adding *What can we do to overcome these obstacles?* would ask learners to come up with a problem–solution argument or policy action plan. And so on.

Sometimes curricular materials provide EQs. These questions often get at curricular goals, and sometimes get at enduring understandings and threshold knowledge. But they also typically fail to be edgy enough to engage students. So we must be cautious about prepared EQs. Skilled teachers often generate EQs for units and SQs for activities or readings, keeping the needs of their particular students in mind. Also, in guided inquiry, the learners must be inducted into how to generate essential questions in collaboration with the teacher and then with each other. It's essential to democracy, to watching television and reading the newspaper, to voting, and to making decisions at the personal level and grocery store that our students come to see the big cultural questions that are at play in our conversations, and how various people and interests are served or undermined by our answers to them. Therefore, we must apprentice learners to identify topics of cultural and disciplinary conversations and to generate compelling essential questions about these.

The "must-make move" activities in this chapter *prime* and *orient* by framing the unit topic with a personally compelling and socially significant focus, and activating what learners already know and care about in regard to this problem.

Principles of an Effective Essential Question

- Compels your students and makes them excited to pursue the inquiry (After all, the question is *for* them, and must connect them personally to the inquiry itself and to applications of the inquiry in the world.) (P-O)

- Requires and rewards learners to develop consciously held threshold knowledge that will help them meet standards and the expert disciplinary knowledge they represent (W-E-R)

What is a researchable question?

- Significant—personally and socially

- Relevant—personally and socially

- Debatable—there is no single obvious answer; there are different perspectives at play

- Data available—data can be found or developed

- Not so general as to be undoable

- Not so specific that it can be answered quickly

What must students know and be able to do to address questions?

- Read and compose a variety of texts and data sets

- Think and inquire like a historian, ethicist, scientist, mathematician, or other expert

- Think more as experts do in the professions/communities of practice

- Construct, represent, share, and use knowledge

ESSENTIAL QUESTIONS MOVE 1: COMPARING EQS TO DEVELOP CRITICAL STANDARDS

A great way to help learners generate EQs is to consider model exemplars, then compare or rank them. This process requires learners to formulate and practice using critical standards of what makes an essential question most powerful and useful, and primes them to generate questions that meet these standards. Our ultimate goal here is to prime and orient students to notice personal connections to conversational topics in current events, popular culture, literature, and the disciplines, issues, and questions they revolve around. Whenever learners watch the news, read a book, or are faced with a hot topic, we want them to be primed to consider the problem that is at play and how this could be framed as an EQ, and we want them to be oriented to see the stakes for different groups and how they personally might consider and address the central problems. Let's look at the process for comparing EQs:

Step 1: Introduce students to two questions related to your unit—one that tends to encourage information retrieval, and one that meets the criteria of an essential question.

> *What are the universal human rights?* vs. *What justifies and defines a "right" as universal, and how has this evolved over time?*

> *What do psychologists say are the three most important aspects of personality?* vs. *What are the most essential aspects of my "me-ness," and how does this compare to others in different times, places, and situations?*

Step 2: Ask students to identify the differences between the questions, and to identify what learners would have to do to answer each one.

Step 3: Ask students to identify the best EQ, along with their criteria for an effective EQ and SQs. In addition to any criteria they come up with for an effective and engaging EQ, ask learners how well the two EQs do the following:

- Honor a "reality principle" by addressing the learners' and users' concerns and points of view (how well the EQ primes learners)
- Help learners name what areas of personal interest connect to the text or topic (P)
- Provide emotive force, intellectual bite, or edginess that address learners' point of view (P)
- Help learners identify why and how the question matters to them right now, and to the world (O)
- Offer uncertainty and debate; are open-ended; are contended; legitimize multiple perspectives and possible answers; invite dialogue vs. monologue (O)
- Address the "heart of the discipline" studied and essential disciplinary knowledge (O)
- Are nonjudgmental and nonleading
- Are succinct and pointed
- Show that context matters, that concrete situations are part of problems and situations (O)
- Require diverse learners' mindful engagement and contributions (O)
- Lead to new questions asked by the students (O)
- Encourage learners to continue thinking about data and context (other people, eras, and situations) beyond this inquiry (O)
- Highlight that knowledge is constructed and that people play an active role in this construction (O)

A natural extension of the previous comparison activity is to rank longer lists of EQs and then revise less effective EQs to more nearly match the critical standards.

Step 4: The teacher and learners can brainstorm what makes an EQ less effective and what could be done to make it more effective. The teacher can model how to revise a question and then engage and mentor small groups of students to do the same. Common problems with questions include

- Merely information retrieval
- That they can be answered with a Google search and so are information driven; they do not require creating data or constructing new understandings
- Phrasing to encourage a yes/no answer, which does not require justification
- Begging the question (i.e., assuming a particular position or conclusion to be true)
- Leading
- Being too generic or, conversely, too narrow and specific

It may be important to highlight that EQs are *not*

- Answerable through information retrieval; they require operating on information to see patterns and implications, and often require developing new sets of data through critical inquiry on the part of students
- Questions whose answers can be understood quickly in one day or even one week
- Questions whose answers can easily be agreed upon

The following are some examples of *revising* problematic essential questions.

Topic: Civil Rights

Questions: How did we win the fight for civil rights? (Begs the question)

What universal rights do some groups (women, racial groups, ethnic groups) still not have access to? (Primarily information retrieval)

Revision: What are basic human rights, and how can they best be secured and protected for particular groups in the United States?

Topic: Identity

Question: Who am I? (Generic)

Revisions: What do I think is most worth fighting for? Where do I most belong, and why? What most makes me into me?

Topic: Relationships

Question: Where do our marriage customs come from? (Information retrieval)

Revision: What is necessary to developing a healthy, long-lasting, and fulfilling relationship in the 21st-century United States?

Topic: Survival

Question: Why is it bad that animals are going extinct? (Leading)

Revision: What flora and fauna will survive, and why?

Step 5: The teacher can provide students, working independently or in their learning groups, with additional examples of EQs that are not effective and ask them to revise them, or to generate SQs to effective EQs. It's also a good idea to create and continually update an anchor chart of questions that are and are not effective EQs (see Figure 7.3 for an example).

■ **FIGURE 7.3: QUESTION EXAMPLES: WHAT'S THE DIFFERENCE?**

ESSENTIAL QUESTIONS	NOT ESSENTIAL QUESTIONS
How do the arts shape, as well as reflect, a culture? How do the arts contribute to social change?	What common artistic symbols were used by the Inca and the Maya?
How can we prepare for the next pandemic?	What were the causes of the 1918 Spanish flu epidemic?
How is the food industry affecting our health and our environment?	Why are humans attracted to fat, sugar, and salt?
What are the causes and effects of poverty, and what can we do to address the problem of poverty?	What key event sparked the Great Depression?
What are civil rights, and how can we best protect and promote them?	What was the importance of Dr. Martin Luther King Jr.'s "I Have a Dream" speech?
Who is a true friend?	Who is Maggie's best friend in the story?

ESSENTIAL QUESTIONS MOVE 3: RANKING, THEN REVISING, EQS

Teachers can think aloud about a list of questions like those that follow, or a list generated in class. The think-aloud should highlight how critical standards are applied to evaluating and ranking the essential questions and, by extension, how they might be revised.

IDENTITY/PERSONAL COMMITMENT

- What is identity? (This is likely to be too general for learners. It is a deep issue of human psychology and may not offer them a way in. A specific SQ about an aspect of identity may offer a way in.)

(Continued)

- What do I stand for, and why? (Is this personally compelling? If so, does it get at the reasons behind personal commitments and their relationship to identity? If so, this could be ranked highly.)

- What is your identity worth? (This is too general and "far from home.")

- What do psychologists agree are the three most important aspects of personality? (This is information retrieval and oversimplifies expert knowledge.)

- Who am I? (This might be too generic to get learners started; how can it be made more specific and closer to home?)

- Why are you totally unique? (This could be interpreted as leading or as answerable with pat clichés instead of helping students to deep thinking.)

Students can then be asked to help the teacher with another think-aloud, and proceed to working in pairs or triads to evaluate and consider potential revisions of EQs from additional lists such as the following.

CIVIL RIGHTS

- Can teenagers help the fight for civil rights?

- What choices and options do we have in the face of injustice or oppression, especially when others hold the power?

- What causes people to act against the interests of others?

- How are genocides and mass violence made possible?

- How do individual choices inadvertently affect social justice?

- What determines who is included or excluded in any situation?

- Where do prejudice and bias come from?

- Under what conditions can art and music (or protest) work for social change?

LOCAL STUDIES

- How do we create a strong community?

- How can teens effect change within their communities?

- Do teens feel like valued members of their communities?

- How can young people be involved in community life?

- What is the importance of local knowledge?

- Where does local knowledge (of history, etc.) reside, and how can we get at it?

- Is the Boise River the lifeblood of Boise? (or any other local waterway, natural feature, industry, etc.)

- Why is it important to protect the Boise River? (or any other local feature, industry, etc.)

MATH

- Was geometry discovered or invented? (or any other kind of math)

- How can we best figure rates of decay? (or any other kind of problem)

- How much space do we need? (works well with area and geometry but also has more global meaning)

- How can we predict if we will win? (probability; has connections to social justice, gambling, etc.)

- How much will my decisions cost me? (financial literacy and probability; works well with rational number units, specifically in middle school with decimal operations as well as interest ideas)

- How do I get the better deal? (ratios and proportional thinking)

- What story do the data tell us? (data analysis)

(*Note:* The companion website at http:// resources.corwin.com/EMPOWER-secondary contains additional lists of EQs for ranking and revising from different content areas.)

ESSENTIAL QUESTIONS MOVE 4: GENERATING EQS FROM SCRATCH

Once students have experienced some of this kind of deliberate practice, they may be ready to identify and examine a topic, theme, or concept in curricular materials that can be usefully framed as an EQ. The teacher can model how to brainstorm EQs and SQs and begin involving learners (I do/you help and you do together/I'll help) in the process using the following strategies.

Students can use these prompts to generate lists of questions in small groups, share with the larger class (on charts as a Gallery Walk, for instance), and work to revise these questions (while visiting a chart with questions, in small groups, or as a class) to make them more personally compelling, socially significant, open-ended, and so forth.

5 *W*'S AND 1 *H*

Use the six typical queries that newspaper articles address, especially *Who? What? Why?* and *How?* The questions *Where?* and *When?* can also be very useful to think about the contexts that affect our answers.

Examples: *Who has been effective in promoting civil rights, and how did they do it? How has the most significant civil rights progress been achieved?*

(Continued)

(Continued)

QUALITATIVE/COMPARATIVE

Add a qualitative or comparative word such as *good, best, most, greatest, most effective,* or *most defensible* in front of the theme or concept. Questions about quality require us to make and justify our judgments. They also typically require defining a concept like "leadership" or "civil rights" and even "effectiveness" or "influence" and then to apply these definitions.

Examples: *Who was the most effective civil rights leader? Who was the greatest president/military leader/policy maker? What are the most influential inventions/movies/works of art in the area of civil rights (or any other area)? What characteristics do (the most) effective leaders have?*

ANALOGIES

Questions framed as analogies can be helpful to us, as they ask us to connect something we may know about already to something new, using our current resources to develop new resources.

Examples: *How do civil rights movements compare to public service advertising campaigns? How are cells and their operations like modern cities/cell phone networks/the water cycle?*

IMPACTS

To foreground why the question matters, select key words that elicit a focus on impact, effect/affect, how, why, if, and so on.

Examples: *How does the loss of civil rights protections affect different groups in society and society as a whole? How does the loss of a job affect one's future earning power and quality of life? How do/might genetically modified organisms affect the safety of our food supply?*

WHAT IF? AND *UNDOING* QUESTIONS

Ask *What if?* questions that pose alternatives to current reality or to history. It is a powerful move to "undo" history and to consider how things could be different, or to "undo" a text and ask how its meaning would be different if the author had made different moves or choices.

Examples: *What would U.S. and world history be like if the American Revolution had never happened? How would U.S. and world history be different if the South had won the Civil War, or the Nazis had won World War II? What if there were no public schools? What if there were no environmental regulations? What would happen if we lost our capacity to purify our drinking water?*

APPLICATIONS

Focus attention on how learning can be used and applied in one's personal life as well as in one's future work with the issue or in the discipline being studied.

Examples: *How should what we know about the history of enslavement/civil rights/ poverty in the United States inform our current thinking about government policy (about taxes, gun control, reparations, etc.)? How can we apply what we've learned to solve a particular problem like monitoring water quality/feelings of personal safety in our school and community?*

ETHICS/FAIRNESS

Ask questions with an ethical edge about what we should do with knowledge or what kinds of knowledge and applications we should pursue. Using the word *should* is often helpful. Stems can include variations on *To what degree is it fair to . . . ? How fair is it to . . . ? When should . . . ?* and *What are the costs and benefits of . . . (ethically/ functionally)?*

Examples: *Under what conditions should the United States consider imposing sanctions on countries that abuse human rights, and what kinds of sanctions would be most effective in specific cases? To what degree and in what situations should we use what we know about genetic manipulation, bioengineering, nuclear energy, nuclear weaponry, and other technologies? What are the costs and benefits of working to genetically modify or clone humans? Colonize Mars?*

IMPROVEMENT QUESTIONS

Both application and ethics questions can be phrased as improvement questions.

Examples: *How can we create a safer, more bully-free school? How can we make our school more welcoming and supportive to new students/refugee students and their families? How can we improve our school lunches to make them healthier?*

COMMUNITY CONNECTION QUESTIONS

How can we link community and global issues with the EQs? Connect current events and burning local issues to the topics you are pursuing. For example, where we live in the western United States, water rights are often in the news; this can lead to questions that are personally engaging and socially significant. And at the time we are writing this chapter, students are demonstrating across the country for stricter gun control. This can easily be connected to a study on civil rights.

Examples: *How does water availability and quality affect our community and quality of life? How can we rank the rights that different people, flora, and fauna have to fresh water? What are the effects of student protests and walkouts on the issue of gun control (or any other issue)? What protests are most effective at effecting policy changes, and why might that be?*

DEGREES/CONDITIONS/UNDER WHAT CIRCUMSTANCES

Adding *under what conditions* or *to what degree* or *under what circumstances* to a question can make it more complex and debatable.

(Continued)

(Continued)

Examples: *Under what circumstances might rebellion against established authority be justifiable? Under what conditions might government justify the invasion of personal privacy?*

VISUAL PROMPTS

Look at images related to the inquiry. These might be a museum of iconic photographs, short YouTube videos, or a collage of visuals. Focus on what you notice; try to identify personal connections, big ideas, contact zones/conflicts, and emotional charges; and then use these to brainstorm questions.

(Note: The Questioning Circle technique in Chapter 11 provides another way to generate "dense essential" questions requiring the use of learner background, newly developed knowledge from reading and classroom activity, and world connections/applications.)

Through all such activities, it is important to prime, orient, and apprentice students into the position and capacity of questioners who can notice topics and frame generative essential questions that require seeing multiple points of view. It's sometimes helpful to first ask learners to articulate their SQs relating to an established EQ and eventually to ask their own EQs that can guide thinking and behavior throughout learners' lives.

ESSENTIAL QUESTIONS MOVE 5: GENERATING EQs BY CONNECTING TO NATIONAL AND STATE STANDARDS

Of course, we all are required to teach to articulated standards. We are also required—at least ethically—to teach the threshold knowledge of our discipline so our students can proceed to be independent learners and practitioners who can use what we teach to pursue future studies and to navigate their way in the world. Hopefully, standards match up with threshold knowledge—and this is typically the case with next-generation standards. When they do not, we need to add threshold knowledge to the mix by teaching how to enact mental models of expert practice.

Here are some ways to use standards to help generate EQs:

- Ask an EQ that requires and rewards meeting a particular standard, or even several standards. Justify how the EQ will require and reward meeting that standard. For example, *What is a healthy relationship?* requires defining, finding examples and nonexamples, evidentiary reasoning, and inferencing in reading, all throughlines of the Common Core State Standards and Next Generation Science Standards. *What are civil rights, and how can we best protect them?* is a two-pronged question that requires the moves just mentioned and then an argument of policy or problem–solution.

- Reframe a required standard, topic, or text so that it matters to the students and to society.

- *Who will survive?* is a question of evolutionary biology that is compelling to learners and important for society and the environment. It requires meeting many standards for argument, evidentiary reasoning, and using crosscutting science concepts like seeing patterns and causality.

- Most national and state standards can help guide EQs. Think about why a particular standard was considered important enough to be a standard. Consider the heart of the standard and what is required to meet it. Ask: *What do my students need to know, understand, and be able to do to meet this standard?* Consider an EQ that invites and requires them to engage in this learning.

- Think about the central principles and the threshold knowledge of the discipline. What questions drive the discipline, research, and expert practice? For example, in social science: *How have disempowered people throughout history worked to improve their condition?* In political science: *What is the effect of different forms of gun control on personal freedoms and security around the world?* In public policy: *How can we figure out the effects of current gun policies on our school?* These kinds of questions will require and assist your students to think more like historians, artists, musicians, writers, and so on.

PLC connection

Work in teaching teams or departments to generate EQs for professional development, school improvement, or policy making, using ideas from this chapter.

POWERFUL PLANNING: ESSENTIAL QUESTIONS, DEEP UNDERSTANDING, DEMOCRATIC DISCUSSIONS

Knowing how to notice topics and reframe them into EQs and SQs is an expert skill set of all inquiry, research, and knowledge development in all domains and disciplines. It is also a basic skill set of democratic living. Essential questions not only work to build interest and to frame learning as a challenge to be addressed but also lead to conceptual understanding and strategic facility with *threshold knowledge.* EQs get at epistemological questions like *How do we know?* Questions of "why learning matters" and "how learning can be applied" get at the big *So whats?* that so compel learners. EQs motivate and support the

sustained engagement and deliberate practice over time that is necessary to deep learning and understanding.

When we frame our civil rights unit with the EQ *How do we best promote and protect civil rights?* our students see immediate personal and community stakes. The EQ is referenced every day, and students track what they are learning and how they will apply it. This creates the curricular coherence so important to all learners, but especially any who struggle. They can now consciously build capacity step by step and identify how they are getting smarter and more capable over time. Our EQ also directly leads to culminating projects and activities like arguments, historical timelines, dramas, and museum exhibits that develop and share understanding of the strategies, movements, and conditions that can produce gains in civil rights. The process also leads directly to social action and service learning projects that promote civil rights in our school and community (see Chapter 15). Our own students undertake these projects with a deep commitment, engagement, and joy. Essential questions are indeed "essential" to focus learning and give it deep purpose, and to transferring that learning to the ongoing conversations and activities that create knowledge and make a difference in the world.

Transferring Our Learning: What to Remember When Priming and Orienting Students' Activities Through Essential Questions

- Engage students in devising questions that matter in the here and now.

- Help students to experience how the question relates to their past, present, and future experiences.

- Prime learners for engagement by identifying contact zones—those aspects of a question that elicit debate and different perspectives.

- Identify and teach the threshold knowledge, disciplinary knowledge, expert strategies, and ethical considerations the question requires.

- Find real audiences for the problem-solving knowledge students create; share students' written, oral, and other projects that address the EQ as widely as possible both in and out of school.

Lesson: Rating and Revising Essential Questions

Unit: How do we protect and promote civil rights?

ENVISION the destination
(Where are learners going, and why?)

GOAL *What kind of thinking is targeted?*	EVIDENCE *What product(s) will serve as proof of learning?*	MEASURES OF SUCCESS *What's the standard and quality-assurance tool?*	STAKES *Why will learners buy in?* *What's the "why" behind the learning?*
✓ Application of skill/strategy ✓ Self-assessing/reflecting	✓ Performance assessment: Open-ended essay/writing, products (e.g., role-audience–format-topic [RAFT]), concept map ✓ Structured/unstructured observation	✓ **SIMPLE:** √−, √, √+ on levels of achievement generating essential questions ✓ **CHECKLIST:** Assess if product contains essential characteristics/features	Use ESSENCE as a guide for buy-in. Your lesson should have one or more of the following: ✓ E-S: Emotional spark/salience (i.e., relevance) ✓ S-E: Social engagement (i.e., collaboration) ✓ N: Novelty (i.e., new concepts and skills) ✓ C-E: Critical/creative exploration opportunities
Generate essential questions for a unit's cultural or disciplinary conversation, problem, or issue so that the unit topic is framed as a productive challenge to be addressed or problem to be solved. Generate subquestions of the essential question that are personally compelling and socially significant.	1. Students generate essential questions and subquestions for multiple possible topics from the subject area, current events, and their personal lives. 2. Students generate possible essential questions and subquestions for the topic of civil rights.	Are the essential questions and subquestions personally compelling, and are they socially and disciplinarily significant? Do they require and reward the learning of threshold knowledge: major concepts and strategies useful across a lifetime? Do they point to significant culminating projects in terms of compositions, collaborative multimedia work, social actions, etc., that will address the problem framed by the essential question?	**E-S:** Students participate in generating personally compelling and emotionally edgy essential questions. **S-E:** Students collaborate in rating and revising questions. **N:** The strategies are likely to be new as is the notion of framing topics as problems to be solved. **C-E:** Learners apply this to their own reading, viewing, and life experiences.

MAP out the path to expertise/mastery
(How would an expert deconstruct and approach this task, step by step?)

TWITTER SUMMARY *(3 bullets max)*	MENTAL MODELS, PROCESS GUIDES	A MODEL OF GOOD WORK LOOKS LIKE . . .	DIFFERENTIATION AND LAYERING
Expert readers, thinkers, and problem solvers see texts and even events as turns in cultural or disciplinary conversations about salient issues and problems. Essential questions express these as issues to be considered or problems to be addressed.	Essential questions are personally compelling and socially significant. They organize the work of disciplines.	*This is a big debatable question without an obvious answer that is personally compelling and socially significant and will contextualize the learning of threshold knowledge.*	Levels of assistance: Assist peers to rate and revise essential questions Various groupings Multiple models provided, more mentoring as needed More deliberate practice mirroring mental model Continual procedural feedback

(Continued)

POWER through your lesson
(What is the sequence of initial major must-make instructional moves?)

PRIME	ORIENT	WALK THROUGH (and check for understanding)	EXTEND AND EXPLORE	REFLECT
Introduce students to two different questions such as "What are the five most important aspects of any person's identity?" and "What are the most essential aspects of my 'me-ness,' and how does this compare to others?" Ask students to identify the differences, and then ask them to explain what a learner would have to do differently to answer each question. Introduce a second set of questions closer to the unit topic. Ask students to identity the differences between the questions, and then ask them to explain what a learner would have to do differently to answer each question. Ask them which question is closer to what experts would ask, which requires more knowledge construction, and which would be most interesting for them to pursue.	FRAME today's lesson: "As we have been discussing, one of the most important skills an expert learner, a disciplinary expert, or a citizen can develop is the skill of framing topics as issues to be addressed or problems to be solved. "Today, we'll first learn how to generate the kinds of essential questions that frame the work that experts and disciplines do. "Second, we'll work on generating an essential question and subquestions that are totally interesting to you, that are important in our culture and everyday lives, that can frame our next unit on civil rights . . ." Students will consider the essential questions and subquestions that have been shared in the priming. Students will discuss what each essential question and subquestion would help them to learn; what kind of knowledge would have to be developed to answer each one; what kinds of culminating projects, social actions, and service learning could address each question; etc. Students will consider the purposes and payoffs of pursuing each question.	ASK students to brainstorm the criteria of a good essential question, based on their comparisons. CHECK FOR UNDERSTANDING: Students categorize their list of criteria and explain them. MODEL: Teacher provides a think-aloud of how he or she might generate a list of essential questions for another unit (e.g., on identity) and looks at major issues and how to revise. CHECK FOR UNDERSTANDING: Ask students, *What did you see me doing? What strategies helped me generate essential questions? Notice issues and revise to correct for these.* GUIDED PRACTICE: Small groups of students read through assigned sections of the ranking and revising essential question activities (see the companion website for lists of essential questions for ranking and revising). They then rank the questions, correct issues with questions, and choose which one they think would be the most effective essential question and which would be good subquestions. DIFFERENTIATE: If some students are struggling, provide more models, work with them to assist, or have other successful groups assist. DEBRIEF: In roundtable presentations, have students share, discuss, evaluate, and revise questions from peers.	DELIBERATE PRACTICE/ ARTICULATE CONSCIOUS AWARENESS: Small groups of students practice generating a list of potential essential questions or subquestions for the civil rights unit or a reading in that unit. Learners provide their own think-aloud as they generate essential questions and subquestions. Learners rate and revise the questions they have generated, identifying which one works best for them as an essential question and why, and which questions might serve as useful subquestions. Then learners provide a process analysis that reviews and describes what they did to ask essential questions, and how they monitored and self-corrected. Learners apply strategies for generating essential questions to current event topics in the newspaper or school, personal life issues, free reading books, etc.	Summarize what you learned. Why is it important? What are essential questions that are/could be pursued in other classes learners are taking—both in general and in particular units? How can you use what you learned in other classes, at home, in your favorite activities, etc.? HOMEWORK EXTENSION: Identify essential questions explored by a favorite movie, a favorite television series, newspaper articles, historical or scientific debates, etc.

online resources — Visit **http://resources.corwin.com/EMPOWER-secondary** for lists of essential questions for ranking and revising.

Chapter 8

PREPARING STUDENTS FOR SUCCESS

Priming and Orienting Learning Through Frontloading

> **ESSENTIAL QUESTION**
> How can we activate and build student interest and background knowledge to prepare learners for success with new challenges?

Earlier in his career, Jeff often dove right into a unit by asking students to read the first chapter of a book or play for the next day. He now knows that this is akin to pushing his own children down a hill on their first bike ride without a helmet or any preparation. He would never have done such a thing! Instead, he first made sure they had tricycles so they could learn how to pedal and steer. When it came time for a bike, there were huge training wheels. And when that momentous day came to take off the training wheels, he ran next to the bike as long as necessary to protect his daughters into success. He took all of the necessary steps to prepare his daughters to learn and master a new skill.

See *Lesson Plan Canvas* on page 127

In our civil rights unit, we do the same thing—we prepare our students for success by activating and building on their prior interests and background knowledge. Asking the subquestion *How does this school violate your civil rights, and what can we do about it?* primes students through an immediate personal connection to the topic of inquiry. We continue frontloading by brainstorming a list of all the ways our school might be said to violate civil rights, then move to our larger community and country. By then, we arrive at the version of the real essential question: *What are civil rights, and what can we do to protect and promote them?*

Because civil rights is a complex topic, we continue frontloading the unit with a survey (also known as an opinionnaire) that primes students' prior knowledge and orients the students by building background for learning about related issues. Through responding to statements related to civil rights issues, supporting their responses with evidence from the world and their own experiences, and then applying reasoning to the evidence, students are deliberately practicing evidentiary reasoning and data analysis. They are oriented to begin reflecting on the consequences and ramifications of issues and positions related to the essential question. This shows them that the inquiry is about them and about the world they live in, and that what they learn can immediately be talked about, thought about, and applied to their lives and the world.

Students will return to these responses throughout the unit and reflect on how the reading, writing, and discussion they engage in reinforces and/or changes their thinking about the statements in the survey. The statements in the survey allow students to connect the inquiry to their own immediate, personal experiences but also shift them toward thinking of the experiences of others through their reading of the news, discussions at dinner, hallway conversations, and so on.

Throughout the unit, we continue to use frontloading to prime, orient, and prepare students for success whenever we think a significant challenge is offered by a complex activity or reading.

HOW FRONTLOADING FITS INTO EMPOWER

Frontloading *primes* learning by activating prior knowledge and interests, and *orients* the learning for students by providing purpose and motivation for inquiry. We design frontloading activities to activate and build on prior knowledge and interest, to arouse more interest and curiosity about the topic, to bridge gaps, to begin addressing less developed conceptions, and to provide students with opportunities to begin practicing new expert reading, composing, and problem-solving strategies.

Frontloading also allows learners to experience small wins at the beginning of an inquiry as they prepare for success with more complex learning later in the unit sequence. Throughout our civil rights unit, we regularly ask students to support their reasoning with evidence from the text and their lives—when they read for theme in a series of images and support their analysis with evidence from the visuals (see Chapter 9), when they analyze symbols in their think-alouds of excerpts from *Number the Stars* (see Chapter 10), and when they write micro-arguments and provide feedback to their peers (see Chapters 13 and 14). We set students up to practice these expert strategies of applying reasoning to evidence through low-stakes writing and discussion in the survey frontloading activity.

The most powerful time to teach is *before* a significant new learning challenge is taken up. We need to prepare learners for success instead of waiting to remediate. No parents would ignore preparing their children for success with the challenges they foresee the children facing when they learn something new like biking, driving, or dealing with finances. Teachers likewise need to make sure learners know the purpose, payoffs, and stakes of the learning plan so that they can begin to develop the motivation and strategies for leaning in to the challenges that will inevitably come up. The process of frontloading is about exercising proactivity instead of reactivity. It's learning how to mindfully climb and descend the hills on one's bike, instead of picking oneself (and students!) up at the bottom of a hill after we've all already crashed.

SUCCESSFUL FRONTLOADING: A MENTAL MODEL

A successful frontloading activity will activate and connect to students' prior interests and background knowledge. These resources will then be recruited in ways necessary to prepare students for success with the next learning challenge. Further, frontloading sets the terms of the inquiry and debate, shows the stakes, illuminates the purposes and payoffs, and provides a template that can be returned to in order to consider how various characters and authors are weighing in and how personal attitudes and knowledge are being confirmed, deepened, tested, developed, and changed throughout the inquiry.

In this chapter, we show how frontloading strategies initiate the guided inquiry process by getting students to begin asking pertinent questions, seeing different perspectives, and practicing with the concepts and strategies of experts.

Principles of an Effective Frontloading Activity

- Activates and/or builds on the students' prior knowledge, interests, and personal connection to the unit inquiry question, theme, text, or topic (P-O)

- Works to motivate students for reading and inquiry regarding the inquiry question, theme, text, or topic (P-O)

- Sets personally compelling and culturally significant purposes for reading and learning (P-O)

- Works to focus and organize student inquiry throughout the unit (i.e., it can be continually returned to in order to help students set purposes for their reading; identify what authors, experts, and characters think; consolidate their learning; clarify what they are coming to know; and monitor their learning progress) (W-E-R)

FRONTLOADING MOVE 1: SURVEYS

Surveys are quick and engaging ways for students to "draw a line in the sand" to show what they currently think or feel about issues pertaining to the inquiry and essential question. Surveys also demonstrate that there are differing perspectives on the issues surrounding the inquiry—that the inquiry delves into a contact zone of contended positions. Surveys are great frontloading activities because they require, assist, and reward students to activate background knowledge and make connections to prior experiences and interests regarding the topic at hand. Surveys require consideration of alternative and contrasting points of view, developing social imagination. The experience also calls for students to support their opinions with evidence from their lives, which means they are practicing analytical thinking and evidentiary reasoning, two throughlines of next-generation college and career readiness standards worldwide (and skills we ask students to apply throughout our throughline civil rights unit).

(Continued)

(Continued)

Surveys provide students with opportunities to revise their thinking based on exploring multiple perspectives. As you can see in the civil rights survey provided in Figure 8.1, the survey can be returned to during and after reading to discuss how characters, authors, or historical figures might respond to the statements or to see how students' own thinking has been reinforced or changed by their reading and learning experiences. In this way, surveys work as a template for building and tracing changes in understanding throughout a unit and for monitoring the perspectives of other authors, characters, and oneself throughout the inquiry.

In creating the survey for our civil rights unit (Figure 8.1), we started by brainstorming a list of statements related to our inquiry. We were looking for statements that included clichés as well as different cultural values and ideas. We like to start by searching quotation sites like Bartleby (www.bartleby.com), The Quotations Page (www.quotationspage.com), or BrainyQuote (www.brainyquote.com) for quotes related to the essential question and/or themes. We then revise the statements to be more controversial by adding absolutes or qualifiers. Sometimes we also search news sites for current events related to the inquiry question and write statements related to what people are talking about around issues in the news.

■ **FIGURE 8.1: FREEDOM AND SECURITY SURVEY**

How Can We Best Protect and Promote Civil Rights?

Directions: Next to each statement below, write SA if you strongly agree, A if you agree, D if you disagree, and SD if you strongly disagree. After you complete this task, choose one item that you feel strongly about and write an explanation of your thinking at the bottom of the page. Be sure to support your opinion with evidence from people you know, the world, and/or your own experience. Consider how you can explain to others how that evidence supports your position (claim) on the survey item.

STATEMENT	WHAT I THINK (BEFORE READING/BEFORE THE UNIT)	WHAT AN AUTHOR, CHARACTER, HISTORIAN, SCIENTIST, OR HISTORICAL FIGURE THINKS (AFTER READING)	WHAT I THINK (AFTER READING/AFTER THE UNIT)
One person can't really make a difference on his or her own.			
If I see someone hurting or bullying another person, I should immediately move to stop it, even if I could be harmed.			
The government has a right to know what people are reading and posting so it may determine who might be a threat.			

STATEMENT	WHAT I THINK (BEFORE READING/BEFORE THE UNIT)	WHAT AN AUTHOR, CHARACTER, HISTORIAN, SCIENTIST, OR HISTORICAL FIGURE THINKS (AFTER READING)	WHAT I THINK (AFTER READING/AFTER THE UNIT)
Profiling, or searching people because they are of a certain ethnicity or religious group, should never be done.			
Everyone should have the same rights no matter what.			
Civil rights should not be automatic; they must be earned and deserved.			
You don't need to worry about the government looking at your cell phone data if you aren't doing anything wrong.			
People who are a serious threat to the government should be able to be held in prison without being charged.			
For the most part, people learn from the past and don't repeat their mistakes.			
It is okay to sacrifice the rights of one or a few for the freedom of many.			
Some people deserve to have their rights taken away.			
Select a statement that you feel strongly about and use it as your claim (what do you want others to believe?), support it with evidence from the world or your life (why do you say so?), and explain how the evidence supports your claim (so what?).			

Before finalizing the survey, we revise statements to make sure they are debatable, meaning it is likely that some students will agree and some will disagree, and also defensible, meaning there is evidence to support both for and against. We also check to make sure the statements are interesting in that they introduce a new, deeper, or more complex perspective about some angle on civil rights issues. You can also revise the statements so they are a fit for your particular students, always thinking about the best way to hook the interests of your students and engage them in conversations around issues that matter to them and the social worlds they inhabit.

FRONTLOADING MOVE 2: WHERE DO I STAND?

Where Do I Stand? (also known as Four Corners) works well as a follow-up to a survey but can also stand on its own as a quick frontloading activity. Like a survey, this activity primes and orients students through discussion of controversial concepts that they will explore in the unit. Students also practice complex processes like making claims, supporting reasoning with evidence, listening and mirroring, summarizing, and addressing opposing viewpoints and reservations to their own thinking. The process is also a powerful way to stimulate discussion and to motivate students to further explore emerging topics throughout the inquiry unit.

To do this activity, teachers can select two or three statements (from a survey or elsewhere) that might be particularly controversial for the students. Put four signs in the corners of the room: Strongly Agree, Agree, Disagree, and Strongly Disagree. Read one of the statements and invite students to go stand by the sign that reflects their response to that statement. Give students a few minutes to discuss why they chose that response with the others in the same corner. Invite one student from each corner to summarize why their group selected the response they did. Open a discussion, inviting students to respond to the other groups. You can also do this through discussion dramas such as a "radio show," which may involve students taking on various roles to share their perspective (see Chapter 13 on discussion strategies). During the discussion, invite students to move to another group if their thinking is changed by the discussion. We often invite those specific students to explain why their thinking was changed. Some examples of controversial statements follow:

Essential Question: *What are civil rights, and how can we best protect and promote them?*

- Children need their civil rights protected more vigorously than any other group.

- You can almost always trust authorities to protect your civil rights.

- If your civil rights are violated, the best course of action is to first address this with the person or group who violated them.

Essential Question: *How can we best deal with trouble?*

- A good friend will always tell you when you are wrong about something.

- The best way to deal with trouble is to ignore it if you can.

- You can't learn anything unless there is trouble; it's necessary to learning.

Essential Question: *How can we contribute to the sustainability of our planet?*

- The United States should be responsible for making sure other countries take action to reduce carbon emissions.

- It is absolutely essential to the future of our planet that everyone start using public transportation/recycling/eating only organic food.

- Nuclear power is the most environmentally responsible way to meet our energy needs.

FRONTLOADING MOVE 3: DRAMA/ACTION STRATEGIES

Where Do I Stand? is an example of a low-stakes drama or action strategy. Jeff's book *Action Strategies for Deepening Comprehension* (Wilhelm, 2013a) features a full chapter on drama/action strategies for frontloading. One such strategy is to use *trigger letters* (e.g., from an anonymous student suffering from bullying). Learners take on the role of guidance counselors, safety resource officers, or community members who brainstorm how they might help address the problem (this kind of in-role discussion is known as a forum drama and can be most useful for frontloading). Teachers can also write *scenarios* that introduce a story or cultural event related to the inquiry that students can role-play to explore how they would deal with that conflict or issue.

Primary sources, YouTube videos, and incident reports relevant to the inquiry can provide the premise for a drama frontload. For example, students can be cast in roles as American colonists who are seeing the Declaration of Independence for the first time and being asked in a town meeting, "What dangers and possibilities do you now face?" Some of the students could be cast as Tory sympathizers. What is their point of view? *Value cards* that correspond to the inquiry can be passed out to students. The values represented might include ideas like health, respect, friendship, wealth, competence, freedom, love, family, political power, fame, willingness to serve others, and artistic talent. Students are given three cards and asked to go around the classroom to make trades for the values that are most important to them. A discussion debrief about the motivation for the trades follows. How the trades relate to the unit theme (e.g., how they reflect values consistent with or at odds with civil rights) can also be explored. Then students are put into roles (perhaps as literary or historical characters they will read about) to redo the activity, later explaining how their activity and thinking has changed after being in the role. There are hundreds of such activities.

Drama/action strategies work when they are adequately framed (i.e., primed and oriented). Proper framing requires that students know

- What they are meant to experience and learn through the drama activity and why this is important
- The context and circumstances of the drama
- The roles and viewpoints the students and teacher will take on in the drama
- What is expected in the allotted time—how they will start and what deliverables they will produce (e.g., they will have traded for new value cards and be able to explain what informed their trades and what this reveals about their deepest values and commitments)

FRONTLOADING MOVE 4: SEE-THINK-WONDER

To start a See-Think-Wonder, we select visually striking and compelling images related to the topic of inquiry. The images are connected in a way that provides students with opportunities to notice patterns within each image and across the different ones as they view more images. When creating a See-Think-Wonder, we search the internet for compelling images related to our topic and/or essential question. Flickr (www.flickr.com) is a great site for finding free, creative, and provocative images. The Library of Congress (www.loc.gov) is another great site with lots of primary source images and photographs. Students can also always be asked to bring in, share, or post new images that they think contribute something related to the inquiry question. They can create a Gallery Walk or museum of images to stimulate further noticing, thinking, and wondering.

When students view each image, we have them jot notes on a notecatcher or in their writer's notebooks with the following prompts, which mirror the trajectory of inquiry—establishing facts, seeing patterns and relationships among the facts, figuring forth, and theorizing from what has been learned:

- What do you see? (data/key details)
- What does it make you think? (inferencing and explaining data/reasoning)
- What do you wonder about when you look at this image? (questioning for further inquiry)
- Write about an experience from your own life that this reminds you of.

A variation on this strategy is to have students do a quick-write response to political cartoons, paintings, YouTube videos, or other visuals about what they notice, why they noticed that (using rules of notice), and what that noticing makes them think and wonder. See Chapter 9 for more on Rules of Notice.

Figure 8.2 shows an example of a collection of images for See-Think-Wonder, and Figure 8.3 shows a See-Think-Wonder notecatcher, filled in with notes from viewing the images that relate to the resettlement of Japanese-American citizens during World War II in Figure 8.2.

■ **FIGURE 8.2: HOW CAN WE BEST PROTECT AND PROMOTE CIVIL RIGHTS?**

Image Sources: left: Pierce/Library of Congress via pingnews; middle: Hikaru Iwasaki/NARA via pingnews; right: Hikaru Iwasaki/NARA via pingnews.

SEE	THINK	WONDER
• Crowds of people with suitcases • People are nicely dressed • Trains • Newspapers	• They look unhappy • This reminds me of people getting on trains to concentration camps	• Where are they going? • Are they going willingly or being forced? • Was this in the United States or another country? • Was there a war? • What does this have to do with civil rights?

FRONTLOADING MOVE 5: RANKINGS

Rankings are another way to prime and orient learning. Rankings should relate to key issues, situations, characters, themes, questions, items, and ideas that will be raised in the readings throughout the inquiry. Rankings require reasoning because you have to justify the thinking behind the ranking. For example, in the ranking activity for leadership (see Figure 8.4), as students share their individual rankings, they should be prompted to explain what they are learning about leadership and how this is helping them progress toward an extended definition of leadership—what elements are definitely required, what traits are disqualifications, and so on.

■ FIGURE 8.4: RANKING: WHAT MAKES A GREAT LEADER?

Rank the following activities in order of those that require and demonstrate the most to the least "true" leadership. Be sure to consider: What makes you say so? So what?

_____ Secretary of class

_____ First-string basketball player

_____ Reporter for school newspaper

_____ Best grade point average

_____ Crosswalk guard

_____ Part in school play

_____ Member of ski club

_____ Community service organizer

_____ After-school job at fast-food emporium

_____ Volunteer at hospital

Source: Adapted from Smagorinsky, Johannessen, Kahn, & McCann, 2011.

Ranking scenarios is another powerful frontloading option. To create a scenario ranking, begin by brainstorming key situations, characters, themes, questions,

(Continued)

(Continued)

items, and ideas that will be raised in the readings for an inquiry. Then, decide on the area of focus for the scenarios. Ranking scenarios might focus on issues, scenes, or events in the readings (e.g., what makes a good parent for texts like *The Watsons Go to Birmingham* and *To Kill a Mockingbird*); descriptions of characters; or actual events that occur in the novel students will read. Teachers then write three to five scenarios. This part isn't easy, and it can be helpful to write them with students or colleagues. We try to make sure that each scenario has both positive and negative elements so that the ranking is debatable. We often revise scenarios after we try them out with students if one emerges as a clear winner or loser and we need to make them more debatable.

Have students rank the scenarios and then discuss in small groups or as a class. We have also used Where Do I Stand? as a follow-up to ranking scenarios by having students stand in the corner with the scenario that they ranked as highest or lowest. As students learn throughout the unit, they can revise their rankings and/or add elements to the ranking activity.

Scenarios are substantive but relatively short, so students can read and rank them quickly. These scenarios are longer than the statements from a survey or controversial statements, so they require different skills like identifying key details, summarizing, making inferences, and supporting reasoning with evidence from a text. It's important that there is no clear answer for the best or worst scenario so students must find data and apply reasoning to the data. It's also important to provide students with opportunities to discuss their rankings in various group configurations and revise their rankings based on their discussions (see Chapter 12 for more on using sorting/ranking activities in collaborative group structures).

As part of our civil rights unit, we asked students to rank scenarios before reading the story "My Son the Fanatic." An example is shown in Figure 8.5. You could use these for any other text exploring issues of going too far in literacy, science, social studies, or any other subject area. (This survey is adapted from student Rebecca Morlo, based on real events reported on in the news.)

■ **FIGURE 8.5: RANKING SCENARIOS: WHAT MAKES SOMEONE A FANATIC?**

Each of the following extracts from an article describes a person who might be considered fanatical. Read each extract and rank them from the one that describes the least fanatical person (1) to the one that describes the most fanatical person (5) according to your opinion. Make sure you can support your opinions by explaining what in each text makes you judge the person that way (evidence) and by explaining "so what?"—why that evidence leads you to that conclusion (reasoning). You'll be sharing your arguments in groups and then with the whole class.

1. A highly passionate Justin Bieber fan jumped on stage to be with his idol while Bieber was performing in Dubai. The man somehow got on stage and grabbed his idol during his performance of "Believe." He wanted to be as close to Bieber as possible. It was an intense moment as the singer and his security team tried to deal with the surprising attack. Bieber's guards ran to his aid and swarmed the fan, who threw down the grand piano on stage in an attempt to evade the security team, which was finally able to contain him. Thankfully, no one was hurt in the random attack.

2. Tyler Cruise, a passionate fan of the soccer team Arsenal, started a fight with other fans of a rival soccer team after Arsenal's defeat by West Ham on the opening day of the season. When his favorite team lost the game at the Emirates Stadium on Saturday, he and his friends went for a beer to The White Swan pub in Islington, just around the corner from the Gunners' stadium. When some

rival fans entered the pub, Cruise and his companions started a brawl because of their disappointment over Arsenal's defeat. Large groups of supporters gathered both inside and outside the pub while bottles, glasses, and chairs were thrown. Only when the police arrived could the fight be stopped.

3. Tyler Rigsby, of Columbus, Ohio, was hospitalized after a marathon-playing session of *Call of Duty: Modern Warfare 3*. His family reported that Rigsby had been playing for at least four days, possibly even five. Rigsby only left his room to pick up snacks, use the bathroom, and take a quick shower. On Tuesday morning, his mother, Jessie Rawlins, decided to bring him to his aunt's house. "It's like he was looking at me but he wasn't there. It was like he was looking through me," Jennifer Thompson, Rigsby's aunt, told WCMH. "We were talking and I heard a thump and I looked over and he just fell." Rigsby had collapsed. His mother said he turned very pale and his lips became blue. Then he collapsed two more times. Medics were called, and Rigsby was taken to the hospital where he had an IV attached to him to replenish his fluids. He was diagnosed with severe dehydration.

4. Mother of five Nannette Hammond has splurged over $494,000 on plastic surgery to transform herself into a real-life Barbie. Her procedures included a breast lift, lip fillers, Botox, veneers, semipermanent makeup, hair dye, nail extensions, and daily visits to her at-home tanning salon. To top off her look, she even has the pink Barbie car. Hammond, 42, from Cincinnati, Ohio, loves to show off her plastic look by uploading racy snaps of herself on Instagram—that are all taken by her children.

5. Ayla Özgül, of Oklahoma City, refused to remove her headscarf in school due to religious reasons. The school imposed the ban in the summer break to reassert the neutrality of the state school and counter what teachers said was rising Islamist radicalism reflected in the wearing of headscarves. The 15-year-old girl insisted on wearing the scarf because of her religious belief and did not want to give in to the force of the school, despite repeated meetings with different teachers and the principal. Schoolmates of Özgül started to get angry at her because she was not giving in and was constantly the center of attention in class. One day, when Özgül was on her way home, some of the girls in her class grabbed her headscarf to end this, and Özgül got furious and started to fight them. She only stopped when she got her scarf back.

POWERFUL PLANNING: FRONTLOADING, ENGAGING STUDENTS, PRIMING FOR NEXT STEPS

When teaching our civil rights unit, Jeff really looks forward to hearing students' responses to the surveys and experiencing the lively Where Do I Stand? discussion that follows—discussion that often continues as students leave class (and that comes up again and again throughout the course of the unit). He has even had other teachers approach him and ask, "What are you teaching right now? The students didn't want to stop talking about it when they came to my class!" When students are primed and oriented, the major hurdles to motivation and engagement and the productive struggle of learning have been overcome. Now it's go time. Even though many frontloading activities take a bit of extra time to prepare, they are always engaging and meaningful for students (and *fun*!). Perhaps most importantly, they prime and orient learners, preparing them for success, and are an essential element of powerful teaching.

Notice how the frontloading activities featured in this chapter are so flexible and easy to adapt that they could work in a variety of contexts and for a variety of inquiry topics. They work not only to activate and build interest but also to build conceptual understanding and support high-road transfer. We provided these examples to show the wide range of possibilities for priming and orienting learning by stimulating student interest, sparking curiosity, and beginning to build conscious competence and knowledge about concepts and procedures that can be built on through the assignment sequence. As you work to create your own frontloading activities, consider which moves will have the most impact for the learners in your classroom as well as which ones will best accomplish your learning goals.

Transferring Our Learning: What to Remember When Priming and Orienting Through Frontloading Activities

- Design activities so that they mirror the process of inquiry by engaging students in examining different kinds of data.

- Ensure activities require students to activate prior experience, knowledge, personal connections, and interests so these can be used as resources for learning.

- Connect activities to the deliverables that are required during the unit.

- Consider how the activity could be reused throughout the unit to reveal and track changes in understanding.

Lesson: Survey

Unit: How do we protect and promote civil rights?

ENVISION the destination
(Where are learners going, and why?)

GOAL	EVIDENCE	MEASURES OF SUCCESS	STAKES
What kind of thinking is targeted?	*What product(s) will serve as proof of learning?*	*What's the standard and quality-assurance tool?*	*Why will learners buy in?* *What's the "why" behind the learning?*
✓ Interpretation ✓ Explanation/reasoning ✓ Application of skill/strategy ✓ Perspective taking ✓ Self-assessing/reflecting	✓ Constructed (discrete task, long/short response, graphic organizer) ✓ Structured/unstructured observation	✓ **SIMPLE:** √−, √, √+ on discrete facts/skills ✓ **CHECKLIST:** Assess if product contains essential characteristics/ features.	Use ESSENCE as a guide for buy-in. Your lesson should have one or more of the following: ✓ E-S: Emotional spark/salience (i.e., relevance) ✓ S-E: Social engagement (i.e., collaboration) ✓ N: Novelty (i.e., new concepts and skills) ✓ C-E: Critical/creative exploration opportunities
Activate student background knowledge and make connections to prior interest. Begin supporting claims with evidence and reasoning to get at explanatory principles about what promotes and protects civil rights.	In speaking and writing, students can cite personal connections and social significance of civil rights issues. They can begin to support their claims with evidence from their lives and the world and reasoning that applies rules and values. In speaking and writing, students use sound evidentiary reasoning by connecting evidence to claims through warrants that apply values, principles, and/or expert rules of thinking, interpreting, and problem-solving.	The argument provider has a clear position on the response to each statement. Provides evidence from the world or life that answers the question, *What makes me say so?* (regarding the position/claim), and that is reasoned about (So what? Explaining the evidence). Listeners can mirror the claim, data, and reasoning back and hear corrections, demonstrating active listening. Listeners engage in conversation and are willing to shift their position if convinced by the evidence/reasoning provided.	**E-S:** Students respond to statements that apply to the inquiry on civil rights. **S-E:** Students engage in conversations in varied configurations (partner, small group, or full class). **N:** Being invited to openly respond to statements—agreeing or disagreeing—and justifying thinking is a novel experience for many students. **C-E:** This shows learners that the inquiry is about them and about the social worlds they live in, and that what they learn can immediately be talked about, thought about, and applied to their lives and the world. The process also requires students to make and support their opinions with evidence from their lived experience, which means they are practicing thinking analytically and using evidentiary reasoning.

MAP out the path to expertise/mastery
(How would an expert deconstruct and approach this task, step by step?)

TWITTER SUMMARY *(3 bullets max)*	MENTAL MODELS, PROCESS GUIDES, HEURISTICS	A MODEL OF GOOD WORK LOOKS LIKE . . .	DIFFERENTIATION AND LAYERING
Experts respond to statements they hear, deciding where they stand relative to the statement and supporting their response with evidence from their lives and the world and reasoning that reflects rules of thinking and interpreting used by experts.	• Claim, evidence, and reasoning for argument • Mirror and uptake for active listening • Development of conceptual understanding through reflective listening and response to many perspectives	*Crew or learners can identify personal connections and real-world applications of learning.* *Claim, data, reasoning—response to reservation for argument*	The number of items on the opinionnaire provides students with flexibility in time—some students may take longer to think about the responses to the statements, while others might respond very quickly. Students do not have to respond to all the statements in order to participate in the discussion. Further, the written explanation of one response provides students with an opportunity to rehearse their responses in writing before presenting in conversations with peers.

(Continued)

POWER through your lesson

(What is the sequence of initial major must-make instructional moves?)

PRIME	ORIENT	WALK THROUGH (and check for understanding)	EXTEND AND EXPLORE	REFLECT
Explain to students that today they will be discussing some statements that are related to the unit inquiry question, *What are civil rights, and how do we best promote and protect them?* or *How can we balance freedom and security?* Note that responding to these questions will help students begin thinking about their opinions on issues they will further explore during the unit and that those opinions are likely to be refined or changed based on reading, writing, and discussion they will do throughout the unit. Note that these issues are highly significant and objects of current cultural conversation.	Explain that students should read through the statements and then, next to each statement, write SA to indicate strong agreement, A for agreement, D for disagreement, and SD for strong disagreement. Ask them to consider what makes them say so—what is it in their experience that informs their response? Further explain: "After you complete this task, choose one item that you feel especially strongly about and write an explanation of your thinking at the bottom of the page. Be sure to support your opinion with evidence from your experience." Tell students they will be sharing their thinking with others, and they will test their thinking against the authors and characters they will read about during the unit.	MODEL: If students have completed a survey like this, it is likely they will not need a model. If they haven't, provide a model by responding to one statement and justifying with evidence and reasoning. Introduce the practice of engaging in a small group discussion with a focus on supporting claims with evidence and reasoning. Guide students to discuss their responses to the statements on the opinionnaire. Explain to students that they can start discussing their responses with a partner or in small groups (ideally 3 or 4 to a group). Remind them that they should discuss each statement, indicate their level of agreement (this is a claim), share what evidence from their lives makes them say so (this is evidence or data), and explain why this evidence supports their level of agreement (this is reasoning). Also let students know that they should feel free to change their responses if they are convinced by the evidence and explanations provided by their group members for a different point of view. Circulate the room as students discuss, providing questions, prompting, or redirecting students as needed.	DELIBERATE PRACTICE/ ARTICULATE CONSCIOUS AWARENESS: Lead a whole class discussion about a few of the more controversial statements that students seem to have a range of strong opinions on. This discussion gives them an opportunity to see what others think, to respond to reservations, and to see that people have different perspectives on the issue. It also offers them the option to change their mind based on more convincing evidence or more compelling or logical reasoning. For the Where Do I Stand?/Four Corners follow-up, select 2 or 3 statements from the survey that were particularly controversial. Read one of the statements and invite students to go stand by the sign that reflects their response to that statement (Strongly Agree, Agree, Disagree, Strongly Disagree). Give students assembled by each sign a few minutes to discuss why they chose that response. Invite one student from each corner to summarize why their group selected the response they did, providing evidence and reasoning. Open up to discussion, inviting students to respond to the other groups. Invite students to move groups if their thinking is changed by the discussion. We often invite those specific students to explain why and how their thinking was changed.	Process analysis that reviews and names the role of evidence in supporting students' claims. Ask students to return to their writing at the bottom of the opinionnaire. Give students this writing prompt: "Now that you have discussed these statements with peers using evidence from your life and hearing evidence from theirs, how has your response to the statement you selected been refined or changed? How did the discussion impact your thinking on the issue? What does this experience make you think about the role of evidence and reasoning in conversations you have outside of school?" As students are responding, remind them to discuss specifically the role of evidence and reasoning in strengthening or changing their claim. Collect their reflection as an exit ticket.

PART 4: WALKING THROUGH, EXTENDING, AND EXPLORING

ENVISION   MAP   PRIME   ORIENT   WALK THROUGH   EXTEND/EXPLORE   REFLECT

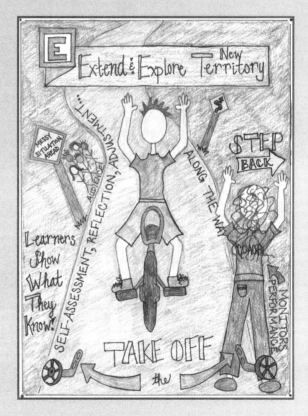

Chapter 9

SEEING IS BELIEVING—AND UNDERSTANDING

Walking Students Through With Visualization Strategies

> **ESSENTIAL QUESTION**
> How can we use visualization strategies to develop
> and then share our evolving understandings?

Many years ago, Jeff was a seventh-grade teacher doing the research into adolescent reading that became *"You Gotta BE the Book"* (Wilhelm, 2016). He noticed that a defining difference between his highly engaged and accomplished readers and those who were less engaged and accomplished was this: Successful readers visualized what they read and developed mental representations or maps of both event sequences and conceptual understandings. The less successful readers didn't visualize at all. As one boy responded: "What do I see when I read? I see nothing! Nothing but words!"

See *Lesson Plan Canvas* on page 149

In follow-up studies (Wilhelm, 2013b), Jeff found not only that using visual strategies to support reading led to greater engagement and success as a reader, but also that visualizing a character, scene, idea, or mental model of a phenomenon allowed even struggling readers to make inferences, engage in analysis, and answer higher-order questions. Jeff realized that he'd been essentially asking struggling students to reflect on experiences he'd never helped them to have, and that visualization was a necessary part of that experience. The struggling students had the capacity for higher-order thinking; they just hadn't been helped to master the prerequisites to it. Helping them to visualize was the answer to a vast array of comprehension issues.

In our civil rights unit, we want students to attend to how a variety of text types (novels like *Number the Stars*, speeches like "I Have a Dream," civil rights photographs, protest songs and political ads, etc.) are structured for meaning and effect. Since our own students often struggle with knowing what details are most important to notice, then connecting the details they notice so that patterns can be established and interpreted, we use visual strategies to introduce them to "rules of notice" that can be transferred to any other kind of text (Wilhelm & Smith, 2016). Visual texts are immediate and concrete and provide a great entrée to using and practicing rules of notice and how to interpret what is noticed. Because our learners struggle with identifying main ideas and themes, we have students produce picture maps that require them to depict what a text is about (topic), the patterns of key details, and then the main idea expressed by this pattern of key details about the topic.

Other visual strategies in this chapter are used to tie what is noticed in a text to an interpretation of some kind, like an assessment of a character's courage or state of maturity. In this way, visual texts help our learners do what experts do to interpret the deep meanings and effects achieved by a particular construction of text (i.e., the specific patterning of details and moves), and help them to develop social imagination as they infer character and character development.

VISUALIZATION STRATEGIES CAN APPRENTICE LEARNERS TO DEEP UNDERSTANDING

Visual strategies can assist and apprentice students to deeper understanding and expertise with all kinds of concepts, reading and composing strategies, genre and text structures, and various problem-solving processes (see, e.g., Wilhelm, 1995, 2016; Wilhelm, Smith, & Fredricksen, 2012). They can make abstract concepts and hidden processes immediately visible, concrete, and available to learners. And don't forget that experts capture and express their understanding and processes of meaning making through visual maps and mental models (Ericsson & Poole, 2016). Visualization strategies can therefore help us all with some of our most intractable teaching challenges because they provide such immediate and powerful models of how to understand a difficult concept or engage in a complex process.

But there's another layer. Take a moment to consider the types of texts you encounter in your everyday life as you read the news, search for teaching tools, scan social media, and otherwise go about your day. What are the different text types you encounter in your job and social life? News articles are usually accompanied by images and/or videos; online resources for teaching include images, graphical representations of information, maps, charts, and checklists; your social media newsfeeds likely contain a mixture of written texts with political cartoons, graphs, videos, and images. Reading visual texts, on their own and in conjunction with other texts, is a necessary part of literacy. We must understand how to read, critique, and compose these kinds of visual and multimodal texts in order to successfully navigate the information we encounter on a daily basis.

Cognitive research shows that learning proceeds from the concrete to the abstract, and from the visual to the nonvisual. And then, too, our next-generation standards ask learners to read and compose a wide variety of multimodal texts. The visualization activities that follow show how multiple modalities can be used to explore the topic of an inquiry, but also to apprentice students into new ways of reading, composing, and problem solving.

Universal design for learning (UDL) provides a path to designing instruction that best meets the needs of *all* learners, and visuals are an essential part of this process. Using visuals hits all three of the primary UDL principles: multiple ways for engagement, expression, and representation. Visualization strategies help learners who are more visual to use their strengths and build on these in ways that develop increased capacities with verbal and other modalities. Through their immediate accessibility, visual strategies can help engage English language learners and those who struggle with verbal language. Visualization also helps more verbal students to widen their learning repertoire and deepen understanding. Using visuals is a democratic move in the classroom for assisting all students to greater capacity and access.

And, of course, it's worth mentioning that reading and creating meaning through visuals can be great fun! Teachers and students will find the activities in this chapter to be enjoyable and engaging, all while providing meaningful learning experiences and developing expert strategies for reading and learning. (Note well that this is not true of all work with visuals, which can be "school-ish" throwaways instead of "tool-ish" work toward transformed expertise.) This enjoyment stems in part because most of these techniques encourage risk-taking and can be pitched within different learners' zones of proximal development. Students know they can complete these tasks; at the same time, the required mental processes move their thinking forward in preparation for more complex tasks in the future. More enjoyment comes from developing conscious competence and outgrowing oneself. Cognitive research shows that enjoyment and having fun while being assisted to meet a challenge leads to greater engagement and deeper learning (Smith & Wilhelm, 2002, 2006; Wilhelm & Smith, 2014).

The research also shows that a developing sense of competence is highly motivating. With visuals, one receives an immediate and visible sign of accomplishment (Csikszentmihalyi, 1990; Smith & Wilhelm, 2002, 2006; Wilhelm, 2013b). Hidden processes of expertise are made visible and available. All of this contributes to engagement and to evolving competence and capacity over time.

HOW VISUALIZATION STRATEGIES FIT INTO EMPOWER

Visualization strategies can be used to *prime* and *orient* learners by activating prior knowledge and piquing interest, preparing students for success by providing new necessary background knowledge and highlighting purpose; this is illustrated in the See-Think-Wonder activity in Chapter 8. In this chapter, we focus on visualization strategies that apprentice learners into new learning by providing a *walk-through* of deliberate practice of new skills. Remember from Chapter 1 that *walk-through* is the crux move of apprenticeship. Through visualization, the teacher can model for students and then mentor them to deliberately practice the learning of powerful concepts and processes. Students are able to develop and use new mental models of expertise that can inform reading, composing, speaking, and problem solving through more accessible visual texts before applying the mental models in more complex written or multimodal texts and data sets.

In this chapter, we show how must-make visualization strategies can work to provide practice with noticing and interpreting, as well as making connections and seeing patterns in order to make meaning of a text or any set of data. These strategies are crucial to providing the walk-through and mentoring pieces of apprenticeship.

Remember, too, that the hallmark of expert understanding is that it can be captured in a visualized mental model of a concept or a map of how to do a process. Understanding is visualized in a flow chart of a process, mind maps, analogies, or another model that translates and transmediates the understanding into a usable visual form.

Principles of an Effective Visualization Activity

- Motivates students to explore an issue related to the topic of inquiry and/or to deliberately practice a key reading, composing, problem-solving, or discussion skill (P-O)

- Supports students in immediately activating or building background around a conceptual topic and/or in practicing a skill (P-O)

- Assists learners to notice and represent key ideas and patterns of meaning in novel ways (W-E)

- Invites learners to move beyond a text/data set/experience to create new meaning (W-E)

- Provides conscious and deliberate practice with a threshold strategy and expert mental model of reading, composing, or problem solving (W-E)

- Moves students toward independence in understanding an important concept or applying an expert strategy (W-E-R)

- Supports students in mindfully using expert strategies and mental models for comprehending complex texts and data sets and developing conceptual understandings (W-E-R)

- Increases retention and moves students toward internalizing expert mental models through creation of a different mode (this process of translating meaning from one modality to another is known as *transmediation* and is a sign of deep understanding) (W-E-R)

- Gives students opportunities to reflect on and name their learning, and consider future applications (R)

VISUALIZATION MOVE 1: RULES OF NOTICE WITH VISUAL TEXTS: READING FOR MAIN IDEA USING THE TOPIC COMMENT STRATEGY

Rules of notice are general sets of cues that help us know what an artist or author wants us to notice and then interpret (Wilhelm & Smith, 2016). They help readers make moves like identifying key details in a visual text and then in other texts and data sets. We teach learners how to use what the noticed key details have in common to identify the *topic* of a visual text, and then teach them how to identify *comments* that the pattern of details makes about the topic. The topic is a general subject of the text (expressed in a noun phrase), and the comment is a main idea of the text (communicated by naming a pattern of key details and expressed by a verb phrase). Main ideas can always be expressed as topic comments. A complete, downloadable list of rules of notice can be found on the companion website at http://resources.corwin.com/EMPOWER-secondary.

Here's what the process for rules of notice with visual texts looks like:

Step 1: Provide a visual; model using the rules of notice to identify key details. Ask: *What are the key details in this picture, and how do we know?* (This is a literal-level, or "on the lines," question; see Chapter 11 for more about questioning.)

Step 2: Review how rules of notice direct attention to what is most important: generalizations/direct statements of meaning, calls to attention, ruptures/ surprises, reader response triggers, and so on. (See Smith & Wilhelm, 2016, for additional model lessons like this using iconic paintings and photographs, and modeling how to use rules of notice to direct attention; see also Chapter 10 for an overview of rules of notice.)

Step 3: Model identifying a topic of the text by considering what all the details have in common. Ask: *What is a general subject or topic/topic of conversation that all of the most significant details pertain to?* (If students struggle, we might tip them off to the context: for example, that this is a photo of the integration of the Little Rock public schools.)

Step 4: Model looking for how the key details are structured and patterned to communicate meaning. Ask: *What are the patterns of details about the topic?* (inferring by figuring forth and connecting dots into various patterns; see more in Chapter 11 about these "between the lines" questions). Bonus question: *How do we know these are the most crucial details and crucial patterns?*

Step 5: Model identifying a comment that is being made about the topic through the patterning of key details. Ask: *What is a topic comment or point about the topic expressed by the pattern of details?* This is a "between the lines" question: *What implicit point is being made about the topic? And beyond the lines?* (topic comments/generalizations about the world expressed by the text).

A rules of notice think-aloud, described in Chapter 10, models how to use the rules to notice key details and then to identify topics, and how details are organized to make a comment about a significant textual topic. By extension, this process of noticing patterns of significant data and "figuring forth" from these patterns is the basis of all evidentiary reasoning and inferencing.

In creating this rules of notice visualization activity for our civil rights unit, we began by searching for iconic images related to civil rights. Our goal was to select an image that required students to do a close reading in order to select key details, name a topic based on what the key details have in common, and then identify a comment (theme or main idea) being made about the topic based on the patterns across key details. Then we narrowed the images by focusing on ones that were particularly compelling and also sufficiently complex so that students had plenty of details to process and analyze.

(Continued)

We used the infamous "Little Rock Scream" photo (Figure 9.1), but you can use any photo that has a lot of details for students to analyze. In this photo, a young black woman is walking to Little Rock Central High School on September 4, 1957, clutching her books to her chest, with a crowd of yelling, jeering white people surrounding her. When viewing this photo, students might focus their analysis on the two central figures in the image (the rule of notice here is a call to attention through positioning), noticing the contrast between the seemingly calm demeanor of the black woman in the forefront and the enraged expression of the white woman behind her (the rules of notice here are rupture—a shift or surprise—through contrast, and reader response through emotional charge). The three figures closest to us in the image are carrying books, and those farther away are not (more rules of rupture). Other students might focus on the faces of others in the crowd (some are stoic, others are distracted, and some even seem to be enjoying themselves; the accumulation of contrasting details is a rule of notice through rupture) or even the details of the neighborhood behind the crowd (these are general calls to attention about setting, which situates the action).

■ FIGURE 9.1: THE SCREAM IMAGE

Source: Will Counts Collection: Indiana University Archives.

As a follow-up to this lesson, we would provide a second related visual (or even several related visuals) connected to the inquiry topic and model how to identify commonalities and contrasts between the visuals and how they might work together to convey a more complex theme. We would eventually move on to modeling and mentoring students through the topic comment process with short written texts and numerical data, eventually having them apply the strategy with a longer written text (full articles, short stories, or an entire novel).

VISUALIZATION MOVE 2: PICTURE MAPPING

A picture map requires students to notice key details from a text and the connections among these key details and then to visually represent the details, their overall patterning, and, most importantly, the meaning (topic comment) this patterning of details implies (Wilhelm, 2013b). The details students are asked to include depend partly on the purpose of the inquiry: the key concepts they are learning in the unit that are necessary to addressing the inquiry question.

Using the picture map, learners *walk through* the skills of (1) identifying key details and capturing the connections among them in order to (2) identify topics, then (3) identify patterns of key details in order to identify main ideas and make deeper meaning of the text. Over time, the teacher should gradually scale back support for creating picture maps after students have had opportunities to practice in varied contexts with varied levels of support. For example, early on the class can work together with the teacher's direction to create one picture map for a shared reading, then students can create picture maps about the same or a new text in small groups or partners, and then they can create picture maps about different texts in small groups, jigsawing to teach others about what they have read. Eventually, learners can create individual picture maps in response to texts they read. When they can do so, they demonstrate proof positive that they can read for main ideas and justify these with evidence from across a text, an accomplishment that less than 10 percent of our graduating seniors currently achieve.

Here's what picture mapping looks like, step by step, followed by examples of different types of picture maps:

Step 1: Invite students to mark or list each key idea about the topic as they read, paying attention to the key detail clues that have been studied:

- Calls to attention
  - Titles, direct questions, emotional charges, repetition
  - Quotes, lists, numbers
  - Positioning: First and last sentences of the text, and of paragraphs, which often signal a new key idea
  - Highlights, italics, bullets, bold print
- Direct statements of meaning/generalizations
- Ruptures: Surprises, shifts, changes in focus or emphasis
- Your intense responses and questions as a reader

Step 2: Remind students to determine the topic of their reading by identifying what all the key details have in common:

- Create a drawing that symbolizes the topic with a *visual* (no words allowed!).
- Symbolize each key idea with a picture or a symbol—do this as simply as you can!
- Show the relationships and the patterns of the key details.

(Continued)

Step 3: Once students feel more comfortable, they can

- Demonstrate several key ideas with one symbol or picture
- Show connections between ideas or progressions of ideas to display the organization or structure of the text (e.g., through a timeline, flow chart, family tree, or Venn diagram)

Step 4: Have students identify the main idea (topic comment) expressed by the article; in other words, have them show what all the key details work together to communicate, and create a symbol of that main idea.

Step 5: Invite students to share their picture map and tell someone else what each picture/symbol means and how the pattern of details works toward communicating a main idea. They should ask their partners what they think and get procedural feedback.

Step 6: Reflect: What are the actions that follow for us based on what we have learned?

PICTURE MAP FOR INFORMATIONAL TEXT, ESSAY, OR ARTICLE

Picture maps are particularly powerful for nonfiction texts in supporting students in the expert mental model of determining main ideas based on identifying key details and topics (what all key details pertain to), then noticing and interpreting the underlying structures and connections between key details about the topic.

Figure 9.2 shows a student picture map for the article "Teen Snooze Time." The Zs at the top identify the topic of sleep, the left-side images show the key details about what follows when you don't have enough sleep, the right-side images reflect getting enough sleep, and the < symbol demonstrates both the text organization of compare/contrast and the topic comment that *Getting enough sleep* (topic expressed in noun phrase) *leads to greater health, productivity, and quality of life than sleep deprivation* (comment about the topic expressed in verb phrase).

■ **FIGURE 9.2: PICTURE MAP FOR "TEEN SNOOZE TIME"**

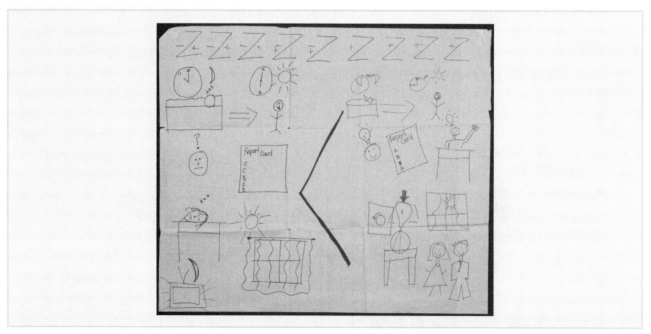

PICTURE MAP FOR NARRATIVE TEXT (SHORT STORY, NOVEL, OR EXCERPT)

Picture maps for novels or short stories can be used to divide and conquer or jigsaw (see Chapter 12 for more on jigsaws) key topics within a longer text to explore the role of various ideas, motifs, themes, or recurring topics. For example, in our throughline unit on *Number the Stars*, we focus on civil rights and our essential question, but teachers might also want to have students explore other themes/topics in the text. To do so without taking up too much class time, students could be divided into groups to create picture maps for various topics/themes explored in the novel, dividing and conquering a wide range of topics such as friendship, courage, identity, lies/dishonesty, fear, and so on.

In the picture map in Figure 9.3, cultural traditions of importance from *Things Fall Apart* were portrayed. Students were challenged to include an important quote from the book about cultural tradition and to use color to emphasize meaning. The student who created this is expressing that cultural traditions (topic) impact the decisions people make in their lives in both good and bad ways (comment).

■ **FIGURE 9.3: PICTURE MAP FOR CULTURAL TRADITIONS IN** *THINGS FALL APART*

PICTURE MAP FOR SUMMARIZING A UNIT

At the end of a unit, a picture map can be created to summarize the learning from various texts and experiences throughout the unit. The picture map in Figure 9.4 is a summary of different texts about censorship. The students are expressing that the topic is the First Amendment and freedom of speech, and the comment is that the problems of applying the First Amendment to censorship issues are just getting worse and are "tearing our country apart!"

(Continued)

(Continued)

■ FIGURE 9.4: CENSORSHIP PICTURE MAP

EXTENSIONS FOR ANY PICTURE MAP

- Find quotes to support the key details, topic, or theme you pictured.

- Provide a meaningful title for your visual.

- Present your picture map to another group, explaining how your picture map captures the key details, topic, and organization of the text, and how those work together to create deep meaning (main idea/topic comments) and effect.

- Create a Gallery Walk of picture maps and have viewers identify the topic picture, key details, pattern, and topic/comment/theme pictures.

- Jigsaw reading different texts and share picture maps to represent what you have learned that relates to the inquiry. Use a notecatcher to capture what you learn about the inquiry from different picture maps.

VISUALIZATION MOVE 3: THE FEVER CHART

A fever chart (also called a time-series chart) is a graphical representation of how a variable changes over time. The purpose of a fever chart assignment is to track important changes in a character, situation, force, or concept over the course of reading a text or a series of texts. The fever chart tracks the evolution of a character (or idea) through a journey by helping students identify important moments in each character's narrative in real time and the causes of particular changes or movements. The cause of change, in return, offers valuable cues to theme and an author's generalization about life.

When creating fever charts, students should be positioned as designers. Fever charts can be designed to track a variety of elements in a text—relationships between characters, mental and emotional changes for individuals, crises and stress levels, progress toward a goal (like achieving civil rights or justice), family status, level of power, and so on. Once students have selected the element(s) they will track, they set up a visual with a y-axis and an x-axis. On the y-axis, they place a scale that relates to their chosen element, and on the x-axis, they place a measurement of time (chapters, paragraphs, passage of time, changes in situation/setting, etc.).

This strategy can be used to track literary elements like character, setting, and plot, but also to track concepts, forces, and trends in other content areas. The process for creating the fever chart can be adjusted to give students opportunities to apply the expert mental model they are focusing on in the unit of study. For example, pausing at selected points in the text to make predictions for future data points requires them to do so based on data trends they have noticed so far in the reading, a key strategy for reading a text or indeed any data set.

Here are the steps for helping students to create their own fever charts:

Step 1: Based on purpose, text, and available time, decide if students will create a simple or complex fever chart. (Once students are familiar with the technique, we favor the complex charts.) And decide on grouping configurations (e.g., small groups, partners, or individuals).

Step 2: Articulate the expert mental model or skills students will apply in creating their fever chart (typically, this involves analyzing and inferring, seeing patterns and relationships, identifying cause and effect or problem–solution trends, etc.).

Step 3: Brainstorm with students a list of elements they could track over the course of reading one text or multiple texts and why this would be worth tracking.

Step 4: Provide a model for students, or have them help you to create one. For the model, students can create a fever chart based on personal experience, like levels of stress in a school day. If this chart is related to the unit, so much the better!

Step 5: Support students in selecting what elements to track in their fever charts and in justifying what might be learned through tracking of the relationship between these elements.

Step 6: Support students in deciding what will be represented on the x- and y-axes. Articulate what type of data students will use to support where points are placed on the chart (direct quotes from the text, paraphrased evidence, inferences from data, etc.).

As always, and consistent with culturally responsive teaching and restorative practice, students can first do a personal example, such as a fever chart of their energy or stress level throughout a school day or school year, their feelings of esteem or success over time, or their civil rights status over time. Students can then track the changes in a chosen character or concept over the course of a text or series of texts (e.g., the level

(Continued)

of Annemarie's courage throughout *Number the Stars* [Figure 9.5], or Hamlet's level of sanity [Figure 9.6]). Students can draw a quick fever chart such as those shown in Figures 9.4 and 9.5, or a more complex chart that requires them to provide specific textual examples to support the placement of items and to explain causes for character change.

■ **FIGURE 9.5: FEVER CHART FOR *NUMBER THE STARS***

Here is a basic example of a fever chart tracking Annemarie's courage throughout *Number the Stars*. Students are asked "What makes you say so?" to help them cite data for where they plotted the points on the chart.

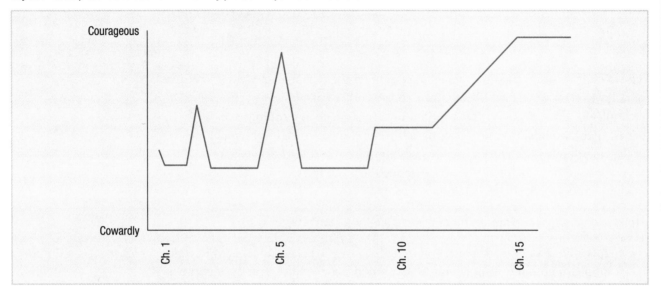

■ **FIGURE 9.6: FEVER CHART FOR *HAMLET***

Here is a basic example of a fever chart tracking Hamlet's sanity over the course of the play, but the basic idea can be expanded and modified in a number of ways.

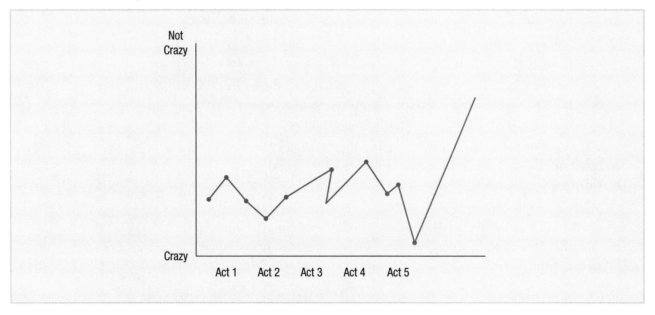

The fever chart format supports students in representing the progression of changes in the chosen aspect throughout a reading. They can also see relationships between two salient elements as well as other patterns, which can motivate them to explain patterns that may promote understanding or be revealing of theme and main idea. Charts such as those for Hamlet and Ophelia, or for Annemarie and a civil rights figure such as Martin Luther King Jr., can be compared to see what they reveal about a particular theme like dealing with stress, or about how character can promote civil rights.

Consider, too, using fever charts in other disciplines, such as the following:

Historical Texts:

- Relationship between the writer or speaker's emotion/tone and the metaphors used
- Relationships between entities involved in any kind of conflict, issue, or alliance
- Strength of political parties or social trends over time tied to events and other causes
- Strength of the economy over time related to various events and forces
- Relationship between technology (or other forces and innovations) and overall progress or social regression on various metrics like health, psychic health, and bullying

Scientific Texts:

- Scientific theories over time (e.g., about evolution or climate change)
- Scientific progress over time (e.g., in terms of effective medical care)
- Relationship between technological invention and various kinds of progress or regression, like environmental degradation

VISUALIZATION MOVE 4: GRAPHIC ORGANIZERS FOR ORGANIZING INFORMATION

A graphic organizer, when properly used, is an expert strategy to *walk through* the process of purposefully selecting information, applying the organizer to see categories and analyze relationships, and then planning forward for how the information can be organized and represented in writing or speaking. Graphic organizers can be used during reading to identify and organize key information, as a place for note-taking during class discussions or activities, and/or as planning tools for an essay or other culminating product. Many easily accessible graphic organizers are available in curricula, in books, and on the internet, and they are easy to create based on the specific skills or expert mental model you are focusing on in your unit of study.

What's most important is that the graphic organizer you select or create is used *to do work*. Graphic organizers are too often used as a throwaway project or to mirror presented information; however, it's important to remind ourselves and our students that a graphic organizer can be a transformative knowledge artifact that gets work done

(Continued)

(Continued)

for developing understanding and to support the composing process. In this section, we highlight how graphic organizers can be used toward specific knowledge-making purposes (vs. repeating what is already known) and making the knowledge internally persuasive instead of authoritative.

The following steps are useful when teaching students how to use a graphic organizer:

Step 1: Identify the purpose of your graphic organizer. What information will students need to gather and organize to meet the purpose? (E-M-P-O)

Step 2: Verify that the graphic organizer aligns with instructional purposes and expert mental models for text and data structuring (describing, defining, sequencing, comparing, classifying, multiple causality/cause and effect, etc.). (P-O-W)

Step 3: Walk students through the graphic organizer, explaining how to use it and modeling an example of how you choose and enter data. Foreground the purpose and payoff of using the graphic organizer to both notice and organize data into a particular thought pattern to answer a question or to reveal data patterns. (P-O-W)

Step 4: Provide students with the support they need to design and complete the graphic organizer (or do another one on their own), moving from collaborative partner or group work to individual work. (W)

Step 5: Make a plan for supporting students in interpreting what the graphic organizer reveals, and moving information from graphic organizer to creating a product. (W-E)

Step 6: Reflect with students on how graphic organizers can be used in future situations to reveal data patterns. (R)

Jerome Bruner (1986) argues that "To perceive is to categorize, to conceptualize is to categorize, to learn is to form categories, to make decisions is to categorize" (p. 13). What he means is that *each kind of informational text structure embodies a specific pattern of thinking with and through categories.* Teaching students how to understand, produce, and use informational text structures means that we are teaching them how to think with these categorical patterning tools.

Graphic organizers are tools for helping to understand and use such structures of thought. Graphic organizers mirror the ways experts come to see patterns and express them. Each specific pattern for thinking with and through categories is a kind of mental model. Learning each of these models gives students a unique and powerful way to organize data and to put those data to work. Figure 9.7 walks you through some basic graphic organizers.

In *Get It Done* (Wilhelm et al., 2012), Jeff and his co-authors explore how basic graphic organizers reflect specific patterns of thinking.

TASK	CENTRAL QUESTIONS	TOOL/PICTURE
Definition	How can we define this term, idea, or concept? How can we define it in a context of use?	Frayer Chart Circle Map
Description	What adjectives, specific clusters of adjectives, or adjectival phrases would best describe this thing?	Bubble Map
Comparison	What are the similar and different qualities of two things? Which qualities are most salient or significant in this context, and why?	T-Chart; Venn Diagram; Double Bubble Map
Classification	What are the coordinating and subordinating categories of this topic? What are some individual examples of each?	Issue Tree or Tree Map/Concept Map
Sequencing	What is the sequence of events? What are the steps in a process?	Flow Chart

(Continued)

■ **FIGURE 9.7: (CONTINUED)**

TASK	CENTRAL QUESTIONS	TOOL/PICTURE
Process Analysis	What are the causes and connections behind a sequence?	Flow Map of sequence + sub-boxes with causes 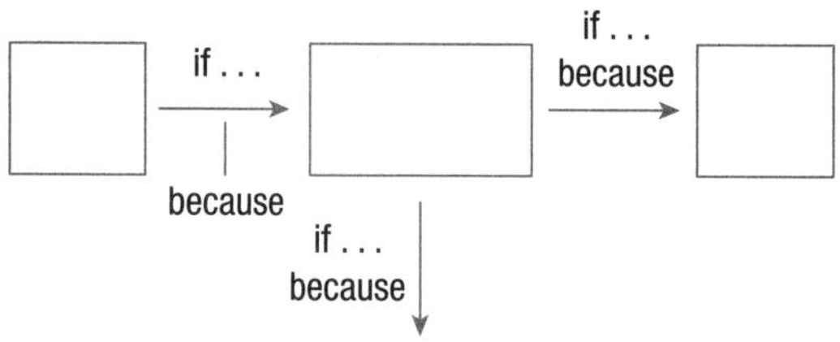
Analogizing	What is a powerful analogy or guiding metaphor to connect the known to the new?	Bridge or Teeter-Totter Map 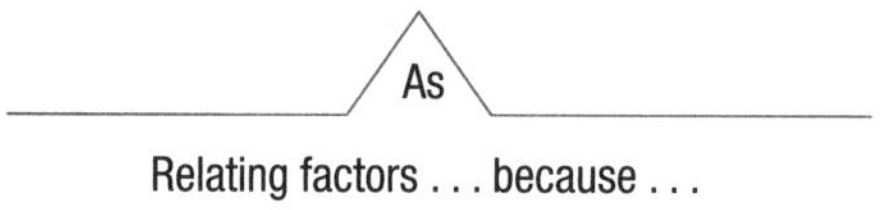 Relating factors . . . because . . .
Seeing Relationships	How are the qualities of different examples related? How are they explanatory of different effects?	Semantic Feature Analysis 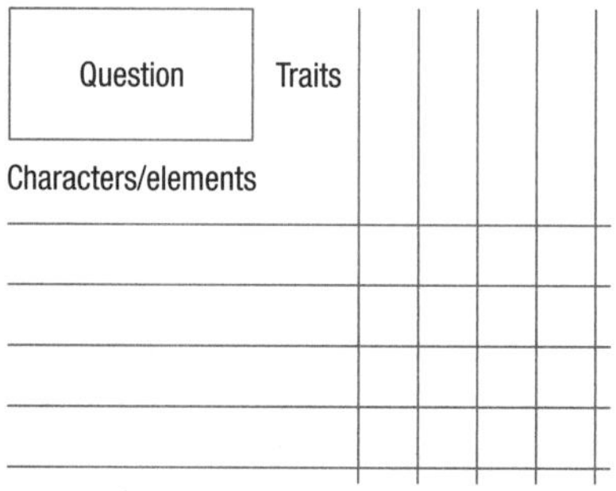
Causality	What are the multiple causes and effects of any outcome?	Multi-Flow Map 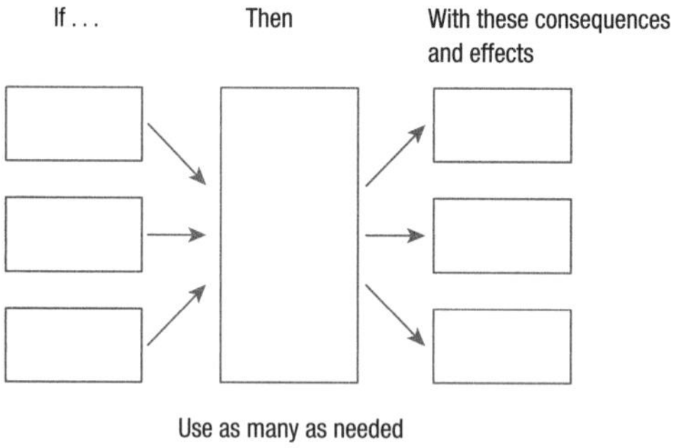 Use as many as needed

You can and should move beyond the basics and experiment with graphic organizers to get even more specialized kinds of work done. Following are two additional options that may serve as inspiration for how you can adapt graphic organizers to apprentice students for your specific purposes.

GRAPHIC ORGANIZER FOR ANALYZING SETTING

The graphic organizer shown in Figure 9.8 is set up as concentric circles to illustrate how each level of setting is nested within a larger setting, and that these levels of setting interrelate and affect each other in various ways that invite or disinvite certain kinds of character activity (Smith & Wilhelm, 2009).

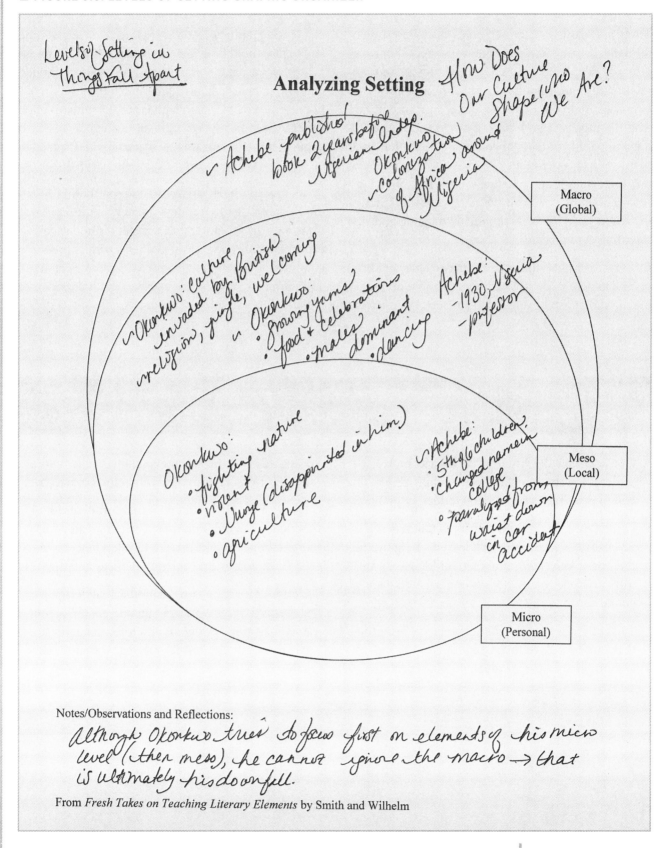

Analyzing Setting

Levels of Setting in Things Fall Apart

How Does Our Culture Shape Who We Are?

~ Achebe published book 2 years before Nigerian Indep.

Okonkwo colonization of Africa around Nigeria

Macro (Global)

~ Okonkwo: Culture invaded by British
~ religion, jingle, welcoming
~ Okonkwo: growing yams
• food & celebrations
• males dominant
• dancing

Achebe: -1930, Nigeria -professor

Okonkwo:
• fighting nature
• violent
• Nwoye (disappointed in him)
• agriculture

~ Achebe: 5 th. 6 children, changed name in college
• paralyzed from waist down in car accident

Meso (Local)

Micro (Personal)

Notes/Observations and Reflections:

Although Okonkwo tries to focus first on elements of his micro level (then meso), he cannot ignore the macro → that is ultimately his doonfall.

From *Fresh Takes on Teaching Literary Elements* by Smith and Wilhelm

POWERFUL PLANNING: MAKING MEANING WITH VISUALS

There are many ways to use visuals to support student thinking, develop new strategies and ways of knowing, promote deeper conceptual understanding, and represent and share what has been learned. It's essential to make sure that the process and product are in line with the processes and skills of expert meaning making and with instructional goals. Students often need permission to experiment with a variety of approaches, but once they have practice with visual tools and representations, they can come up with all kinds of interesting and fun ways of visually tracking and representing complex ideas.

In our civil rights unit, we use the reading of visual images to help students learn rules of notice and interpretation that can be applied to any text. We use fever charts and graphic organizers to track data across time and to placehold those data for analysis that can reveal causes, trends, and comparisons and lead to extended definitions, classifications, and other forms of composition. By the end of the unit, for example, students often create museum displays with various visuals or video documentaries about areas of special interest related to civil rights (Wilhelm, 1995; Wilhelm, 2013b).

Reading visual texts and visually representing learning supports learner independence because it is a clear way of teaching for transfer—students apply expert mental models to visual texts with appropriate amounts of support, gradually decreased over time, and ultimately transfer those expert mental models to longer, more complex written texts.

Transferring Our Learning: What to Remember When Designing Visual Activities to Walk Students Through Their Learning

- Consider how the visualization activity moves students toward independence in applying a complex skill or expert mental model.

- Design the visualization activity so that it is immediately accessible to all learners by activating their prior knowledge and then building on it in ways that lead toward deeper understanding and your own unit goals.

- Target the use of new mental models of expertise that can inform reading, composing, speaking, and problem solving through more accessible visual texts before moving to applying the mental models in more complex written texts or data sets.

- Design the activity so that it helps students to notice key details and topics, see new categories or relationships in the data, develop new understandings, and infer main ideas and themes.

- Consider how the visualization activity supports students in identifying, organizing, placeholding, and analyzing key details and interpretations to use in future reading, composing, and problem solving.

Lesson: Reading for Theme: Using Rules of Notice With a Visual Text

Unit: How do we protect and promote civil rights?

ENVISION the destination
(Where are learners going, and why?)

GOAL *What kind of thinking is targeted?*	EVIDENCE *What product(s) will serve as proof of learning?*	MEASURES OF SUCCESS *What's the standard and quality-assurance tool?*	STAKES *Why will learners buy in?* *What's the "why" behind the learning?*
✓ Application of skill/strategy	✓ Constructed response (discrete task, long/short response, graphic organizer)	✓ **SIMPLE:** √–, √, √+ on discrete facts/skills	Use ESSENCE as a guide for buy-in. Your lesson should have one or more of the following: ✓ **E-S:** Emotional spark/salience (i.e., relevance) ✓ **S-E:** Social engagement (i.e., collaboration) ✓ **N:** Novelty (i.e., new concepts and skills) ✓ **C-E:** Critical/creative exploration opportunities
Apply mental model of expert reading for main idea, aka topic comments/authorial generalization or theme: • Identify general topics and subtopics • Identify crucial details and ideas expressed (use rules of notice) • Keep track of patterns—repeated subjects, words, phrases, images, etc. —and connections between details • Develop working theory regarding author's purpose—see and interpret implied relationships • Explain how this text is structured for meaning and effect	After viewing and discussing the image, students work in partners or small groups to identify the topic or general subject of the text, identify the key details and pattern of these details, and use these to articulate a topic-comment (main idea or theme expressed about the topic by this pattern of key details). The topic is expressed as a noun phrase/subject of the topic-comment sentence. The comment is expressed as a verb phrase that presents a main idea expressed by the text about the topic.	Did students write a general statement of theme and back it up with evidence from the image? √– = Statement of topic-comment/theme is general and/or only names a topic of the image. No evidence from the image to back up statement. √ = Obvious statement of theme. Naming of key details, but explanation of patterns across them is not entirely clear. √+ = Clear and defensible statement of—topic-comment/theme. Naming of key details from the image and patterns that led them to the statement of theme. Students might name and justify a theme that isn't immediately obvious.	**E-S:** Visual is eye-catching and intriguing. **S-E:** Partners/small groups engage in discussion and collaboration on statements of theme. **N:** Applying a reading skill to a visual rather than a written text is likely to be a novel experience for students. **C-E:** Learners will apply this analysis of visuals to their own reading, viewing, and life experiences.

MAP out the path to expertise/mastery
(How would an expert deconstruct and approach this task, step by step?)

TWITTER SUMMARY *(3 bullets max)*	MENTAL MODELS, PROCESS GUIDES, HEURISTICS	A MODEL OF GOOD WORK LOOKS LIKE . . .	DIFFERENTIATION AND LAYERING
Expert readers identify topics, key details, analyze patterns across details, and name main ideas or themes based on patterns. Rules of notice support students in knowing what to notice and interpret in all kinds of texts, including visuals.	The process of noticing patterns of significant data and applying interpretations based on those patterns is the basis of all evidentiary reasoning and inferencing. Topic key details, pattern of key details—work together to express a comment about the topic.	*I know that detail X is important because it uses rule of notice Y, and it connects to these other details in these ways . . . to express this comment about the topic*	Teacher modeling as necessary Various groupings Collaboration on statement of theme and justification Provide copies of the image for students

(Continued)

POWER through your lesson

(What is the sequence of initial major must-make instructional moves?)

PRIME	ORIENT	WALK THROUGH (and check for understanding)	EXTEND AND EXPLORE	REFLECT
Explain to students that expert readers identify themes or main ideas in the texts they read. Today they will be learning a go-to process for analyzing theme, but rather than practicing with a written text, they will be practicing with a single image.	Remind students that we have been exploring the question *How can we best protect and promote civil rights?* "Throughout the unit, we will be continuing our discussion around civil rights by reading a range of texts to see what others have to say about the topic. Today we will be learning a strategy for making sense of what possible meanings an author is trying to convey. We will apply this strategy to all the texts we read and view in this unit, including *Number the Stars.*" "Today we are going to start with an iconic civil rights image."	Project the image on the screen and/or provide a copy of the image. MODEL: The rules of notice to identify key details. Ask students, "What are the key details in this picture? How do we know?" CHECK FOR UNDERSTANDING: Invite students to discuss in partners, identifying and writing down additional key details. MODEL: Identifying a topic of the text by naming what the details have in common/patterns across. Ask, "What are other general subjects or topics that the significant details relate to?" CHECK FOR UNDERSTANDING: Students are invited to talk with a partner and then share out other possible topics based on key details. MODEL: Looking for how the key details are structured and patterned to communicate meaning. Ask, "What are the patterns of details about the topic?" CHECK FOR UNDERSTANDING: Students work in partners to identify additional patterns. MODEL: Identifying a comment that is being made about the topic through the patterning of key details. Ask, "What is a topic comment or point about the topic expressed by the pattern of details?" After each modeled example from the teacher, students work in partners or small groups to practice applying the strategy. GUIDED PRACTICE: Students work in partners or small groups to name a theme/main idea based on their topic comment analysis. Students justify their theme/main idea with explanation of the key details, patterns across the details, and how those patterns lead to a theme.	Provide students with additional images or short texts and have them work alone or with a partner to apply the process and articulate a statement of theme and key details. Present across groups. If offering the homework extension, have students trade images and apply the process.	How might you apply the topic comment strategy to other texts you read or images you encounter? HOMEWORK EXTENSION: Find an image that is related to our topic of inquiry and that would be interesting for a classmate to analyze, and bring it to class the next class period.

Chapter 10

NAVIGATING NEW TERRAIN

Walking Students Through With Think-Aloud Strategies

> **ESSENTIAL QUESTION**
> How can we use think-alouds to make public and model the secret stances and strategies of experts?

A few years ago, after suffering a stress fracture from marathon training, Rachel decided to take up weight lifting to vary her workouts and to build strength in the hopes of avoiding future injuries. Having never successfully lifted weights in her life, Rachel turned to her husband, a weight lifting expert, to learn. In their first training session, Rachel's husband walked her through the major lifts, modeling each lift while she watched and took notes. But he didn't do this modeling in silence. He moved through each lift slowly, "thinking aloud" and naming the moves he was making, the invisible muscle cues he was paying attention to, and any other things he was attending to in order to complete the lift safely. After modeling and thinking through each lift several times, Rachel got under the bar (with somewhat lighter weights!) and replicated the process with her husband's help, naming what she could remember as he jumped in to name anything she forgot. Over the course of the next several training sessions, Rachel was gradually doing more of the naming, eventually being able to complete each lift on her own and name all of the moves, muscle cues, and other important considerations. Now she is able to go to the gym with conscious competence and safely complete all of the lifts on her own, silently naming the cues in her head as she does so. Rachel uses this same process for teaching students how to approach reading an unfamiliar text type or for trying out a new writing approach. For example, in analyzing a poem, Rachel models her own reading processes, thinking aloud as she reads the first several stanzas. She then invites students to contribute their own responses as a whole class or with a partner and, ultimately, on their own in written or spoken analysis of a stanza or entire poem.

Think-aloud strategies are a "must-make move" for teaching students to use expert strategies and mental models through cognitive apprenticeship. (See Wilhelm, 2013c, for a book-length treatment of how to use this technique.) In a think-aloud, the teacher models, names, and describes the process of using expert moves to address any kind

See *Lesson Plan Canvas* on page 170

of challenge. Next, the teacher mentors and monitors students' progress as they name and use these specific reading, composing, and problem-solving strategies. In the same way as Rachel's husband was moving her toward independence in safe strategies for lifting weights, the goal is moving students toward independence in consciously applying focal strategies to their own learning. Think-alouds can be used to teach the reading or composing of any genre, or for any problem-solving process you are focusing on. Think-alouds support students in applying the same meaning-making moves as experts.

For example, expert readers apply a range of approaches to noticing and interpreting textual cues and moves. They freely respond to a text while they are reading—with ongoing observations, questions, connections, and more—as cued by significant details or moves in the text. When appropriate, expert readers also apply text- or task-specific skills and approaches to making meaning of a text as they read. In reading a short story, they might notice and then analyze the author's use of symbols or figurative language (task-specific strategies). In reading a scientific argument, they might notice and build scientific vocabulary; evaluate data, data collection methods, or scientific reasoning; or analyze data sets (text-specific strategies). In a historical text, they might compare accounts of an event across multiple primary texts, or gather key details to summarize an event from different perspectives (discipline- or community-specific strategies). But whenever an expert reader reads any kind of text, she always attends to the general topic under consideration, the key details expressed (see Figure 10.1).

■ FIGURE 10.1: MENTAL MODEL OF EXPERT READING

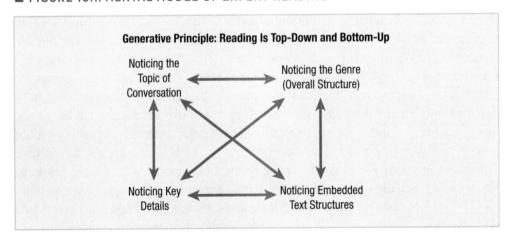

Often we take for granted that secondary students already "know how to read" because they are able to independently read and comprehend texts that are within their zone of actual development (Vygotsky, 1978). But complex texts may include genre features, structures, words, and other text conventions that learners are unfamiliar with; a complex text can also simply be a text type that students don't yet know how to navigate. The text may place demands upon a reader (or composer of that text type) that he or she does not yet know how to meet, that are in the zone of proximal development. This textual complexity is why we must actively teach reading in every subject at every grade level. When learners are reading or composing a text, or completing any kind of task that is just beyond their current capacity, assistance is necessary. This assistance is what Vygotskians call "teaching."

Thinking aloud is an instructional move that assists learners to do *with assistance* what they *cannot yet do alone*. Teachers can use think-alouds to support students in reading and composing more complex texts, reading and composing unfamiliar genres, or applying more sophisticated expert mental models to any problem-solving task (like safely lifting weights). Similarly, thinking aloud can help learners apply a range of approaches for pursuing inquiry: questioning, problem framing, planning, task decomposition, finding and generating data, analyzing findings, organizing ideas, choosing vocabulary, representing and presenting findings, and so on.

For example, in our civil rights unit, we read complex visual texts, speeches, a novel, and many other complex and carefully structured texts. We use thinking aloud to model and support our learners to navigate these texts, and to do so in a way that develops new capacities like exercising social imagination and perspective taking, and using new strategies like inferring character, noticing and interpreting symbols, identifying theme, and composing arguments of analysis and interpretation. We also think aloud to help learners turn insights into commitments and action through advocacy and service. Thinking aloud is a must-make move for teacher modeling and then for learners to deliberately practice and consolidate new strategies.

In this chapter, we focus on must-make expert reading stances like taking the participant and then the observer stance, and strategies like using context clues to make meaning of an unfamiliar text or analyzing an author's use of symbolism to convey meaning. We also explain and provide examples of think-alouds that focus on a range of reading approaches and expert mental models. We show how think-alouds can be used to mentor students to independent application of any sophisticated reading, writing, or problem-solving strategy.

HOW THINK-ALOUD STRATEGIES FIT INTO EMPOWER

In a think-aloud, the expert who is modeling the process is essentially *mapping* out a process, answering the question, "How would an expert deconstruct and approach this task, step by step?" Think-alouds *prime* and *orient* the learner—they foreground purposes, payoffs, and the necessary use of prior background knowledge as the path to creating new understandings and knowledge. When learners experience a model think-aloud, a *walk-through* is provided that opens up the path, showing the process for developing understanding to address the demands of that particular problem, data set, or text. When learners can name and mirror this process, they are apprenticed into greater expertise and conscious competence.

The moves in this chapter focus on thinking aloud as an apprenticeship *walk-through* in which the teacher models the skill or strategy, then provides scaffolding and mentoring as students think aloud in partners or small groups, and finally move to independence as they apply the skill on their own. Students also *extend* and *explore* the use of the strategy in their own independent task completion, and continually *reflect* on the journey. In reflecting, they name what's been learned and areas for growth in further applying the mental model so that they will eventually transfer the approach to later experiences, both in school and out.

Principles of an Effective Think-Aloud

- Focuses on purposefully supporting students in reading or composing a more complex text, reading or composing an unfamiliar genre, or applying a specific reading, composing, or problem-solving strategy to a new and challenging task. The think-aloud is pitched in the learners' zone of proximal development. (E-M)

- Focuses on a relatively short process, episode, or text; excerpt of a longer text; section of a piece students are reading or composing (introduction, conclusion, abstract); data set; or problem. (E-M)

- Begins with the "expert" (teacher early on, students later) foregrounding the purpose and payoff of using the think-aloud to make reading/composing/problem-solving processes visible, and of using it to learn specific new strategies. (P-O)

- Continues modeling the strategy and the use of the mental model but gradually moves students to independence in applying the skill or strategy through the use of mentoring and monitoring. (W-E)

- Walks students through specific and transferable moves of readers, writers, and problem solvers, naming and modeling how to do them until learners take over the process together and then alone. (W-E)

- Reflects real-world expertise, focusing on meaning-making moves that experts apply in navigating a complex task. (W-E)

- Provides students with an opportunity to experience applying the expert strategy and mental model, naming it, and reflecting on how it works, so they are likely to achieve high-road transfer of its use to future experiences, both in and out of school. (W-E-R)

THINK-ALOUD MOVE 1: CUED THINK-ALOUD TO TEACH A NEW PROCESS OR STRATEGY

A cued think-aloud is an approach that focuses on teaching students to apply one specific strategy, like making inferences based on noticing and interpreting connections between key details, or evaluating evidentiary reasoning in an argument, noticing and analyzing figurative language, making predictions based on previous detail patterns, evaluating narrator reliability, noticing and interpreting symbolism, and so on. It's important that teachers identify the focal strategy based on understandings that are central to the overall inquiry and the text/data/problem at hand, that learners have not yet fully mastered. In other words, a cued think-aloud should always be (a) about a strategy necessary right now and (b) pitched in the learners' zone of proximal development. Teachers plan cued think-alouds based on immediate points of need and on specific grade-level standards focused on in a unit.

For example, in our civil rights unit, identifying and analyzing symbols is a key move for making meaning of *Number the Stars*, especially the final chapter in which symbols are an important part of the meaning and help communicate the theme of the whole novel. Much of the commentary about how to promote and protect civil rights is communicated through symbolism, so our learners need to know how to notice and interpret symbols to get the book's full contribution to our inquiry. For a cued think-aloud, we begin by selecting a short text or an excerpt from a longer text that is a good fit for the strategy we are focusing on; ideally, the excerpt provides a *concentrated sample*, in which the strategy will be used several times.

For any reading strategy think-aloud, it is ideal for students to have the text side by side with a place to annotate and keep a written account of their thinking (see example in Figure 10.2). Students can alternatively keep a written account of their thinking in a notebook or on a separate sheet of paper laid next to a text, or use sticky notes stuck to the part of the text they are responding to.

If students are new to applying the skill or strategy, we make it easier by highlighting text cues for them, underlining key words and phrases that constitute the tip-offs that a detail or move must be noticed. As they gain more practice with responding to cues and learn the rules of notice for them, we gradually release responsibility until eventually learners are independently identifying key words or phrases related to the strategy. (Complete rules of notice can be downloaded from the companion website, http://resources.corwin.com/EMPOWER-secondary.) With a new complex strategy like symbolism, it is often helpful (as well as culturally responsive and restorative) to do some preliminary frontloading that starts with students' familiarity with symbols in their own lives (e.g., asking them about religious symbols from their culture, or the meaning of various flags, and then proceeding to cultural fables that make use of symbolism). For example, before completing the cued think aloud below, students will have practiced the mental model for reading symbols (recognizing an object or symbol as symbolic, identifying the symbolic value, inserting the symbolic value in a way to contributes to its meaning) with various symbols they might encounter in their own lives.

The process for a cued think-aloud is as follows:

> Step 1: Once students have been primed for success, start by reading aloud the first section of the text and modeling your own think-aloud, explaining how you knew to notice cues to a particular convention (such as symbolism), and then interpret the meaning and effect of how the convention used this strategy (e.g., the cultural connections made by the symbols, and the contribution of symbols to the local- and global-level meaning of the text).

(Continued)

Teachers often skip this first step, but this modeling move is essential for student understanding. It's helpful to tell students to take notes or highlight, too, because in the next section of the text, you can continue to read aloud, pausing at key words and phrases and asking students to jump in with their responses, naming what they noticed and attempting interpretations of their own.

Step 2: Students then continue through the next section with a partner or in small groups, making sure to at least stop and comment on underlined words and phrases (the "cue" that there is something important to notice).

Step 3: After completing the cued think-aloud, students reflect in speaking or writing about what they learned, and brainstorm ideas for applying the strategy later in the reading, or in new reading or composing contexts.

The sequence in our EMPOWER canvas lesson plan for this chapter leads learners through the gradual release of responsibility for analyzing the significance of symbols in the last chapter of *Number the Stars*. The ultimate goal is that students will move forward with noticing and interpreting symbols in order to make meaning of the texts they encounter in the future. The last chapter of *Number the Stars* is used for this cued think-aloud (Figure 10.2) because it is a concentrated sample of symbolism and the symbols are directly connected to the meaning of the text as a whole, but teachers can create cued think-alouds like this for any excerpt in the novel (or any other reading).

■ **FIGURE 10.2: CUED THINK-ALOUD EXAMPLE: EXCERPT FROM THE LAST CHAPTER OF** *NUMBER THE STARS*

NUMBER THE STARS BY LOIS LOWRY	
The war would end. Uncle Henrik had said that, and it was true. The war ended almost two long years later. Annemarie was twelve.	I notice the number 2 because numbers can be symbols. But in this case I think it just means two years. I also notice Annemarie is 12. Numbers are a symbolic marker and call to attention, and I think this number is a symbol. I connect this to world knowledge because I know that 12 is the age when people with religious upbringings become confirmed or have their bat or bar mitzvahs. The age of 12 was when Jesus realized who he was. So this shows Annemarie achieving some kind of adult understanding or responsibility through her ordeal, I think.
Churchbells rang all over Copenhagen, early that May evening. The Danish flag was raised everywhere.	Churchbells are a symbol of joy and celebration or of alarm of danger. It's clearly celebration here. May is the month when spring begins. Seasons are often symbolic calls to attention. The author mentions this because May is the time of rebirth and Denmark is being reborn into freedom. The dark cold winter is over. The flag and anthem are fairly obvious symbols: They are direct statements of national pride—pride that had to be suppressed but now can be expressed.

People stood in the streets and wept as they sang the national anthem of Denmark.

Annemarie stood on the balcony of the apartment with her parents and sister, and across on the other side, she could see flags and banners in almost every window. She knew that many of those

apartments were empty. For nearly two years now, neighbors

had tended the plants and dusted the furniture and polished the candlesticks for the Jews who had fled. Her mother had done so for the Rosens.

"It is what friends do," Mama had said.

Now neighbors had entered each unoccupied, waiting apartment, opened a window, and hung a symbol of freedom there.

Peter Neilsen was dead. It was a painful fact to recall on this day when there was so much joy in Denmark. But Annemarie forced herself to think of her redheaded almost-brother, and how devastating the day was when they received the news that Peter had been captured and executed by the Germans in the public square at Ryvangen, in Copenhagen.

I know that positioning can be a symbolic call to attention, like in a painting. Here, people are standing in the streets. I think this shows their pride in being freed, but also shows that they now feel safe because they did not stand around during the Nazi occupation because there were armed guards and threats everywhere.

Annemarie is standing too—so another call to attention through positioning. And she is standing on a balcony, which means she can see and has perspective, so that is symbolic too. And she is standing with her parents and sister—who you are positioned with can be symbolic, and I think this means that they got through their struggles as a family who stuck together and as a community that helped each other, and this shows that. Empty apartments are a rupture and show that there has been loss, and people like the Rosens had to go into hiding. Emptiness can also show possibility that something will come back.

There is a rule of three in symbolism, that symbols often come in threes. Plants fit the symbolism of rebirth. Plus it's been two years, so someone must have watered them, which symbolizes how you have to take care of each other to get through trouble. Furniture symbolizes home, so perhaps the Jews will come home now. The polishing again symbolizes that someone took care of things so they would be ready. Candlesticks symbolize light, and they also symbolize the practice of Jewish religion, which is now out on the table again, after it had to be hidden.

Students continue with annotation alone or in partners. Be sure to discuss the symbolism in the final paragraphs as a class as the symbols in the closing paragraphs are essential to the meaning of the text as a whole.

THINK-ALOUD MOVE 2: FREE RESPONSE THINK-ALOUD

While a cued response think-aloud targets a single strategy or a small set of related strategies, a free response think-aloud involves making students aware of the variety of strategies any expert reader (or composer or problem solver) uses when reading or composing a text or solving a problem (see Figure 10.3). It models how experts orchestrate a wide variety of strategies and responses into a whole as they make meaning.

■ FIGURE 10.3: GENERAL PROCESSES OF READING

Whenever they successfully read a text, all expert readers

- Activate background/set purpose of reading
- Decode text into meaningful words and units of meaning
- Personally connect to the content/experience
- Summarize: Bring meaning forward throughout the text
- Ask questions: Factual, interpretive, critical/applicative; intratextual, intertextual, text to self, text to world
- Make predictions
- Visualize story worlds/mental models
- Monitor understanding/self-correct
- Reflect on knowledge; consolidate understanding

Free response think-alouds are useful early on in a unit to assess natural reading/composing/problem-solving responses and strategies learners currently use with the text types or problems that will be part of the inquiry. This kind of think-aloud thus serves as a formative assessment of learners' current strategy use with the kind of texts, data, or problems the unit will provide. This will help you to know how to pitch and differentiate instruction through the unit (more on formative assessment in Chapter 14). At the end of the unit, this kind of think-aloud can be used for students to demonstrate strategic progress.

Some students need to be explicitly taught the elements of freely responding and orchestrating the whole set of strategies and responses necessary to what they are reading, especially when they encounter more challenging or unfamiliar text types. They might read the words, but they don't necessarily engage in decoding, or they might decode but not go to deep comprehension by asking questions, making observations, making connections, or monitoring understanding. Seeing the difference between a free response and a cued response for the same text or excerpt can be helpful, so Figure 10.4 shows a free response activity for the same passage from *Number the Stars*.

The process for a free response think-aloud is as follows:

Step 1: Prime students by having them reflect on the processes they go through when they are reading for fun—what do they think about as they are reading? What makes them pause? Mention that being metacognitively aware of what you do as a reader—especially knowing when a text does not make sense and using fix-up strategies—is the hallmark of expert reading.

Step 2: Orient the learners by reminding them of the goals of the lesson: to practice a free response think-aloud to an excerpt from the text, naming the general process moves as well as other moves they are making as they read. This should foreground that reading is a highly active process of using various strategies to transact with a text's content and structure.

Step 3: Model the free response think-aloud, reading aloud the first excerpt of the chapter, pausing regularly to name and think aloud about the process of reading. Students follow along, annotating as they go. Begin to mentor students by having them jump in with their own responses. It's helpful to model a range of general reading process responses, including setting a purpose, making personal connections, asking questions, making predictions, and visualizing. Provide students with stems to use in their annotation, and model using those stems, such as the following:

- I notice . . .

- The meaning I make of this is . . .

- I can really picture . . .

- This reminds me of . . .

- I wonder why . . .

Step 4: Students then work together in pairs, thinking aloud together for the next sections of text. Circulate the room, monitoring student conversations and providing prompting or questions for students who are struggling. If they need extra support and prompting, use the "say something" strategy: Students pause at the end of each paragraph and take turns saying at least one thing in response to what they just read, using stems or prompts to scaffold responses as necessary.

Step 5: For the final section, students work individually to continue their own free response think-aloud. During this time, circulate the room, assessing students' responses and reminding them to continue keeping a written log of their think-aloud if they forget.

Step 6: Finally, provide a closing writing prompt for students to reflect on the experience and rehearse transfer to future reading experiences. The following prompts provide an opportunity for students to reflect on what they learned from the think-aloud and to share this in pairs or small groups (see Chapter 14 for more on self-assessments for reflection and transfer):

- Characterize *how* you read this excerpt (e.g., visual, questioning, participatory). Be *general*.

(Continrued)

- Identify some of the characteristic *moves* and *strategies* you used (cite *specific* strategies).

- Explain how these moves helped you engage and make meaning.

- Go on to discuss anything else you want to share about your experience.

Another variation on an after-reading reflection:

- Tell me something you learned from pursuing and sharing the think-aloud about each of the following.
  - Yourself
  - Your way of reading
  - Someone else
  - That person's way of reading
  - Strategies for reading
  - The text and its meaning
  - Other texts
  - The world

We also often ask students to write a reflection like the following:

- Now that you've finished the text or excerpt, comment on what you think and feel about the text or excerpt as a whole. Remember, we're interested in any response that you have.

- What did you notice about yourself as a reader as you completed your free response think-aloud?

■ **FIGURE 10.4: FREE RESPONSE THINK-ALOUD FOR *NUMBER THE STARS***

The war would end. Uncle Henrik had said that, and it was true. The war ended almost two long years later. Annemarie was twelve.	First off, I notice that there is a repetition of a quote from earlier in the book. Repetition is a call to attention, so I know it is important. Uncle Henrik said the war would end, and he was right. But I wonder what it is like for a child in an oppressive situation—it must seem like it would never end! So I am thinking of the adult vs. child perspective here. I am also doing a bit of a math problem here: I see that there has been a two-year gap since the end of the last chapter—so I'm being asked to imagine what happened in that gap—and I am guessing that it was more of the same: food shortages, Nazi oppression, helping neighbors.
Churchbells rang all over Copenhagen, early that May evening. The Danish flag was raised everywhere. People stood in the streets and wept as they sang the national anthem of Denmark.	I have lived in Europe, so I know what it is like when all the churchbells ring. And I know that the churchbells can either signal danger or signal joy and celebration. Here it has to be celebration. I also notice a rupture because earlier in the book we learn that any citizen with a Danish flag could be shot, but they have all been hiding those flags for this moment and bring them out! _____ _____

If you have not been constantly reporting on how you are responding to this reading, please do so now for the page you have just read. Remember that we're interested in anything you are noticing, asking, seeing, feeling, thinking, and doing as you read.

Annemarie stood on the balcony of the apartment with her parents	The situation has really changed since you would not have stood outside during the Nazi occupation—you went inside to be safe. Also, she can see her community as she could not before as she stands on the balcony.
and sister, **and across on the other side, she could see** flags and banners in almost every window. She knew that many of those apartments were empty. For nearly two years now, neighbors	People must be hanging banners and flags for the people who are not there, because those people are now free, too, if they are still alive. I imagine the flags being Danish flags and pennants, red and blue.
had tended the plants and dusted the furniture and polished the candlesticks for the Jews who had fled. Her mother had done so for the Rosens.	So people had been taking care of the homes and businesses of the people who escaped or were taken away.
"It is what friends do," Mama had said.	This really grabs me. I know it is a quote, but it is also a one-line, one-sentence paragraph among longer paragraphs. This rupture makes me pay close attention. I think Mama is saying that this is what you have to do for each other in times of trouble, and I ask myself if I would risk my life for my friends, and I sure hope that I would.
Now neighbors had entered each unoccupied, waiting apartment, opened a window, and hung a symbol of freedom **there.**	I imagine the symbol of freedom being peace signs even though I am not sure they had peace signs back then.
This evening, Mrs. Johansen's face was wet with tears. **Kirsti,** waving a small flag, sang; her blue eyes were bright. Even Kirsti	I am like a camera, and I see her face like a close-up. Then I go wider and see Kirsti, who is the younger sister.
was growing up; no longer was she a lighthearted chatterbox of a	This reminds me of how Kirsti almost gave away Ellen earlier in the story and almost got them all in trouble with the soldiers because she talks so much.

If you have not been constantly reporting on how you are responding to this reading, please do so now for the page you have just read. Remember that we're interested in anything you are noticing, asking, seeing, feeling, thinking, and doing as you read.

(Continued)

(Continued)

child. Now she was taller, more serious, and very thin. She looked like the pictures of Lise at seven, in the old album.	This is how the war has changed her.
	I know that comparisons and figurative language are calls to attention: Why is the author comparing Kirsti to Lise, who is now dead from fighting in the Resistance? I think it is because it is up to the younger generation to heal Denmark and finish the work Lise started.

Students continue with annotation with partners or individually and respond to the following prompt at the end: Now that you've finished the story, please comment on what you think and feel about the story as a whole. Remember, we're interested in any response that you have.

If you have not been constantly reporting on how you are responding to this reading, please do so now for the page you have just read. Remember that we're interested in anything you are noticing, asking, seeing, feeling, thinking, and doing as you read.

THINK-ALOUD MOVE 3: RULES OF NOTICE THINK-ALOUD

As Wilhelm and Smith (2016) have noted:

> Authors do specific things to help readers orient themselves to the conversation taken up by a text, to the genre, and the text structures they employ. We have found that we need to teach students how to notice and attend to these *orienting moves*. If we do, students are much more able to enter into texts and make meaning of them. In fact, we have found that they do so with the enthusiasm and joy of a knowing insider, someone who is in the process of developing new forms of expertise. (p. 15)

Wilhelm and Smith use the term *rules of notice* to designate the textual cues readers use to orient themselves to the text in general, and to attend and make meaning with specific details and moves. In a rules of notice think-aloud, the teacher apprentices students through the process of naming what is noticed, naming the rules of notice that served as cues, and naming how meaning is made with what is noticed. All expert reading of any text comes down to knowing how and what to notice, and then how to interpret what is noticed. Rules of notice are important tip-offs to a reader that a detail, idea, structure, or move is important to the meaning of a text or data set, or for understanding and navigating a genre, text structure, or text type. A general rules of notice think-aloud is a more focused free response think-aloud. When you use a rules of notice think-aloud to teach a new strategy or text structure convention or move, as we do here, then it is a kind of cued think-aloud.

Rules of notice fall into four general types:

1. *Generalizations*—direct statements of meaning or reflections on what something means from an author, narrator, or character

2. *Calls to attention*—titles, breakthroughs in understanding, questions, emotionally charged words, metaphors, allusions, figurative language, repetition, and so on

3. *Ruptures*—shifts or surprises of any kind

4. *Reader's response*—anything that causes the reader to pause, to question, to deeply agree, or to experience a strong emotional response

Figure 10.5 shows a sample rules of notice sequence using the opening of Martin Luther King Jr.'s "I Have a Dream" speech.

■ **FIGURE 10.5: ANNOTATED "I HAVE A DREAM" SPEECH**

TEXT EXCERPT	ANNOTATIONS
Note: Boldface text is a tip-off that there is a connection to be made to other words, phrases, or ideas through compare/contrast, repetition or repetition with a twist, or builds or uptakes.	Note: UP and DOWN refer to emotional tone.
I have a dream![1]	[1] *UP—Rule of Notice: Title; Reader's Response: Emotional Charge; Trajectory: Dreams are generally inspiring and lead us to becoming something new and better.*
I am happy to join with you today in what will go down in history as the greatest demonstration for freedom in the **history** of our nation.[2]	[2] *UP—Rules of Notice: Introductions/openings—always set the stage; emotional charge of "happy," "greatest"; repetition of "history" gives a sense of grandeur and significance.*
Five score years ago, a great American, in whose symbolic shadow **we stand** today, signed the **Emancipation Proclamation**. This **momentous decree** came as a great beacon of light and hope to millions of Negro slaves who had been seared in the flames of withering injustice. It came as **a joyous daybreak** to end the long night of their captivity.[3]	[3] *Overall, UP. Emancipation is the "great decree," so we have a repetition of the reference to the 100-year anniversary of the freeing of all American slaves. Trajectory: Beacon of light is positive. Contrast: Immediately followed by flames of withering injustice to show that the hope came out of centuries of persistent injustice—suggestion of heaven vs. hell. Contrast: Joyous daybreak after a long night of captivity—day vs. night—again emphasizing the upwardness after a very long period of downwardness.*
But one hundred years later, the Negro still is not free. **One hundred years later**, the life of the Negro is still sadly crippled by the manacles of segregation and the chains of discrimination. **One hundred years later**, the Negro lives on a lonely island of poverty in the **midst of a vast ocean of material prosperity**.[4]	[4] *DOWN. Rupture/shift signaled by transitional word of "But"—despite promised upward movement, nothing has happened. Repetition with a twist: "One hundred years" repeats "Five Score" (meaning 100) and evokes Lincoln's Gettysburg Address, which begins "Four Score and seven years ago"—this invokes a repetition of Lincoln's most famous works, the Address and the Emancipation Proclamation, and invokes the Declaration of Independence, which Lincoln refers to in the Address. Repetition: "One hundred years later" repeated for effect—we are reminded that a century has passed since the emancipation. Contrast: "island of poverty" vs. "vast ocean of material prosperity"—note end rhyme.*

(Continued)

■ FIGURE 10.5: (CONTINUED)

TEXT EXCERPT	ANNOTATIONS
One hundred years later, the Negro is still languishing in the corners of American society and finds himself an exile in his own land. So we have come here today to dramatize a shameful condition. In a sense we have come to our nation's capital to cash a **check**. When the Architects of our republic wrote the magnificent words of the **Constitution and the Declaration of Independence**, they were signing a **promissory note** to which every American was to fall heir. This note was a **promise** that all men, yes, black men as well as white men, would be **guaranteed the unalienable rights of life, liberty, and the pursuit of happiness**.[5]	[5]*UP. Extended analogy: cashing a check. Repetition with a twist: check, Constitution, and Declaration, which were the checks, promissory note, and promise. Uptake: Declaration and then the "unalienable rights . . ." from the Declaration. This continuous invoking of the founding documents reinforces that the promises of equality and freedom are part of the very founding fabric of the United States.*

Step 1: Prime students by (a) asking learners to brainstorm how emotional movement is used in their own communications when trying to persuade someone of something, and (b) describing the process of the thinking aloud and annotation. Ask learners to brainstorm times that they have imaginatively rehearsed a process, or reported out on a process. Point out that in this think-aloud the class will work to identify structures like comparisons/contrasts and annotate their meaning/effect. They will also designate upward and downward movements (in emotion, tone, and possibility) with arrows and describe in annotation how these movements are a form of comparison/contrast, creating a trajectory serving meaning/effect. They will circle and connect repetitions, connections, and builds/uptakes of previous images/ideas/phrasings, and describe in annotations how these work for meaning/effect.

Step 2: Orient learners by describing the goal of the lesson: in this case, how to notice authorial decisions about structure and how these decisions lead to making meaning. Brainstorm how conscious competence with structuring moves can make a powerful difference to their own reading, and in their own speaking and composing.

Step 3: Begin the walk-through by modeling the process in the first two or three paragraphs, naming what is noticed, naming rules of notice, and naming the unpacking and interpreting (i.e., how meaning is made with what is noticed, especially regarding local and global structure).

Step 4: Mentor the walk-through process by thinking aloud and then quickly involving students in naming what is noticed, naming rules of notice that tipped them off, and naming the unpacking and interpreting. Prompt, ask questions for the next few paragraphs, and check what students have annotated.

Step 5: When you've determined that students are ready, ask pairs or triads to extend the same kind of work to the next paragraphs. To differentiate and provide more assistance to those still engaged in productive struggle, ask students to work with you in a small circle to continue the mentoring process. Monitor those working more independently by walking around the classroom observing, or do so afterward by having students share their responses through exit tickets or other forms of formative assessment such as procedural feedback to the author. (See Chapter 6 for more on procedural feedback and Chapter 14 for more on exit tickets as formative assessments.) For example, students might work to articulate a statement of meaning for the whole speech and how the structural and up/down movements communicated and reinforced this meaning. Or students could jigsaw to share their think-aloud annotations in small groups. (See Chapter 12 for more on jigsaw.)

Step 6: Model how to use the structuring of excerpts to look at overall structuring and trajectory of the whole piece and how comparison/contrast, repetition, builds/uptakes, and other kinds of connections work to shape the piece as a whole and to create meaning and effect. Pose structural generalization questions (see Chapter 11) about how the text was structured to create specific meanings and effects.

Step 7: Ask learners to reflect and consider how they can use the same strategies learned here as they consider talk and texts they encounter during the day, and for future readings of texts, data, or problems in this unit and beyond.

THINK-ALOUD MOVE 4: TALKBACK THINK-ALOUDS FOR REFLECTING ON COMPOSING OR PROBLEM SOLVING: PLANNING AN ARGUMENT

Although this chapter focuses largely on think-alouds for reading, think-alouds are also powerful for teaching students to approach any complex composing or problem-solving task. A teacher can think aloud with any kind of problem solving, or with composing any particular kind of text, highlighting cued strategies (e.g., how data generate a claim in an argument or how reasoning connects data to the claim). The process for planning an argument can be adapted for teaching students how to write in any genre or for teaching them how to approach any kind of problem. At the end of the composing and problem-solving process, learners do a "talkback"—a process analysis describing what they did and why they did it.

(Continued)

(Continued)

Here's what it looks like when planning an argument:

Step 1: Prime students by explaining the goals of the lesson: to synthesize their collection of evidence to begin planning their argument.

Step 2: Orient students to the task by having them take out any data/evidence they have collected to write their arguments—articles they have read and annotated, notes from class discussions, reflective writing, and so on.

Step 3: Using your own set of data/evidence, walk through your own thought process for composing a claim based on all the data/evidence you have gathered. Then model testing the claim to make sure that it is debatable, defensible, and compelling. We have used the PMI (Plus-Minus-Interesting) strategy (de Bono, 1986; see Figure 10.6) to have students test claims to make sure they are debatable, defensible, interesting, and significant (Smith, Wilhelm, & Fredricksen, 2013).

■ **FIGURE 10.6: IS YOUR CLAIM DEBATABLE AND DEFENSIBLE? APPLYING THE PMI STRATEGY**

- 2 minutes: List all the possible pluses that follow from accepting your claim.
- 2 minutes: List all the potential minuses of accepting your claim, including any possible unintended consequences.
- 2 minutes: What makes your claim interesting and significant?
- Restate or revise your working claim: _____
- Talkback Reflection: Talk through how you created your claim based on evidence. How do you know that your claim is debatable and defensible and significant to an audience?

Step 4: Students then go through the process of writing and testing their own claims based on evidence. Monitor as students generate and share their claims with a partner, testing them together to make sure they are debatable, defensible, and compelling.

Step 5: Once all students have a claim, walk through evaluating and then selecting the best evidence to support the claim. Students follow the same process, selecting their own evidence and testing it with a partner. We have used semantic scales (Figure 10.7) to help students analyze their own evidence or evidence their partner has selected. You may download a semantic scale for student use from the companion website, http://resources.corwin.com/EMPOWER-secondary.

online resources

Question: Is technology making us stupider?

Claim: Yes, technology is making us stupider because it is addictive and distracts us from deep thinking.

Evidence: "'Technology is rewiring our brains,' said Nora Volkow, director of the National Institute on Drug Abuse and one of the world's leading brain scientists. She and other researchers compare the lure of digital stimulation less to that of drugs and alcohol than to food and sex, which are essential but counterproductive in excess." (Quoted in Matt Richtel, "Attached to Technology and Paying a Price," *New York Times*, June 6, 2010)

SAFETY OF EVIDENCE/ACCEPTABILITY AND VERIFIABILITY

X——

Is safe, can be agreed upon   Unsafe, illogical, and untrue

BECAUSE: *Dr. Volkow is cited as a top expert on drug abuse and the brain. We can point directly at her quote. We were able to look her up and confirm her as an expert and confirm her viewpoint on technology as addictive, distracting, and something that is rewiring our brains. So this evidence is safe. We can agree she is an expert and that she said and thinks this.*

AUTHORITY OF SOURCE(S)

X——

Positive   Negative

BECAUSE: *The* New York Times *is a credible news source, and Matt Richtel is an award-winning journalist.*

REPLICABILITY OF EVIDENCE

————————————————X——

Repeated/replicable   Not repeated/not replicable

BECAUSE: *The rest of the article cites several other experts who also believe that the brain is being rewired in ways that are highly addictive, that distract us, and that keep us from concentrating or thinking deeply about issues over time. Some of the other articles we read also confirmed this point of view. We did not give this our strongest rating because there are experts who argue that technology makes us smarter in some specific ways like visual acuity and reaction time.*

Relevance of Evidence—ON-POINTNESS

————————————X——

Clearly relates to topic   Does not relate to topic

BECAUSE: *The evidence doesn't directly support our claim that technology is making us stupider, but it is very supportive of that claim if we reason about the evidence to show that most people give in to the addictiveness and are distracted, which keeps them from deep thinking and understanding.*

Validity of Evidence—COLLECTION OF DATA IS SOUND

X——

Sound collection of data   Suspect collection/methodology

BECAUSE: *This quote and the following commentary come from a carefully researched article about the brain and computers, and this is a direct quote from a recognized expert. We assume that the author, Richtel, as an award-winning journalist, tape recorded the conversation and cross-checked the quote and its meaning with Dr. Volkow.*

Sufficiency of Evidence

——————————————X——

Enough evidence to convince audience   Not enough evidence

BECAUSE: *We don't think this quote alone is going to convince our audience of peers who love their smartphones and tablets. But by adding other evidence about the effects of smartphones and technology on the brain, we think that we will have sufficient evidence by showing a pattern of agreement among brain scientists about the negative effects of tech on our concentration and on our deep thinking.*

NOTE WELL: *Students may identify other features that make strong evidence, and those insights can be included in a scale such as this.*

Source: "Analyzing Evidence Semantic Scales" by Rachel Bear, based on explanation and examples from *Fresh Takes on Teaching Literary Elements* by Smith and Wilhelm, 2009.

online resources — Available for download at **http://resources.corwin.com/EMPOWER-secondary**

(Continued)

(Continued)

Have students conclude with a final reflection on their plan for the argument; following are two suggestions. (See Chapter 14 for more on self-assessment through reflection.)

Complete a talkback or written self-assessment:

- How did you select the evidence you will use in the first draft of your argument?
- What is your working claim, and how is it based on the evidence?
- What reasoning (values, rules, etc.) will you apply to the evidence to connect these data points to your claim?
- What do you want to make sure you remember as you start drafting your argument?

And/or reflect and talk back about your process in a conference with a peer:

- Do a talkback think-aloud with a partner, or your partner can use a talkback guide of the mental map for composing this kind of text or solving this kind of problem to prompt your think-aloud about the process.

Talkback guides can be created for any kind of text or problem-solving process to help students think through the specific demands of a task, or for use by peers to prompt the composer or problem solver to think through and monitor his or her process and how well he or she is meeting critical standards. The companion website resources .corwin.com/EMPOWER-secondary contains talkback guides for reading and writing arguments, news stories, and general information texts.

POWERFUL PLANNING:
THINKING ALOUD TO NAVIGATE AND MEET NEW CHALLENGES

Think-alouds are useful anytime students are introduced to a new interpretive challenge such as noticing a textual convention or move (e.g., an unreliable narrator, symbols, or implied relationships that must be inferred), a new text structure or thought pattern (definition, classification, argument of policy, etc.), a new problem to solve, or a new writing task. The think-aloud process is a must-make move to help students toward expertise in new kinds of reading, writing, and problem solving.

In our civil rights unit, we use think-alouds to help students interpret symbolism in various texts, and to use readers' rules of notice for identifying how texts are structured and how this structuring creates meanings and effects. We also use think-alouds to prepare them to compose their advocacy pieces, which are typically a kind of problem–solution argument, and in various other ways to model using new strategies and developing new capacities.

Making visible the step-by-step process of an expert to deconstruct and pursue any task helps develop conscious competence. Students become aware of the meaning-making process and are able to name the steps, eventually internalizing and naturally applying the process to texts and tasks they encounter in school and in their lives. This is the high-road transfer that is the ultimate goal of all teaching and learning.

Transferring Our Learning: What to Remember When Designing Think-Aloud Activities to Provide Walk-Throughs That Lead to Deeper Expertise

- Consider how the think-aloud activity moves students toward independence in understanding and making use of a new complex conception, strategy, or expert mental model that will be immediately useful in the context of the unit, as well as in the future.

- Design the think-aloud activity so that it connects to learners' prior knowledge in terms of the content of the text or data set to be used, and in terms of the processes, purposes, and payoffs of the strategic learning.

- Consider how the think-aloud activity supports students in noticing, interpreting, structuring, and analyzing key details, conversational topics, and text structuring moves to use in future reading, composing, and problem solving.

- Design the think-aloud so that learners consider and rehearse how to apply and extend what they have learned in the near future, both in school and in their lives.

Lesson: Cued Think-Aloud for the Task-Specific Strategy of Noticing and Interpreting Symbols

Unit: How do we protect and promote civil rights?

ENVISION the destination
(Where are learners going, and why?)

GOAL *What kind of thinking is targeted?*	EVIDENCE *What product(s) will serve as proof of learning?*	MEASURES OF SUCCESS *What's the standard and quality-assurance tool?*	STAKES *Why will learners buy in?* *What's the "why" behind the learning?*
✓ Interpretation ✓ Explanation/reasoning ✓ Application of skill/strategy ✓ Self-assessing/reflecting	✓ Constructed (discrete task, long/short response, graphic organizer)	✓ **CHECKLIST:** Assess if product contains essential characteristics/features.	Use ESSENCE as a guide for buy-in. Your lesson should have one or more of the following: ✓ E-S: Emotional spark/salience (i.e., relevance) ✓ S-E: Social engagement (i.e., collaboration) ✓ N: Novelty (i.e., new concepts and skills) ✓ C-E: Critical/creative exploration opportunities
Students will learn to **apply** the process of noticing symbolic tip-offs and then interpreting them by applying a cultural connection as a **strategy** for noticing and analyzing symbols, which is an important mental model for meaning making in any literary text, and is a central **skill** in understanding the final chapter of *Number the Stars*. In this cued think-aloud process, students will **identify** possible symbols, **interpret** their significance, and **explain** their thinking. Finally, students will **reflect** on their responses to the excerpt, **self-assessing** their level of confidence in applying this skill to future texts.	Students keep a written record of their think-aloud through annotations. They also write a brief written reflection/self-assessment at the end of the lesson. The teacher observes student responses during the "we do" portion of the think-aloud and also monitors the students' work in pairs or small groups.	☐ Students can identify people, places, events, and objects that have symbolic significance. ☐ Students can provide a reasonable interpretation of their significance by applying cultural connections and implications. ☐ Students can use the interpretation in a way that fits the text and leads to a reasonable meaning of the text. ☐ Students can explain their process of noticing and interpreting, which is the mental model for interpreting symbolism. ☐ Students feel confident in applying the mental model in future texts and can successfully explain why.	**E-S:** Students often see themselves as passive readers, simply moving through a text to get to the end. This lesson engages them as active readers who are capable of noticing and analyzing symbolic significance. This is a real-world skill that will be applicable to future texts they encounter. **S-E:** Students engage in a collaborative think-aloud in partners or small groups. **N:** Noticing and analyzing symbols in order to make meaning of the final chapter and the work as a whole is likely a new skill for students. **C-E:** Learners can apply what they have learned about noticing and interpreting symbols to movies, pictures, political cartoons, T-shirts, and many other texts in their everyday lives.

MAP out the path to expertise/mastery
(How would an expert deconstruct and approach this task, step by step?)

TWITTER SUMMARY *(3 bullets max)*	MENTAL MODELS, PROCESS GUIDES, HEURISTICS	A MODEL OF GOOD WORK LOOKS LIKE . . .	DIFFERENTIATION AND LAYERING
Expert readers notice and interpret objects, people, events, and places that have symbolic significance. This lesson mentors students into this important mental model.	Process for analyzing symbols (this is the process we will be thinking aloud about): 1. NOTICE: Recognize an object or action as symbolic. 2. INTERPRET: Identify the symbolic value (through cultural connections and considering context). 3. USE TO MAKE MEANING: Insert the symbolic value into the text to make an interpretation—use it to make meaning of the text—in a way that makes sense to that text.	*I know that X (the yellow dress) is symbolic because color is often symbolic and is a call to attention; because it is hidden and gets extended attention when it is brought out, which is a call to attention; and, finally, because it is faded, which is a rupture, and hides Ellen's star of David, which is a surprise. I interpret the dress as symbolizing that Ellen and her family will come home, as the dress came out of hiding, and will be able to be open about their Jewishness.*	Levels of assistance: Teacher uses different groupings, different layers of assistance, and more modeling as necessary for individuals, small groups, or whole groups. Teacher identifies key words and phrases as cues if necessary. Peers assist peers to generate and confirm think-aloud responses. Students engage in more deliberate practice mirroring the mental model and provide continual procedural feedback.

POWER through your lesson

(What is the sequence of initial major must-make instructional moves?)

PRIME	ORIENT	WALK THROUGH (and check for understanding)	EXTEND AND EXPLORE	REFLECT
Introduce the process for recognizing and analyzing symbols. Discuss visual examples in a slideshow of obvious symbols. Students discuss obvious symbols using the process for analyzing symbols.	FRAME today's lesson: "In this unit, we have been discussing the question, *How can we best promote and protect civil rights?* Today we will be reading the final chapter of *Number the Stars* and discussing what the final chapter reveals about the meaning of the book as a whole." "Today we will focus in on one way authors convey meaning, using symbols. Recognizing and identifying symbols is a key move that expert readers make, so we will learn a process for recognizing and analyzing symbols we encounter in texts and in the world."	EXPLAIN: Process for analyzing symbols (this is the process we will be thinking aloud about). 1. NOTICE: Recognize an object or action as symbolic. 2. INTERPRET: Identify the symbolic value (through cultural connections and considering context). 3. USE TO MAKE MEANING: Insert the symbolic value into the text to make an interpretation—use it to make meaning of the text—in a way that makes sense to that text. MODEL (I DO, YOU WATCH): Teacher provides a think-aloud for the first section of the excerpt from *Number the Stars.* Students follow along, adding annotations to their copies of the excerpt. MODEL (WE DO TOGETHER): Teacher reads the next section of the excerpt, pausing to invite students to help with the annotation. CHECK FOR UNDERSTANDING: Ask students, *What did you notice about reading for symbols? What was helpful to you? What was challenging?* GUIDED PRACTICE (YOU DO TOGETHER): On the next section of text, students continue with annotation in partners or small groups. DIFFERENTIATE: If some students are struggling, they can continue working with a partner or in a separate group with the teacher. If some students are ready, they can annotate the final section on their own. DEBRIEF: Full class discussion of the role of symbols in the final chapter. What is the significance of the symbols? What do the symbols reveal about the meaning of the work as a whole?	DELIBERATE PRACTICE/ARTICULATE CONSCIOUS AWARENESS: Close the lesson with a discussion of how students will use the process of analyzing symbols in texts they encounter. How might this be helpful in texts they read in other classes? Or in texts they read in the world—to gain information or for entertainment?	HOMEWORK EXTENSION: Make a list of symbols you encounter in reading, television shows, or movies. Write an 8-sentence essay about which symbol was the most important to the story and why.

Chapter 11

THE QUEST IS TO POWERFULLY QUESTION!

Walking Students Through Expert Questioning Strategies

> **ESSENTIAL QUESTION**
> How do we support learners to independently generate the questions that help them notice, interpret, make, and apply meaning?

When Jeff was teaching seventh grade, he had a student named Tommy. Tommy was reading a story about baseball aloud to Jeff, stumbling over many words. He read that a base runner slid into second base and "kuh-nocked his kuh-nee." Tommy was in seventh grade and did not yet know the silent *k*! Jeff asked him what a "kuh-nee" could possibly be. Tommy replied tersely: "*I don't know. I only read what it says!*" Tommy interpreted reading as literal-level decoding.

See *Lesson Plan Canvas* on page 188

Later in the story, there was a play at home plate where the runner was called out. Jeff asked who had called the runner out. Tommy replied with some heat: "*I don't know! It doesn't say! I'm telling you what the story says, and you keep asking me what the story doesn't say!*" Jeff asked Tommy who calls players safe or out in baseball, a game Tommy loved well. "The umpire!" he almost yelled. "But it doesn't say who's doing it *here*!" Jeff asked Tommy what he was seeing when he read. "*See?! I see words, man, nothing but words!*"

The exchange struck Jeff like a laser. Tommy did not expect texts to make sense, and they didn't because he only read on the literal level, never bringing his life experience to bear on them. He did not know that readers have to bring textual details together, fill in gaps, and add their prior knowledge in order to make inferences and create story worlds or mental models of what they read. One of the many ways Jeff helped Tommy (see *"You Gotta BE the Book"* [Wilhelm, 2016]) to go beyond the literal level of reading and learning was through the use of questioning strategies. (There is a happy ending. By being apprenticed to use analytic phonics in the context of meaningful reading, Tommy learned about the silent *k*. When a new assistant librarian arrived named Ms. Knight, Tommy announced to Jeff: "She's Ms. Silent Knight!")

Traditional forms of informational and authoritative teaching keep students locked in on the literal and factual layers of learning. This, in turn, keeps these students from knowing learning should be meaningful, from experiencing the wonder of reading and of independent problem solving, from the power and joy of extending and exploring, and from figuring forth from their learning to achieve deeper meanings and see new applications that move them into the future.

Answering any kind of inquiry question, such as our essential question about civil rights, requires inferencing when we read any text or data set. It also requires connecting our personal lived experience and knowledge of the world to the new material we are reading or learning. To help our students learn how to make connections and inferences, we use a variety of tools and strategies such as three-level questioning guides, the Questioning Circle, questioning and answering in role, and others that support reading and thinking on these deeper levels.

HOW QUESTIONING FITS INTO EMPOWER

Helping students learn how to generate and answer higher-order questions that move beyond the literal is an absolute "must-make move" of guided inquiry/apprenticeship. Questioning is unquestionably (ha!) a necessary element in the repertoire of an independent learner, problem solver, and meaning maker. Experts use specific kinds of questions to help them notice, to see patterns and connections, to explore, to deeply understand, and then to do powerful work that really matters. This is how students need to be taught and then assisted to use questioning strategies on their own.

Through guided inquiry, educators assist learners in developing strategies and mental models that mirror experts' ways of making meaning. So, any questions asked by teachers must provide models—a *walk-through*—that help students become the ones who know how to generate as well as how to answer different kinds of questions.

Despite their popularity, "text-dependent" questions fall far short of what we're trying to do; they are but one tool in our tool kit. Text-dependent questions only apply to the *current* text. To us, such questions don't apprentice learners into more generative, independent, future-oriented expertise. Ultimately, our approach aspires to show students *how*—how to generate their own questions, how to use questions to pursue specific kinds of understanding, how to use questions to tackle multiple genres of text, how to use questions to notice, interpret, and unpack the data—so when they encounter these challenges throughout a lifetime, they feel equipped with a big toolbox and empowered to use it.

Since questioning to get at deeper meanings and understandings is necessary in every field, it's our responsibility to "pull back the curtain" and show students how the experts do it. In sum, questioning is not just a technique for teachers, nor should it be taught only as a comprehension tool. Questioning is a strategic repertoire that learners can and must develop as they pursue expertise as readers, composers, and problem solvers in any content area or domain.

Questions matter because of how they position and orient us, and what they help us to notice and do and learn in our evolving expertise. When teachers ask all the questions, or when questions focus on the literal level, the implication is that knowledge is static and comes from authority. Literal questions can promote understanding, be useful, and be internally persuasive, *but only if they are in service* of the inferential, critical, and evaluative questions that follow.

In the apprenticeship stages of walking through and extending/exploring, text-level questions modeled by teachers and then generated by students help learners to internalize the *noticing and interpretation* skills of experts. Questioning on multiple levels also assists in deepening understanding, reflecting on one's learning, and identifying and justifying how one knows what one knows, as well as identifying what one might not know *yet* but could know through future inquiry and apprenticeship.

Principles of an Effective Questioning Strategy

- Is planned to teach real-world expertise of the processes/mental map for (1) establishing factual information; (2) inferring the meaning of factual details, as well as inferring the meaning of patterns and connections between details; and then (3) evaluating and applying the generalizations and takeaways of what has been learned (E-M)

- Primes learners to use their background knowledge and orients them to the purposes and payoffs of using the questioning strategy in this instance and in general (P-O)

- Is concretely modeled by the teacher with the use of relevant texts or data sets (W)

- Helps readers see how texts and data sets work to express both meaning and effect, and therefore how we can all compose and structure texts for similar meanings and effects (W-E)

- Rewards learners for using a mental map that combines varied resources for developing understanding—the text or data set itself, one's personal lived experience, and the world/disciplinary knowledge (W-E)

- Mentors students into generating questions of different types and identifying each question type, the work each kind does, and what must be done to answer each kind (W-E-R)

- Leads to deeper conceptual understanding, and will help learners to justify their answers through evidence and reasoning (W-E-R)

- Provides opportunities for learners to reflect on and name their learning and learning processes, and to name ways forward in using the strategies in future situations for particular purposes (W-E-R)

QUESTIONING MOVE 1: THREE-LEVEL QUESTIONING GUIDE

In the vignette opening this chapter, Tommy could not move beyond literal decoding because he did not have a mental model of expert reading that included inferencing and reflecting while building meaning. A powerful technique for assisting readers of any text—visual, written, numerical—is the three-level questioning guide, because it moves learners through the levels of literal, inferential, and reflective evaluation and application questions. These question types are also known as "on the lines," "between the lines," and "beyond the lines" questions. The three-level guide provides support for generating powerful questions that work toward deep understanding and knowing how to find answers to them. Through this gradual release, an expert mental model of reading and how to pursue it with three levels of questioning becomes the domain of the learner and can be transferred across texts and situations. Figure 11.1 walks us through each type of question, as well as examples to prompt thinking.

Let's look at the different types of questions in three-level questioning:

"ON THE LINES" QUESTIONS

These are literal-level questions that have a directly stated answer. In other words, you can point at the answer and say, "The answer is right there!" This is the simplest kind of question. The reader finds the answer directly stated in the text through key details that deepen understanding. Key details are cued by rules of notice (see Chapters 9 and 10 for more on rules of notice, and download the complete list of rules of notice from the companion website, http://resources.corwin.com/EMPOWER-secondary).

"BETWEEN THE LINES" QUESTIONS

These are also known as inferential questions, which can be either Think and Search or Author and Me questions (according to the Question-Answer Relationship scheme [Raphael, 1982]).

- Think and Search: The reader searches for patterns in the text and then connects the dots and interprets the pattern formed by the different pieces of information.
- Author and Me: The reader "figures forth" by inferring additional meanings typically from one crucial and revealing piece of information. This requires connecting the detail to personal life experience or world knowledge that reveals the hidden or unstated implications of the details.

With "between the lines" questions, the questioner may be required to

- Infer what key details imply but do not directly say
- Connect details from different parts of the text into a pattern that reveals meaning, being able to explain the nature of the connections
- Ask an Author and Me question by identifying a textual detail and adding life experience or world knowledge to interpret it by
- Predict or anticipate consequences, what will happen next, or endings

- State underlying motivations and reasons for problems, events, or actions
- Make generalizations about a character, setting, problem, or other aspect of text

"BEYOND THE LINES" QUESTIONS

Also known as critical/evaluative/applicative or inquiry questions, these do not actually require textual details to answer, though the question will be related to a central topic of the text. The reader makes links between a topic of the text and his or her own experience and world knowledge to find the answer. The question is open-ended and promotes rich discussion and deeper understanding. The reader needs to justify the answer with evidence from beyond the text and reasoning about this evidence. *The topic of the text or data generally informs the question but will not be necessary to answering it.*

The questioner may be required to

- Make generalizations or explain rules the text or data implies for human behavior
- Make comparisons to different extratextual events, actions, or ideas
- Make judgments, and consider how far he or she wants to accept, resist, or revise major points that apply to the world
- Make recommendations and suggestions
- Make decisions
- Create alternative endings and explain differences in meaning

■ **FIGURE 11.1: THREE-LEVEL QUESTIONING GUIDE**

QUESTION TYPES AND DEFINITIONS	EXAMPLES (REHEARSE SAMPLE QUESTIONS HERE, INCLUDING EVIDENCE FROM TEXT OR YOUR LIFE NECESSARY TO CRAFT AN ANSWER.)
ON THE LINES (or Right There questions) TIP: This kind of question should highlight a *key detail* (cued by rules of notice) that is important to understanding the text at a deeper level. This kind of question should be in service of the higher-level questions that follow it—between and beyond the lines. To ask this kind of question: • Identify a directly stated key detail that conveys deep meaning or that may be important later on, or identify a directly stated point, generalization/main idea of the excerpt, or what might be a main event or consequential action. **CONFIRM: To confirm this question type, find the answer at one place in the text and point to it in the text.**	Examples of "on the lines" question starters, *if the answers are directly stated:* • **What happened . . . ?** • **How many . . . ?** • **How did . . . ?** • **Who . . . ?** • **What is . . . ?** • **Which is . . . ?** • **When did . . . ?** • **Where was . . . ?**
BETWEEN THE LINES (or Think and Search/Author and Me) **Think and Search questions:** Search for patterns in the text and then interpret or explain the pattern formed by the different pieces of information. TIP: This kind of question should connect key details to reveal patterns that express implied meanings. This can also be called a "connect the dots" question.	Examples of Think and Search question starters: • Why did . . . ? • What was the deep or hidden reason for/implied meaning of . . . ? • Why might X be important? • What might be the implications or consequences of detail/action/result X?

(Continued)

(Continued)

■ FIGURE 11.1: (CONTINUED)

QUESTION TYPES AND DEFINITIONS	EXAMPLES (REHEARSE SAMPLE QUESTIONS HERE, INCLUDING EVIDENCE FROM TEXT OR YOUR LIFE NECESSARY TO CRAFT AN ANSWER.)
Author and Me questions: The reader infers additional meanings from one crucial and revealing piece of information. This requires connecting the detail to personal life experience or world knowledge that reveals the hidden or unstated implications of the detail(s). TIP: This kind of question should help you to interpret the unstated and implied meanings of a detail or event by connecting it to life experience or world knowledge. This involves going beyond what is directly stated to figure out deeper meanings. **CONFIRM: Think and Search questions can be confirmed by pointing to details in different places in the text and explaining how they are connected. Author and Me questions can be confirmed by showing how a detail can be interpreted by connecting it to details and knowledge outside the text, and usually include "you" or "me" in the question.**	**Examples of Author and Me question starters:** • What do you think about . . . ? • How can you explain . . . ? • What is your theory about why . . . ? • How do you think this was similar to/different from X (from another text or the world)? • How would the character/action/etc. be changed if the text were in a different setting or if the situation was changed to/there was a different narrator (or any kind of change) . . . ? • How does this excerpt extend or complicate our understanding from previous understandings or other texts we have read? • Do you think that . . . should have . . . ? • What else could he/she/you . . . ? • How would you . . . ? • Do you agree . . . ? • What do you think would have happened if . . . ?
BEYOND THE LINES (On Your Own: Evaluation and Application questions) TIP: This is an inquiry question that requires generalizations or rules that can be applied beyond the text (e.g., making a claim that is generally true about the world beyond the text, or setting a rule about behavior applicable in the world beyond the text). **CONFIRM: "Beyond the lines" questions can be confirmed by demonstrating how the question is about the world beyond the text and could be answered without information from the text if needed.**	**Examples of "beyond the lines" question starters:** • What is courage/love/leadership (a definition that applies to the world)? • What makes a powerful speech/effective parent, great leader, good relationship etc.? • What actions most effectively promote civil rights? • How might major ideas/rules about the topic be used/applied in our lives? In policy? • How might . . . ? • What effect does . . . ? • In the future/in this different context of . . . what would follow . . . ? • How might I use what I've learned in future readings on this topic? When I encounter particular problems or challenges that I might envision?

The process for guiding students through the three-level questioning guide is as follows:

Step 1: Prime students when you first introduce the three-level questioning guide by asking how they know that they really understand something. Prompt them to think of something they deeply understand and the

178

ways in which they demonstrate deep understanding. Point out that understanding has multiple levels. Continue priming by viewing an excerpt of "Questions Only" from *Whose Line Is It Anyway?* (www.youtube.com/watch?v=tkxRzV3gtDcor) or playing a round of Twenty Questions. Ask students to reflect on and name what kinds of questions generated the most insight or discussion, and how questions can be sequenced so that one question leads to a deeper one.

Step 2: Orient learners by explaining that expert understanding goes beyond facts to the implications of facts, the connections between details, and the deeper meanings and applications of what has been read. Ask learners to consider how often they ask questions that go beyond the literal, and when and why they do so.

Step 3: The walk-through begins by explaining the three question types and how they mirror what expert readers and learners do when they reach for understanding and use; the template in Figure 11.1 can serve well here. Use this guide to model how to use the question types and stems to generate questions of each type. Quickly move to having learners help you, and then to helping each other. Share and provide procedural feedback about power moves and potential moves used by the students.

Step 4: Have students explore and extend the use of the questioning guide by applying it independently to their own reading or learning. Peers and teacher can "Gut Check" the question types with learners and help to revise them as necessary. Throughout, ask learners to reflect on how the different kinds of questions help them develop deeper understanding, and to assess how they have improved in asking higher-order questions.

QUESTIONING MOVE 2: THE QUESTIONING CIRCLE FOR USING MULTIPLE RESOURCES

In the opening vignette, Tommy could not move beyond literal-level questions and comprehension, create a story world, or experience the joy of living through that world because he did not bring his personal and world knowledge to bear on what he was reading or learning.

The Questioning Circle is a strategy (Christenbury & Kelly, 1983) that provides a structured framework for developing questions about a text or data set using personal reality and real-world knowledge. It expresses the expert mental model that reading requires, drawing from combinations of three resources: one's personal interests, questions,

(Continued)

(Continued)

and experience; the text/data itself; and knowledge of the world beyond the text. The Questioning Circle scheme helps students understand the resources they must access to answer particular kinds of questions. This strategy also helps learners think more critically about a text/data/experience and see how its implications can be applied to their own lives and to the world. Most important, the technique apprentices and scaffolds learners toward writing their own questions that draw on all three resources for making meaning with texts, data sets, and experiences.

These three resources must be interconnected for an interpretation to constitute understanding that is respectful of the data, personally compelling, and useful in disciplinary work and out in the world. Questions can require only one resource to answer, but more complex questions will require the combination of two resources. A dense question requires using information from all three resources and constitutes a rich inquiry question that will yield deep understanding and applications. The Questioning Circle also works well in the content areas with data of all kinds and represented in different ways. (See the companion website at http://resources .corwin.com/EMPOWER-secondary for examples of a Questioning Circle in different content-area contexts.)

online resources

Follow the following steps when introducing a Questioning Circle to your students:

Step 1: Prime students by asking them when they have had to figure out something that wasn't directly expressed, or was hidden. Highlight how they use past personal experience and world knowledge to make the inference. For example, how do they figure out the mood of a parent, teacher, or friend?

Step 2: Next, orient students by explaining that making text-to-self, text-to-text, and text-to-world connections mirrors expert meaning making. Highlight that the Questioning Circle will explicitly help them to notice connections, and to generate and explore questions that reveal these kinds of connections. You will also want to emphasize that drawing from extratextual sources of information (one's personal reality and world knowledge) is absolutely necessary for inferencing, for generalizing and applying, and for all other "between" and "beyond the lines" kinds of thinking. In this way, the Questioning Circle assists learners with the movement from the literal to the inferential to the evaluative and applicative.

Step 3: Begin the walk-through by explaining that the Questioning Circle consists of three overlapping areas of knowledge that expert learners bring to bear when reading and interpreting anything:

Knowledge of the text or other material being studied	Text
Personal lived experience, interests, and questions	Self
Knowledge of the world and other texts	World

Step 4: Share the diagram in Figure 11.2 and highlight how questions can require drawing on a single resource, or the combination of two resources. For the highest-order thinking about a text/data set, all three resources are required. This dense question is always an inquiry question with personal and social implications.

■ FIGURE 11.2: QUESTIONING CIRCLE

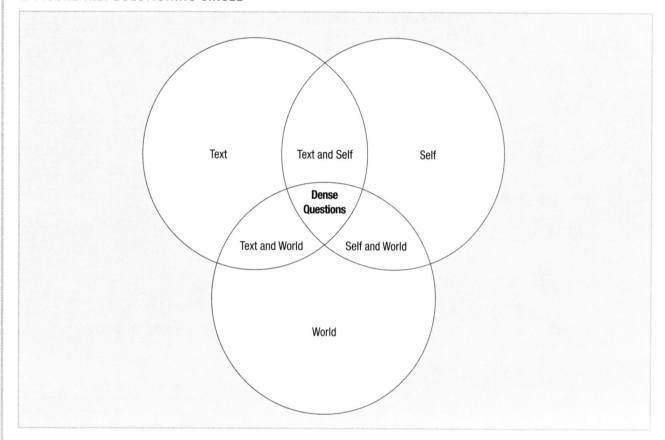

Students need to know how to frame questions of each type, and how to inquire into and reflect upon these complex questions in order to mirror the activity and mental map of an expert reader. (The Questioning Circle requires readers to have read a text or be familiar with new data, and the scheme has particularly strong value for conceptual mental modeling and deep understanding later on in a unit, as our example shows.)

Step 5: Introduce students to the idea that the question provides a path to the answer—that is, in thinking carefully about framing a question, the path to answering the question is explored. The walk-through continues by modeling how to generate questions of each type, and how to confirm (through what you do to answer each question) that it indeed relies on that one resource or combination of resources. Quickly, students are mentored into the process by asking them to help the teacher, then to help each other in pairs or triads to generate questions of each type. You can provide procedural feedback and reflect on what's been learned so that students continue to use it in future reading and inquiries.

(Continued)

(Continued)

The example in Figure 11.3 is from our civil rights unit.

■ FIGURE 11.3: QUESTIONING CIRCLE REVIEW FOR A CIVIL RIGHTS UNIT

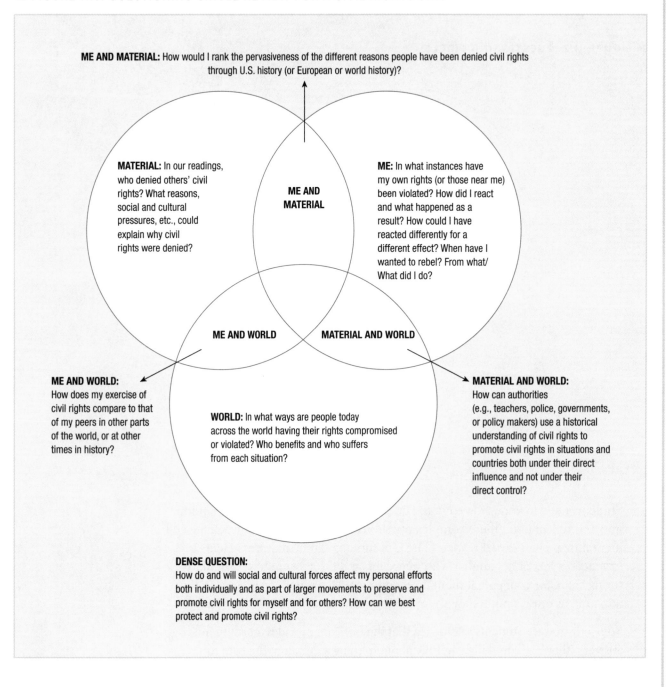

ME AND MATERIAL: How would I rank the pervasiveness of the different reasons people have been denied civil rights through U.S. history (or European or world history)?

MATERIAL: In our readings, who denied others' civil rights? What reasons, social and cultural pressures, etc., could explain why civil rights were denied?

ME AND MATERIAL

ME: In what instances have my own rights (or those near me) been violated? How did I react and what happened as a result? How could I have reacted differently for a different effect? When have I wanted to rebel? From what/ What did I do?

ME AND WORLD

MATERIAL AND WORLD

ME AND WORLD: How does my exercise of civil rights compare to that of my peers in other parts of the world, or at other times in history?

WORLD: In what ways are people today across the world having their rights compromised or violated? Who benefits and who suffers from each situation?

MATERIAL AND WORLD: How can authorities (e.g., teachers, police, governments, or policy makers) use a historical understanding of civil rights to promote civil rights in situations and countries both under their direct influence and not under their direct control?

DENSE QUESTION: How do and will social and cultural forces affect my personal efforts both individually and as part of larger movements to preserve and promote civil rights for myself and for others? How can we best protect and promote civil rights?

QUESTIONING MOVE 3: KEEP! A SCHEME TO UNDERSTAND TEXTUAL ORGANIZATION/GENRE

Imagine taking some papers from your school mailbox. When you pick each one up and skim it, the first thing you're likely to ask yourself is "What kind of text is this?" Is it a memo, an individualized education program (IEP), an advertising flier, a personal note? Your answer in each case will determine whether you read it, how you read it, what you expect and hope to gain from reading, and much more.

In our teacher research (e.g., Wilhelm & Smith, 2016), we have found that proficient readers read texts *as* something—as a type of text that organizes certain kinds of content in a particular way *to do particular kinds of work and engage in specific social actions*. The identification of the genre or text type guides reading of a text (and later composing of that kind of text). Texts, indeed, are structured by thought patterns called *genres* and *text structures*. Yet, few of our students know how to use the rules of notice that would tip them off to the overall genre or embedded text structures that organize the key details of a text, and would help them to navigate and make meaning of that text. Because there are so many kinds of texts, we can't teach the characteristics of all of them. Instead, we teach students a general set of questions they can use over and over again:

K: What *kind* of text is this? What rules of notice help me to identify it? (see Chapter 10)

E: What are the *essential* features of this kind of text?

E: How did the author *employ* these features?

P: What was the author's *purpose* in employing them that way?

!: What meaning and effect did the author want to achieve (i.e., what social actions with what audience and in what situation are the goals of the communication)?

We call this questioning heuristic KEEP! and we have found that these questions are important for readers to ask themselves no matter when (or what) they read. Doing so helps students build knowledge of genre and to use genre expectations to make meaning both as readers and as writers.

EXAMPLE KEEP! ANSWERS FOR THE "I HAVE A DREAM" SPEECH

K: This is a speech. The first sentence tells us that Dr. King is giving the speech to a large and historic gathering.

E: A speech has to be interesting to a live audience that is right there. It has to be a performance. It has to be emotionally appealing. It should rouse people to change understanding and action.

(Continued)

(Continued)

E: Dr. King appeals to notions of fairness and justice. He uses repetition, and uses references to historic documents like the Gettysburg Address, the Declaration of Independence, and the Exodus in the Bible. He also repeatedly uses the metaphor of the check that has not been honored to show the broken promises, and appeal to people's sense of fairness and justice, to charge their emotions and rouse people to action to right the wrongs done to them and others.

P: Dr. King wants to show how long the people have waited and how many promises have been broken to show that the people are impatient and cannot fairly be asked to wait any longer.

!: The message to everyone is that we have to work together *right now* to do whatever we can to address the civil rights issues we see around us—that unfairness to anyone leads to an unfair and unjust society that hurts all of us.

QUESTIONING MOVE 4: HOTSEATING FOR IN-ROLE QUESTIONS AND ANSWERS

Hotseating is a drama technique in which learners are put in the role of a character, an author, or a historical figure (or even a force or an idea). In the role, they ask or answer questions in some kind of context like a news conference, town meeting, interview, or interrogation. Hotseating helps students go further with inquiry-based questioning because it promotes social imagination and has them take the position of a character, to think about what they would ask that character, and/or to think about how they would respond from a different perspective.

online resources

Figure 11.4 can be used to guide students through the process of hotseating. You'll find much more information on roles for questioning on the companion website, http://resources.corwin.com/EMPOWER-secondary.

Your name: _____

Title of assigned reading: _____

In groups of three or four students, choose a character from this text that one (or more) of you will become for the hotseating. The teacher may also assign groups to represent different characters. It is important that the group agree on the following information about the character so that any one of you can go to the hotseat and answer questions from the class in that role. If the information required to answer a specific question is not in the text, then you will have to infer or make an educated guess about it based on what you know from the text, your own life, and the world. All of the following prompts address crucial rules of notice about character and about narrative experience.

Name of character:

Your age and physical appearance:

Your house, city/area, favorite place(s):

Your favorite activities:

Your favorite passions, "soapbox" topics, deepest desires (these may not be mentioned in the text but should be suggested by it):

Your deepest values and commitments (and what makes you say so):

Your main goal (and what makes you say so):

Your biggest problems and obstacles to achieving your goal:

Your biggest influences:

Your greatest strength(s):

Your greatest weakness(es):

One or two words that best describe you—give examples from the text that demonstrate these traits:

Members of your group not being hotseated will be your LIFELINE, your INNER VOICE (telling us the truth if your character will withhold from us, will lie, or has repressed something), AND will get to ask the first two questions. What will they be? You may also choose to question from a specific role. How will your character respond? How do you know that these responses are good ones?

Question 1/from role of _____: _____

Answer: _____

Question 2/from role of _____: _____

Answer: _____

What other questions might the audience of your peers ask? What roles from our inquiry might they play? What will they want to know? How will your character respond, and why will he or she respond that way? Rehearse a few possible questions with your group.

(Continued)

A FEW VARIATIONS ON HOTSEATING

LIFELINE: The hotseated student can get advice from group members if he or she struggles to answer a question. They quickly confer to help the hotseated character know how to respond.

ALTER EGO or INNER VOICE: Each student-in-role could have another student from the group stand behind him or her to play the "alter ego," "inner voice," or "conscience" and, after each response, reveal the character's inner thoughts and feelings that the hotseated character would not reveal in public or may be in denial about or repressing. In this way, the hotseated student says what the character would say in a public interview, but the inner voice says what the character might be thinking and feeling behind the persona or "mask."

CONTEXT: Play out the hotseating in an interview, press conference, trial, debate, or talk show.

GOOD ANGEL/BAD ANGEL: If a character is having a dilemma, other students can visit the character in the role of a good angel trying to help, or a bad angel tempting the character to make the wrong decision. Students can debrief by reflecting on the strategies used and how these exemplify argument strategies (ethos, logos, pathos) and manipulative strategies of persuasion.

WHISPERS: If a character is in deep trouble and in need of help, other students can walk by and provide verbal support and advice. Afterward, students can discuss what comments were most helpful and why. This can be an imaginative rehearsal for real-life response to people suffering problems.

DEBRIEF: After the hotseating, learners review what went well and what moves or answers they would change now that they have had time to reflect. One of the great things about drama is that it's like a tape recorder—one can always "rewind" and redo things, erase, or fast-forward into the future. Too bad real life isn't like that!

Source: Adapted from Wilhelm, J. D. (2013a). *Action strategies for deepening comprehension.* New York, NY: Scholastic.

PLC connection

PLCs, as always, can work together to devise a questioning scheme of some kind to use with students, and to serve as a model for future instruction in questioning. The strategies themselves can be used to look at school data or explore issues important to the community. Hotseating likewise can be used to explore perspectives of community members, refugee parents, and others.

POWERFUL PLANNING:
CREATING COMMUNITY BY ASKING AND LIVING THROUGH QUESTIONS

Questioning is a basic teaching method of all guided inquiry teaching models. It is also a basic learning method for developing understanding and expertise that is used by all manner of disciplinary experts. Questioning strategies (as is the case with all strategies) must be internalized so that questioning can be used flexibly and independently by the learner to develop deeper understanding of different situations and texts. That's where EMPOWER comes in: The principles of apprenticeship and deliberate practice help our learners become familiar with and internalize the questions and—even more important—the expert strategies exemplified in each scheme.

In our civil rights unit, we always use at least two of the questioning strategies shared here, and we always use hotseating to provide a context for questioning in a role and answering from different perspectives. We provide enough deliberate practice with those strategies that the students can use them independently. When students generate questions together, they have rich discussions that explore how to answer the question. When they share their questions and respond to each other, they become a community of practice doing inquiry together.

Transferring Our Learning: What to Remember When Helping Students Walk Through Their Learning by Asking Their Own Questions

- Consider what questioning strategy would be most helpful to learners right now given their needs and current goals. Which one seems "closest to home" and most usable for the purposes at hand?

- Highlight how the questioning strategy reflects a model of expert reading from the literal to the inferential to the reflective, always using multiple resources or perspectives.

- Provide collaborative mentoring and deliberate practice so that students own the strategy.

- Provide opportunities for students to reflect on their questioning and the work that different kinds of questions and questioning schemes do.

- Provide invitations and opportunities for learners to use these strategies in their free reading and in their thinking about other texts and experiences in their lives.

Lesson: Introducing Three-Level Questioning

Unit: How do we protect and promote civil rights?

ENVISION the destination
(Where are learners going, and why?)

GOAL *What kind of thinking is targeted?*	EVIDENCE *What product(s) will serve as proof of learning?*	MEASURES OF SUCCESS *What's the standard and quality-assurance tool?*	STAKES *Why will learners buy in?* *What's the "why" behind the learning?*
✓ Explanation/reasoning ✓ Application of skill/strategy ✓ Perspective taking ✓ Self-assessing/reflecting	✓ Performance assessment: generating questions, reflecting, justifying each type, and answering them ✓ Structured/unstructured observation of students generating and revising questions	✓ **ANALYTIC 1:** Score product against *one* category of a rubric (i.e., generating each question type and explaining how it is that type and what must be done to answer it).	Use ESSENCE as a guide for buy-in. Your lesson should have one or more of the following: ✓ E-S: Emotional spark/salience (i.e., relevance) ✓ S-E: Social engagement (i.e., collaboration) ✓ N: Novelty (i.e., new concepts and skills) ✓ C-E: Critical/creative exploration opportunities
Learners generate questions at three different levels—literal, inferential, and reflective—about a text or data set. They learn to use different literal key details to generate inferential questions that make use of key details, and then to use inferential questions to generate evaluative and applicative questions that generalize and apply what is learned.	Students generate connected questions at all three levels for a current reading such as *Number the Stars.* HOMEWORK: Students generate questions at all 3 levels on free reading, and can explain and justify each type and how each type aids understanding and meaning making.	Does the student have a balance of literal, inferential, and evaluative/applicative questions? Can the student explain what makes each type of question that type, what work each type does, and what is required to answer each type? √– = literal only √ = literal and inferential √+ = literal, inferential, and reflective	**E-S:** Teachers usually ask the questions. Now, students get to sit in the driver's seat. Questioning is a real-world skill with many immediate applications. **S-E:** Students play the question-asking game and do collaborative work. **N:** The strategies are new and powerful. "Questions Only" is a new game! **C-E:** Learners apply this to their own reading and life experiences.

MAP out the path to expertise/mastery
(How would an expert deconstruct and approach this task, step by step?)

TWITTER SUMMARY *(3 bullets max)*	MENTAL MODELS, PROCESS GUIDES	A MODEL OF GOOD WORK LOOKS LIKE . . .	DIFFERENTIATION AND LAYERING
Expert readers read on, between, and beyond on the lines. **OR** Readers "read and figure forth" from the literal to deeper levels of meaning that can be eventually applied to our lives and real-world situations.	• Three-level questioning model guide • Noticing key details using rules of notice to infer/interpret by explaining the hidden meaning of details and the implied connections between details to generalize rules and ideas that can be applied to other situations	*A key detail question that leads to an inference question that makes use of that key detail in some way that leads to an evaluative/applicative question that applies generalizations to personal life and the world*	Levels of assistance: Teacher and peer assistance to generate and confirm question types Different kinds of groupings Use of question stems as needed More modeling as needed More deliberate practice mirroring mental model Continual procedural feedback

POWER through your lesson
(What is the sequence of initial major must-make instructional moves?)

PRIME	ORIENT	WALK THROUGH (and check for understanding)	EXTEND EXPERTISE (PRACTICE) AND EXPLORE NEW TERRITORY (TRANSFER)	REFLECT
PLAY video of "Questions Only" from *Whose Line Is It Anyway?* where contestants must speak to each other *only* in questions. PROMPT students to partner up and try to play for a round. Note what questions work most powerfully, or how questions work together. Note what questions work for particular goals and needs, or that do not work. Note what helps students to generate questions and to think of answers. Students play "Questions Only" for a few rounds. Ask enthusiastic performers or volunteers to compete in front of the class. Reflect on and name what questions generated the most discussion and yielded the most insights.	FRAME today's lesson: "As we have been discussing, one of the most important skills a citizen or an expert in any field can develop is the skill of questioning. Readers need this skill to focus on important literal and inferential information and what this might mean for their thinking, problem solving, and living." "Today, we'll learn how to generate three categories of questions as we read, just as expert readers do . . ." "First, I want you to self-assess your current skills around questioning while reading . . ." Students self-score their current aptitude with questioning: 1. I rarely ask questions while I read. 2. I sometimes ask questions while I read. 3. I usually ask questions while I read. 4. I am constantly asking questions as I read. 5. I ask mostly literal-level questions. 6. I am aware of the different kinds of questions I ask to get different kinds of work done.	EXPLAIN: Three categories of questions: literal, inferential, and evaluative/applicative. CHECK FOR UNDERSTANDING: Have students categorize the list of questions from the beginning-of-unit opinionnaire (because these questions are familiar). MODEL: Teacher provides a think-aloud of how he or she generates questions of each type using question stems and rules of notice and seeing connections inside the text and from the text to issues outside the text, connected to the inquiry. Teacher then does a reflective process analysis of what he or she did, and models how to use the questioning strategies to analyze a different text, visual text, classroom episode, sequence from a sporting event, etc. CHECK FOR UNDERSTANDING: Ask students, *What did you see me doing? What strategies helped me generate questions of each type? Highlight rules of notice.* GUIDED PRACTICE: On the next section of text, have students generate new questions—in triads or pairs (this is for deliberate practice and formative assessment). DIFFERENTIATE: If some students are struggling, provide more modeling, work with them to assist, or have other successful groups assist. DEBRIEF: Share, revise, and evaluate questions students came up with.	DELIBERATE PRACTICE/ ARTICULATE CONSCIOUS AWARENESS: Learners provide their own think-aloud as they generate questions of each type together, then alone for a new text or experience. They articulate what they do to answer each question type and how this confirms the question type. Then learners provide a process analysis afterward that reviews and describes what they did to ask a question of each type, and how they monitored and self-corrected. Learners name the role each level of questioning played to deepen understanding of another chapter of the story, or helped them rehearse for transfer of this kind of questioning to their life and to their next reading.	Summarize what you learned. Why is it important? Self-score yourself on questioning now: What did you learn this unit, this week, or today that affected your score? What do you want to work on next? What is your action plan for doing this kind of questioning in the future? How can you use this questioning strategy in other classes, at home, in your favorite activities, etc.? HOMEWORK EXTENSION: Generate three levels of questions for your favorite fictional television program or movie this weekend.

Chapter 12

SETTING UP LEARNERS FOR SUCCESSFUL COLLABORATION

Walking Through and Extending Expertise With Collaborative Group Structures

> **ESSENTIAL QUESTION**
> How can we set up group structures that assist, require, and reward authentic collaboration?

Rachel recalls some of her first attempts at setting up collaborative activities as an early career ninth-grade teacher. She would come to class prepared with an activity idea like a problem-solving prompt, or a rich set of discussion questions around an intriguing essential question. She would proudly display the carefully crafted prompt or questions on the whiteboard. She would then sit back and wait to see the magical work unfold.

See *Lesson Plan Canvas* on page 204

But instead of jumping into the problem solving or into lively discussions with their partners, quite often students would read the prompt and then spend a few minutes half-heartedly talking with the person next to them before drifting into conversations about their plans for the weekend, or pulling out their phones to text. Or, even worse, they might simply read the prompt, shrug their shoulders, mumble something incoherent, and stare at her in silence, waiting for something to happen or for Rachel to provide the answers for them.

As McCann (2014) points out, it is not enough to move students into classroom activities with a prompt to talk or act. We need structures to focus and assist students to collaborate. Rachel did not yet have a repertoire for structuring collaboration and providing scaffolding to guide the success of group work. She did not yet have a way to design collaborative work for equity that promotes the engagement and learning of each individual in ways that contribute to group learning and the common project of the classroom.

Now, with the help of empowering collaborative structures, Rachel walks around the classroom and listens in as students engage in lively, respectful, helpful evidence-based discussions and problem solving for the entire class period, playing off of her or their own organizing questions (see Chapter 10) or prompts. They follow up with many more questions and generate answers and data from their own lives and experiences; they explore various perspectives and advocate for silenced or oppressed voices. After introducing bigger projects like those that might culminate a unit, Rachel can observe with satisfaction how students work together to decompose the task, divide up roles and responsibilities, and work over time on a problem or group multimedia composition together.

As teachers focus on meeting next-generation standards, the principles of universal design for learning (UDL), English language development (ELD), social–emotional learning (SEL), and inductive/restorative practices are necessary to meeting the diverse needs of all learners are met, it should also be noted that all these initiatives call for increased peer-to-peer collaboration in the classroom. In fact, "the ability to collaborate with others has become one of the most sought-after skills in both education and the workplace," and as collaboration in the classroom "gains new prominence in state standards, researchers and educators are working to understand how to help students gain the skills needed to learn and work in groups" (Sparks, 2017).

Despite the acknowledged benefits of collaboration in the classroom, it can be challenging to set up group structures that assist, require, and reward authentic and engaged "joint productive activity" that leads to the growth of all students that is both academic and interpersonal. Providing students opportunities to collaborate on a regular basis may seem easy in theory, but in practice, helping students learn to collaborate both respectfully and usefully can be much more complicated—and messy—and involve lots of assistance to develop SEL and executive functioning and work toward equity.

MEETING THE CHALLENGE

We can't emphasize this point enough: *Collaboration is a necessary component of apprenticeship and of all deep learning.* Collaboration is a requirement of democratic living and equity work, and it is a requirement of the modern workplace. It is essential to satisfying relationships and a fulfilling life. "Joint productive activity" is a hallmark of transformative teaching and learning and of expert communities of practice (Tharp & Gallimore, 1988). Experts in any field collaborate to develop knowledge. They work in groups to complete tasks, solve problems, elicit other perspectives, make plans, and justify and revise their thinking. Just like experts, students need regular and routine practice working with varied group structures, group configurations, and tasks. Essential elements of SEL are learning how to effectively collaborate, invite other perspectives, respectfully disagree and navigate challenges, be accountable, uptake and use each other's ideas, lead, and listen.

Collaborative group structures are a crux move in guided inquiry with cognitive apprenticeship because setting up a successful group structure is essential for students to apply a key concept or skill in the "we do together" phase. But students also need modeling and deliberate practice with collaboration in order to develop awareness, see from the perspectives of others, and experience success. In other words, if students don't know how to collaborate, then we must teach them. McCann (2014) points out that "Vygotsky (1986) reminds us that learning is social" but "this does not mean simply that students should engage in a lot of small-group activities, although that would be better than having few or no opportunities to work collaboratively with classmates" (16). When students are learning protocols for collaborating in groups, it can be tempting to skip the "I do" and "we do together" steps; resist this temptation. (Note that many of the discussion strategies in Chapter 13 involve modeling and mentoring and gradual movement toward independence with collaborative dialogic discussion.) Once students have learned protocols for collaboration, they will be able to keep improving their capacity as part of daily classroom practice and will move from collaborating with partners to working in small groups and with varied partners. Learning how to collaborate is a profound achievement in itself, and collaboration leads to deeper and more significant learning and more satisfying and reciprocal relationships.

SETTING UP SUCCESSFUL COLLABORATIVE GROUP STRUCTURES

One important factor of planning regular opportunities for collaboration involves thinking carefully about how you set up the learning space in your classroom. We realize that classrooms are often constrained by factors beyond your control—room size, number of students, tables versus desks, and so on. However, if at all possible, set up the classroom so that students can easily move between different group configurations. You will want to make it as easy as possible for students to turn and talk to a partner or to move desks into groups of four or five so they are facing each other. If all desks are facing the front of the class, this expresses that only the teacher is worth listening to. When students face each other in various ways, this expresses that learning will require the active participation of everyone and responsiveness to the needs of all.

We often have our students sit in quads and number the desks as 1, 2, 3, and 4 so students can quickly talk with a face buddy, elbow buddy, or crisscross buddy or do a "stand and deliver" by standing up when their desk number is called to provide a response or to ask a question of the group. (Just standing up puts more blood and glucose in the brain!) Also, consider the overall arrangement of the room, access to wall space for hanging chart paper, and room for students to move between desks for standing conversations in small groups or with partners. Finally, we always use pair, triad, or small group discussions instead of or before large group discussions. This promotes safe sharing and provides the opportunity for everyone to share.

HOW COLLABORATIVE GROUP STRUCTURES FIT INTO EMPOWER

In terms of EMPOWER, standard collaborative routines provide students with opportunities to experience *walk-throughs* that support collaboration as well as deeper focal conceptual and strategic learning. Learners are also invited to *extend* and *explore* expertise about collaboration and unit goals through deliberate practice with collaborative reading, composing, and problem-solving tasks.

In our civil rights unit, for example, we regularly structure classroom activity so that students spend the first chunk of class time writing reflectively about a civil rights issue that has come up in our reading, their experience, or current events. They then work in pairs, sharing their writing or discussing questions they have crafted themselves. They might search through the novel or articles they are reading to find textual evidence to support their thinking. They then move to a group of four and gather around chart paper to pool their thinking from their partner groups. They might craft a new question, insight, theory, challenge, or visual of the relationships among the data they have found. Finally, the last chunk of class time is spent in a Gallery Walk, with one student from the group of four staying with their chart to explain the group's thinking to other students as they move from poster to poster, adding their own thinking and questions. In the last few minutes, students go back to their desks, individually writing a reflection on how the lesson has added to or changed their thinking.

In this chapter, we provide examples of group structures that support students in having productive and meaningful collaboration. These moves illustrate how teachers can set students up for success in having meaningful conversations, solving problems, and creating artifacts of shared knowledge.

Principles of an Effective Collaborative Group Structure

- Provides students with a compelling problem or task to address that is immediately interesting and serves the inquiry. (P-O)

- Provides students with a clear focus for what they will be discussing or doing in their groups. The purpose is connected to the essential question for the unit of study and/or the central focal skills and concepts. It is also helpful to give students something to *talk around*: a data set, a prompt, an artifact, an image or collection of images, a quote, a list of items, an excerpt from a text, an article, etc. (P-O)

- Provides students with clear and explicit directions for their role(s), as individuals and as a group. Be clear about what steps they should complete, their deliverable, and how much time they have to produce the deliverable. It is extremely important to keep a rigorous pace with time limits for collaborative activities; you might want to project a timer and give regular updates—for example, "One more minute to have a deliverable to share!" Doing so supports students in staying focused and on task. (You can always provide more time if you observe that students need it. But when there is no "drop-dead" deadline, students tend to meander and waste time.) (W-E)

- Encourages full participation from *all* students. All students should be necessary to the work, and all students should contribute to it and be able to name their contribution. (W-E)

- Asks students to monitor how well they elicited, respected, and responded to various perspectives and contributions and reflect on how to progress in these areas. Asks how the collaboration helped them to see others, their perspectives, and their social worlds to foresee future possibilities. (R)

- Makes it clear to students what they should make or produce and be able to share in the time they have, and why that deliverable will be useful to the whole class. Accountability is essential to an on-task and successful collaborative activity. If possible, require both an individual and a small group deliverable for each collaborative activity (this promotes the synergy of personalized and community learning) along with quick reflections on the process and ways forward. (R)

COLLABORATIVE GROUP STRUCTURE MOVE 1: GALLERY WALK

A Gallery Walk is "a useful way to have students share their ideas and work, get responses to these, see patterns across other students' work and responses, and provide the stimulation for both formal and informal discussions" (Wilhelm, Wilhelm, & Boas, 2009, p. 86).

There are a number of ways to set up a Gallery Walk (also known as Stay and Stray), but the basic idea is for students to work in pairs or small groups to create a visual of their thinking or response to a problem, typically on chart paper or a whiteboard. The visualization ideas from Chapter 9 work well for Gallery Walks. The visual can be a response to a teacher-created question, a student-generated question, a prompt or challenge, or a problem to be solved (e.g., of how different stakeholders are interacting around a civil rights issue, or a visual theory of heat flow to explain why an attic is warmer than a basement). The visual is then displayed on the wall or laid out on tables. Students are provided with opportunities to view and respond to what other groups have created, adding ideas and looking for patterns, common threads, and differences and keeping track of new ideas or questions and challenges that are raised.

It's important to structure the preparation and the Gallery Walk itself to ensure that all students are necessary and fully participate. In the EMPOWER canvas for this chapter, this is accomplished through several key moves:

Step 1: Provide a focus for the Gallery Walk or negotiate one with students. For example, after reading Chapter 10 in *Number the Stars* and various historical and informational texts on Denmark during World War II, students work in pairs to identify challenges to achieving civil rights in an atmosphere of oppression

(Continued)

195

(Continued)

and ways to address the challenges. Alternatively or additionally, learners could be asked to craft higher-order (between or beyond the lines) questions focused on civil rights challenges in *Number the Stars*, or even across the different texts read (and one's personal experiences), and gather evidence to answer these. (See Chapter 10 for more on creating between and beyond the lines questions.)

Step 2: Students work individually and then in partners to generate a list of insights, connections, or questions about the focus. This provides each student with a peer thinking partner and invites full participation. The pairs rehearse potential answers to any of their questions.

Step 3: Students move to the small group of four or five with ideas to bring to the conversation based on their pair work.

Step 4: Learners share their thinking and then plan their visual display on chart paper or a whiteboard. They create a visual display of their thinking about the focus. This display often portrays different and even competing ideas.

Step 5: One student stays and explains the visual display to others while the rest of the group members circulate around the room to other displays and respond in ways they feel comfortable (talking, adding insights or comments on a sticky note that they initial, etc.).

Step 6: Students return to their home group, and each learner has the chance to explain something significant that was learned during the Gallery Walk. We might ask them to record this insight on a sticky note that they initial.

Step 7: Learners respond to an exit ticket to reinforce mindful practice and accountability and provide formative assessment data to the teacher:

> How has creating your display and viewing the displays of others impacted your thinking about this lesson's focal challenge and about our essential question, *How can we best protect and promote civil rights?* How would you assess your own participation in the groups you worked with: What did you do well, and how do you know? What do you want to do even better next time, and what's your action plan for doing it?

COLLABORATIVE GROUP STRUCTURE MOVE 2: THINK-PAIR-SHARE

Think-pair-share is a quick and easy way to provide students with opportunities for oral processing of questions, challenges, and new ideas. It should be a regular, even daily part of classroom practice in which students are given a clear, relatively simple collaborative task and then turn to talk with a partner. They can then share with a different partner or as part of a larger group, record responses for later use, and so on.

If students sit in quads (two desks facing two other desks), then the think-pair-share can be prompted by asking students to talk to their face buddy, elbow buddy, or crisscross buddy.

Some sentence frames to cue students in to think-pair-share include

- Now, turn to an elbow partner and discuss this issue/question/problem/ prompt/dilemma/controversial statement . . .

- Find another pair nearby and tell them what you think about/how you responded to . . .

- Get up and talk individually to someone from a different group about . . .

- Deliverable: Be prepared to write down a major takeaway from your discussions, or to share your ideas with another group or the whole class.

The think-pair-share (or think-triad-share) configuration lends itself to full participation because the exchange is relatively short, low-stakes, and in partners. A group of two (or three) gives an invitation to talk and support for doing so—even for our English language learning (ELL) students and most reluctant students.

Short response and questioning guides can also help prompt student responses and subsequent discussion in think-pair-share or larger group discussions. These guides prime and orient learners, preparing them for success with subsequent discussion. The guides also can work to support deliberate practice with threshold knowledge moves. Here are some examples:

Say Something: In this activity (Short & Harste, 1996), one person reads or makes a contribution, and his or her partner "says something" about the contribution or what has been read. Roles are then reversed. This guide is very easy and low-stakes.

Say Something About . . . : Prompt students to "say something about" a key detail, an important concept or word, or a connection from the selection to the inquiry, world, or personal experience. Depending on the text, students can be prompted to say something about a particular text aspect, like a key detail, the genre or text structure, a symbol, a point of view, an interesting insight or perspective, or the warranting of evidence.

Paraphrase Passport: This is often used in National Writing Project meetings. To speak during a small (or large) group, you must start by paraphrasing the contribution of the last speaker. A variation is to allow students to question or extend the previous comment. This requires active listening and encourages uptake—recognizing, addressing, and responding to or building on others' ideas.

COLLABORATIVE GROUP STRUCTURE MOVE 3: JIGSAW

In a jigsaw discussion, students are given or select a text (or excerpt from a text) to read, a topic to explore, or part of a problem to solve (McLaughlin & DeVoogd, 2004). The jigsaw is structured so that each student works in two different small groups, each with a specific task focused on full participation and a clear deliverable. The first group is students' "home group" that is typically assigned and heterogeneous, and the second is an "expert group" that students typically have some choice about joining. They start off in their home group to explore and discuss a particular general prompt or question. Then they proceed to an expert group to look more deeply at a specific aspect of the topic, to do a shared reading of a text excerpt or data set, or to focus on a specific angle or aspect of the problem to be solved.

For example, home groups could read the same text and then discuss the question, *What are general conditions and capacities of individuals and groups that contribute to the growth of civil rights?* They could then self-select into different expert groups to focus on a more specific aspect of the reading, or to read about or review different texts or additional data—for example, how the abolition of apartheid and growth of civil rights was achieved in South Africa, or how civil rights legislation was achieved in the United States. Then they return to their home group to report back, sharing new insights from their expert groups. This individual report-out is a crux move in the group structure, as it ensures full participation from all students through accountability to the peers in their group. No one else in the home group knows what they know, and what they know is necessary to the inquiry and perhaps an immediately ensuing activity. As each student reports out, the other group members have a process for recording what they are learning and a final, individual, "bringing it all together" task.

This group structure scaffolds a reading or problem-solving task by having students work in small groups to share ideas and strategies. But a key move here is the accountability when they move to mixed groups and, ultimately, in the individual response.

In preparation for the jigsaw and in keeping with the principles of UDL, the texts can be distributed randomly to students, students can choose the texts they read, or the teacher can match the texts to specific students based on ability (color-coded copies come in handy). The teacher can select texts of varied length, complexity, or type (a mix of written and visual texts) to allow for differentiation, providing less complex options for ELL students, students with disabilities, or struggling readers and more complex options for advanced students.

Students can use a graphic to capture notes about their thinking and evidence shared in their jigsaw groups. In the activity shown in Figure 12.1, students read their assigned text in their expert group with a focus on the author's use of evidence to support a claim. They then report out on their text to their home group. The graphic organizer provides a place for students to take notes as they listen to the reports of their peers and becomes a tool for them to return to later as they select evidence from the sources to support their own claims.

Jigsaw Note-Catcher

Article Title and Student Expert	Purpose of the Article	Most Logical, Relevant Evidence (Hervis moves)	Notes About Possible Limitations of Evidence and/or Source
Title: "Tip of the Day: A New Food Pyramid." Name of Student Expert: John	To illustrate that healthy food is based on the Harvard food pyramid. Also to show that what's healthy changes w/ time	• illustrating → french fries = vegetable • authorizing → Harvard • illustrating → food pyramids	1. use sparingly refined grains, red meat, and butter 2. whole grains are equal to fruits and veggies. These facts seem questionable in my experience
Title: "It's not just fast food..." Name of Student Expert: Megan	To show that getting rid of fast food restaurants would not stop childhood obesity	• countering: shut off supply but they still eat at home • illustrating: "western diet" example • extending: "the result:"	This seems like a reputable source because the author is a certified dietician.
Title: "Yes to poptarts" Name of Student Expert: Jennifer	To argue that bake sales are better than selling pre-made items.	• illustrating → children buy 2-3 bags • illustrating shared opinion about food companies • illustrating → high fructose corn syrup	I might question this source because there is no information about the author.
Major Takeaways/Synthesis	Defining what is healthy is complicated and there is no consensus in the scientific community. Also you can't force people to be healthy.		

THINKING HATS: A DRAMA DISCUSSION VARIATION ON JIGSAW

In Thinking Hats (De Bono, 1985), each member of a group uses a specific parallel thinking process about an issue. The process assists with mindful focus and productivity. Each hat divides thinking about an issue into a clear function, responsibility, and role. Each thinking role is identified with a symbolically colored "thinking hat." By mentally wearing and switching "hats," learners can easily focus and then reframe and redirect their thinking and the direction of a collaboration.

In a drama extension of Thinking Hats, each learner might discuss a focal issue from the perspective of a particular group who may have been affected by the issue. For example, in studying *Number the Stars*, Thinking Hat groups might include the Johansens (or typical Christian Danes), the Rosens (or Jewish Danes), German commanders, German soldiers who are not Nazis, members of the resistance, or Swedes who are helping Jewish refugees. Each group could respond to the inquiry question, *How can we best work for civil rights and social justice given our interests and the constraints of our situation?* They could then report out with the answers each perspective might offer, given their particular

(Continued)

(Continued)

interests and constraints, or create a chart or visual display of their answers. Students then return to their home group and share what they learned in the expert group.

Thinking Hats promotes powerful collaborations by accessing different angles and unique roles and perspectives related to the common project. Following are some possibilities for this strategy:

- The White Hat symbolizes clarity and calls for information that is already known, established, and needed—in other words, "the facts, just the facts."

- The Yellow Hat signifies optimism. Under this hat, one explores only the positives and probes for value and benefit.

- The Black Hat signifies the devil's advocate and explores the underside of a situation or why something may not work. Black hats identify difficulties and dangers; but beware overuse!

- The Red Hat symbolizes emotions: feelings, hunches, and intuition. Under this hat, one expresses emotional charges and feelings, sharing fears, likes, dislikes, loves, and hates.

- The Green Hat signifies creativity and growth; sees new connections, new possibilities, alternatives, and new ideas; and asks, "What if . . . ?" The Green Hat takes every opportunity to express possibility, new concepts, and new perceptions without any editing—let it rip!

- The Blue Hat is the manager of the overall thinking process and of the contributions of the other hats. It's the control mechanism that ensures that executive function guidelines are observed.

COLLABORATIVE GROUP STRUCTURE MOVE 4: SILENT DISCUSSION

In Silent Discussion, students write responses to teacher-generated questions or compose their own questions and responses. They then "silently" pass their paper (though this can also be done online in a Google Doc) so that the next learner can respond with additional insights or further questions. The fact that there is no talking during a silent discussion is by design and really puts the focus on promoting full participation during collaboration. A silent discussion is an easy entry point for students to practice collaboration, especially reluctant students—and there is the added bonus of limiting airtime for students who normally dominate the conversation.

Students begin either by folding their paper in quadrants and responding to a prompt or by writing a question of their own in the first quadrant, then composing a response to the question, in a short amount of time. When "time" is called, each student passes his or her sheet to the person to the left or right, who reads the question and the response to it and adds something new—building on, disagreeing with, revising, extending, or shifting thinking. This is repeated until everyone in the group has responded to each question in a separate quadrant. A variation is to have each student add a new follow-up question for the next person to respond to.

Note that this protocol focuses on the Three Level Reading Guide strategy from Chapter 11.

Step 1: Each member of the group (typically made up of four learners) takes out a clean sheet of paper and folds it in four.

Step 2: On the top of the sheet, each member composes a "between the lines" question (see Chapter 11 for more on questioning). On the back of the sheet, each member composes a "beyond the lines" question that prompts seeing text–text, text–world, or text–self connections, or that poses subquestions of the essential question.

Step 3: The members pass the sheets around the group, silently answering the questions, one student per quadrant. Responders could also compose more between or beyond the lines questions for others to respond to, especially if they feel the initial question has been sufficiently explored.

Step 4: The members continue to pass the sheets around until they receive their sheet back.

Step 5: The members read over the responses on their sheet and then discuss all responses orally with the group.

Silent discussion supports preparation for collaboration, collaborative thinking, and reflecting. It also provides a safe space for those who are less confident responding in larger groups. A variation on the silent discussion protocol is shown in Figure 12.2.

■ **FIGURE 12.2: VARIATION ON SILENT DISCUSSION QUESTIONING PROTOCOL**

Quadrant 1	Quadrant 2
Write a self, self–world, or "on my own" question that relates to the essential question, *How can we best promote and protect civil rights?*	Read the question in quadrant 1 and respond here with your own thoughts, reactions, questions, or shared feelings.
Quadrant 3	**Quadrant 4**
Read the question in quadrant 1 and what is written in quadrant 2 and respond here with your own thoughts, reactions, questions, or shared feelings.	Read the question in quadrant 1 and what is written in quadrants 2 and 3 and respond here with your own thoughts, reactions, questions, or shared feelings.

SILENT DISCUSSION EXTENSION: PASS-AROUNDS

Another form of silent discussion is the pass-around. This is useful when students are working on an I-search paper, a typically informal and personal research paper about a topic that is important to the writer, or some other kind of independent inquiry, personalized learning, or composing project. They write their topic or question or need at the top of a sheet with a request for resources, perspectives, and thoughts and then pass it around the classroom. Each learner adds an idea, question, or resource that might help the author or researcher with his or her work. When the original student retrieves the sheet, he or she should have many new ideas for moving forward.

COLLABORATIVE GROUP STRUCTURE MOVE 5: RANKING AND SORTING ACTIVITIES

Ranking and sorting activities lend themselves to successful group collaboration because they give students a clear problem to solve with an artifact to talk around. These activities facilitate collaboration by providing students with scenarios, objects, or manipulatives to organize in some way, requiring group collaboration and decision making based on individual reasoning. This process has never failed us. Give a small group or a pair of students an envelope with images, a list of items, a collection of very short texts, or a collection of quotes. Then, provide a task to complete: categorizing the quotes, grouping the items, ranking the significance or truth value of the items, and so forth. Finally, circulate the room and listen in as students actively work together to complete the task.

Another strategy for ranking and sorting is List-Group-Label, where students are provided or come up with a list of items related to the topic of inquiry, group them, and label the groups based on a system they negotiate together. Another ranking and sorting activity is to give students a list of items or texts to classify, like pictures of insects or mathematical equations. This provides great practice in classification and articulating the basis of the classification, both of which are necessary to scientific and mathematical thinking.

In a unit that explores poetry, students might be given a collection of short poems and group them based on themes, language, or style, or they might rank them in order of expressive power or some other quality. For an argument unit, students might be given a collection of evidence, or gather evidence themselves, and then group the evidence based on how they might use it in their arguments. Teachers could create any variation of these activities with items related to their topic of inquiry, but the basic idea is to provide students with tangible items to move around and "talk around" in their groups.

Other examples of ranking and sorting activities include

- Ranking and sorting historical events
- Ranking and sorting characters in a novel or short story
- Ranking and sorting mathematical concepts
- Ranking and sorting causes of specific phenomena

PLC connection

Use one of the activities from this chapter to collaborate on addressing or learning more about a current challenge or initiative undertaken by your team, department, or school.

POWERFUL PLANNING: COLLABORATING TO EXTEND EXPERTISE AND ACHIEVE DEEPER UNDERSTANDING

When teaching our civil rights unit, we use collaboration every single day. We take this a step further by connecting the notion of collaboration to the conditions for achieving civil rights. The same can be done in any subject area: studying symbiosis in biology, alliances in social studies, complementarity in math, and so on.

Just like other skills we have discussed in this book, students should be taught to work collaboratively in groups using the steps of cognitive apprenticeship. Routinely providing opportunities to solve problems through structured collaboration moves learners toward the independent skills they will need to successfully engage in other collaborative discussions and projects—in school and in the world. The setup and scaffolding for these collaborative group structures is key. Setting students up with a specific purpose, clear steps, roles and responsibilities, strategies for navigating difficulty, and a challenging but doable deliverable will work toward full participation and memorable learning opportunities that extend beyond what individual learning experiences can bring. Teaching and supporting collaboration is worth it. As Vygotsky (1978) maintained: in cooperation the child is always a head taller than herself. In other words, we are always smarter when working with others—we are always in our zone of proximal development and moving toward greater expertise.

Transferring Our Learning: What to Remember When Walking Through and Extending Expertise With Collaborative Group Structures

- Plan to use collaborative activities to move students through challenges in their zones of proximal development; for example, use collaborative structures when learners need each other to do a complex task they can do together but not yet do alone.

- Provide students with a compelling problem or task that is immediately interesting, serves the inquiry, and requires developing a required strategy or concept.

- Provide students with clear and explicit directions for their roles and responsibilities, as individuals and as a group. Be clear about what steps they should complete and how much time they have.

- Provide structures and scaffolds that will assist them to collaborate, use each other's ideas, navigate challenges, and make use of the focal strategy and concepts.

- Ask learners to produce and then reflect on both an individual and a group deliverable for each collaborative task that requires using focal strategies and concepts.

- Have students reflect on the process and ways forward. Make sure they are able to identify their individual contributions to the collaborative task and that they can name used power moves and potential moves of successful collaboration.

Lesson: Gallery Walk

Unit: How do we protect and promote civil rights?

ENVISION the destination
(Where are learners going, and why?)

GOAL *What kind of thinking is targeted?*	EVIDENCE *What product(s) will serve as proof of learning?*	MEASURES OF SUCCESS *What's the standard and quality-assurance tool?*	STAKES *Why will learners buy in?* *What's the "why" behind the learning?*
✓ Explanation/reasoning ✓ Application of skill/strategy	✓ Constructed (discrete task, long/short response, graphic organizer) ✓ Performance assessment: open-ended essay/writing, products (e.g., role-audience-format-topic [RAFT]), concept map	✓ **CHECKLIST:** Assess if product contains essential characteristics/features.	Use ESSENCE as a guide for buy-in. Your lesson should have one or more of the following: ✓ E-S: Emotional spark/salience (i.e., relevance) ✓ S-E: Social engagement (i.e., collaboration) ✓ N: Novelty (i.e., new concepts and skills) ✓ C-E: Critical/creative exploration opportunities
Collaborate with a partner and then a small group to record insights, and/or craft higher-order (between or beyond the lines) questions and gather evidence from the texts and personal experience to answer these. Then collaborate with other groups to reinforce their thinking or provide new ways forward.	Visual display of insights, and question(s) with responses Exit ticket: How has creating your display and viewing the displays of others impacted your thinking about our essential question, *How can we best protect and promote civil rights?*	Students work together to collaboratively generate insights, generate questions, and gather evidence. Full participation of all group members is encouraged. Students who "stay" at the poster clearly explain thinking and answer questions from peers. Students who "stray" listen attentively and add ideas, and can bring insights back to the home group. Exit ticket response is specific and includes references to the activity.	**E-S:** Teachers usually ask the questions or provide insights. Now, students get to sit in the driver's seat. Insight sharing and questioning are real-world skills with many immediate applications. **S-E:** Students engage in collaborative work with a clear deliverable. **N:** Varied group configurations (partners, small groups, Gallery Walk) are represented. **C-E:** Learners apply this to their own reading and life experiences.

MAP out the path to expertise/mastery
(How would an expert deconstruct and approach this task, step by step?)

TWITTER SUMMARY *(3 bullets max)*	MENTAL MODELS, PROCESS GUIDES, HEURISTICS	A MODEL OF GOOD WORK LOOKS LIKE . . .	DIFFERENTIATION AND LAYERING
Collaboration in various groups leads to generating more ideas from various perspectives and leads to deeper understanding.	Collaboration requires focusing on a shared purpose, pulling one's weight, sharing one's tentative thinking, uptaking others' ideas, being open, and coming to a new deepened or revised understanding.	*Everyone is working together on a shared project and for a shared purpose. Everyone makes visible contributions and uses the ideas of others.*	Levels of assistance: Assist peers to generate and confirm insights and question types—or get help from peers. Different kinds of groups More modeling as needed More deliberate practice mirroring mental model Continual procedural feedback

POWER through your lesson
(What is the sequence of initial major must-make instructional moves?)

PRIME	ORIENT	WALK THROUGH (and check for understanding)	EXTEND AND EXPLORE	REFLECT
Ask students to think-pair-share about what personal life circumstances, or events from the various readings, seem most injurious to achieving civil rights. EXPLAIN to students that by Chapters 9 and 10, midway through the novel, Annemarie has had many experiences that reveal how complicated it can be to promote and protect civil rights, especially during wartime or any context where one is oppressed and marginalized. Also, Chapter 9 is a key turning point in the novel because Henrik begins to treat Annemarie like an adult by revealing some secrets to her. Students gather all the resources from the unit that they might bring to their group—the novel, annotated articles/excerpts, think-alouds, reflective writing, ranking activity, personal connections, etc.	FRAME today's lesson: "At this key turning point in the novel, and after reading a range of other sources related to our essential question, you will collaborate with peers to record insights gained so far in the unit about the challenges and ways forward addressing the challenges to achieving civil rights in different kinds of contexts. You will also be asked to compose a higher-order question(s) and gather responses from the text that pertain to this focus. The deliverable will be a visual display of your insights and question(s) and responses for the rest of the class to view, learn from, and respond to." Students review materials to prepare for collaborative discussions—what initial ideas will they bring to the conversation with their partner? What evidence/data is important to attend to? Individually list some insights and potential higher-order question(s) about *Number the Stars*, or even all the reading and activities thus far in the unit.	ORGANIZE students in partners: Either assign (table buddy) or have students choose. REMIND students of what they learned about keeping track of insights and developing high-order questions (MODEL an example if needed). Circulate the room as students work with partners to generate a list of insights and a higher-order question(s). Once all students have at least an initial draft, ORGANIZE pairs into small groups either by assigning (table groups) or by allowing them to choose. EXPLAIN that they will work collaboratively in their new group to display insights and craft a higher-order question based on their partner ideas and to gather evidence from the novel, other texts, and class discussions to create a visual display of questions with answers. Circulate the room and MONITOR as students create their visual displays, stopping to answer questions or prompt groups that are stuck (or if there isn't full participation from all group members). MONITOR time, allowing sufficient time but maintaining a sense of urgency. Provide frequent reminders of the time left and the deliverable. As time wraps up, ensuring there is sufficient time for both the Gallery Walk and the exit ticket, EXPLAIN to students that they should select one group member to "stay" at the visual display while the others "stray" and view and respond to other visual displays. MONITOR the room as students explain visual displays and add thinking and ways forward on sticky notes. EXPLAIN to students that they will conclude by writing an individual exit ticket to REFLECT on their experience and ASSESS their own participation in their groups.	DELIBERATE PRACTICE/ ARTICULATE CONSCIOUS AWARENESS: Begin the next class period with a full-class debrief of the experience: What was your experience like working collaboratively with partners around this task? What did you have to negotiate? What was challenging? What was enjoyable about it? How did the experience impact your thinking about working collaboratively in the future? How does collaboration figure in to the struggle for civil rights? How does collaboration assist in deepening understanding, in completing complex tasks? How can you use collaboration as a conceptual tool to think about civil rights, and as a procedural tool for getting work done most efficiently in school and in your personal life?	EXIT TICKET RESPONSE: How has creating your display and viewing the displays of others impacted your thinking about our essential question, *How can we best protect and promote civil rights?* How would you assess your own participation in the groups you worked with? What did you do well? What do you want to do better next time? FUTURE REFLECTIONS: How can you monitor and self-correct toward more efficient and respectful collaboration in your academic and personal life? What is your mental model of effective collaboration? What is your mental map for achieving effective collaboration?

Chapter 13

TO SPEAK, TO BE HEARD, TO LISTEN, AND TO LEARN

Extending Expertise With Discussions That Promote Deeper Understanding

> **ESSENTIAL QUESTION**
> How can we promote the most effective classroom discussion that assists students to understand complex texts and problems and to navigate challenges?

James Britton (1983) maintains that "all reading and writing floats on a sea of talk" (p. 11). Many others have maintained that in fact *all learning* floats on a sea of talk—and research supports this (Nystrand, 1997). In the previous chapter, we looked at structuring group work in ways that aid in all kinds of collaborative activities, including talk. In this chapter, we dive deeper into ways to cultivate rich discussion that promotes and extends deep learning and understanding. Dialogic talk is a particular kind of collaborative activity deserving special attention because of its unique power to develop, apprentice, extend, and explore learning.

See *Lesson Plan Canvas* on page 221

Rich discussion that feeds engagement and learning can be challenging to achieve. Jeff recalls asking his seventh graders to discuss the civil rights implications of *Roll of Thunder, Hear My Cry* (a Newbery Medal–winning book about an African American family struggling to survive the Depression and the civil rights abuses of the "night riders"; Taylor, 1976) using a careful question sequence. It was a total flop. Epic fail!

The next day, Jeff used a variation of Quotation Café (a technique where students make inferences and predictions based on different quotes from a book they will read) by bringing in several quotes from reviewers of the book. He asked students to read through the quotes and write a response to the one that most grabbed them, either in agreement or in disagreement. He wanted the students to then pair up to share responses prior to a large group discussion run by a student leader and a discussion mapper (described later in this chapter). One of the quotes maintained that white readers would not understand the book and would find little to relate to. Nearly every student (both white students and students of color) chose that particular quote to respond to. They began to write, some of them furiously. Then one student looked up and practically yelled: "This review is full of crap! We can totally understand prejudice!" Another student exploded: "We experience prejudice and we see it and we feel it ourselves, even when it is against someone else!" The rest of the class cascaded in agreement—and some disagreement. Long story short: Jeff did not say a word for the next 42 minutes while a class of seventh graders ran their own discussion, responding to and building off each other's comments. Every student spoke at least twice.

What made the difference? Jeff's second attempt provided concrete priming and prompting, an emotional edge, and a structure and process to apprentice and walk the students through the necessary steps of preparing for, pursuing, and monitoring an engaged discussion.

HOW DISCUSSION FITS INTO EMPOWER

Vygotsky (1978) maintained that the meaning-making talk we engage in with others to maneuver through problems eventually becomes "inner speech," an internal kind of talk that captures what we call *mental models*: transferable maps that guide us as we expertly read, compose, and problem solve. This inner speech can become so internalized that the maps guide us with automaticity, but they can also be brought into consciousness as needed to productively navigate challenges.

The goal of the EMPOWER framework is for students to become independently and consciously competent (or even expert) using new processes and concepts to complete new kinds of complex tasks. To achieve this goal, learners must develop a new transferable repertoire of strategies that Vygotskians call a *tool kit*. In this chapter, we explore how to give learners a tool kit for developing mastery in leading, listening, participating in, sustaining, and monitoring their own discussions in ways that lead to inclusive community, equity, and deep learning. Any teacher-led discussions should therefore be in immediate service of students deliberately practicing the moves that would allow them to lead and engage in their own respectful and substantive discussions.

A key to guided inquiry/cognitive apprenticeship is the capacity to talk through threshold concepts and processes in service of both understanding and application (i.e., getting work done). This kind of talk helps us to create and flesh out mental models and flexible processes for doing complex tasks. That's why thinking aloud, explaining, and talking through our meaning-making and problem-solving processes each constitutes a powerful move for both teachers and learners (see Chapter 10). Questioning strategies (see Chapter 11) can also focus and frame meaningful talk about how to understand anything in more consciously competent ways. In this chapter, you'll learn how to combine questioning and group structuring strategies in service of apprenticeship through dialogic discussion. Research shows that this kind of dialogic discussion rarely happens in classrooms—it must be consciously primed and oriented, then actively apprenticed and mindfully extended through structures and strategies that promote deliberate practice with the "must-make moves" (Applebee, Langer, Nystrand, & Gamoran, 2003; Nystrand, 1997).

MAKING OUR LEARNING SPACES DIALOGIC

The hallmark of guided inquiry, and of inquiry-oriented discussion, is that it is *dialogic* versus *monologic*. Monologue reflects an authoritative, information transmission approach to teaching and learning. Monologue is interested only in predetermined answers and has no concern for the listener's knowledge, attitudes, goals, needs, and feelings. According to Johannesen (1996), the monologic communicator attempts to "command, coerce, manipulate, conquer, dazzle, deceive, or exploit" (p. 11). This is the information-driven authoritative discourse so typical in school and that works against educational equity, democracy, engagement, and transformative learning.

Dialogic communication, in contrast, reflects a sociocultural apprenticeship approach to teaching and learning. The mental model of dialogue is that of a reciprocal interaction where each person involved plays the roles of both speaker and listener, of participant and observer. In other words, dialogues are communication in which all participants are encouraged to express themselves and is committed to active listening and processing all that is said. Mutual understanding, internal persuasion, and empathy are the results of dialogic communication—even when those conversing are opposed. There is a deep concern and respect for the other person(s), the relationships between them, and the needs of all. In dialogic communication, procedural feedback and feedforward (see Chapter 6) replace pushback, resistance, and critique of other's ideas, because the goal is negotiating meaning and furthering mutual understanding, processes of understanding, expertise, relationships, and a common good. Because of these purposes, an essential element of dialogic discussion is "uptake"—that people respectfully recognize, respond to, and actively address each other's needs and questions, and build on and revise each other's ideas.

To engage in dialogic conversation, learners need strategies to effectively frame and reframe conversational topics, to express ideas that are on point, to listen and summarize prior points, to uptake and build on ideas so that reciprocity and mutual understanding are promoted, to navigate disagreement, and to show respect for different perspectives. And, of course, we focus discussion on the content of the inquiry so that learners create mental maps of the conceptual and strategic territory (of the definition of civil rights, the history of civil rights, how to advocate for oneself and others, how to effectively work for civil rights, etc.). We cannot forget that receptive and careful listening is essential to learning from each other. If students are not yet good listeners, then we must teach and assist them to become better (as is the case with any stance or strategy). In his groundbreaking book *Not Light, but Fire* (2018), Matthew Kay proposes that creating community (Chapter 6) and using techniques such as those featured here are what enable students to usefully discuss significant yet volatile issues such as race. Kay argues that through authentic inquiry and combining dialogue with respect, humility, and ongoing reflection, teachers can make school an energized and safe place for young people to honestly discuss the most urgent and volatile social justice issues that directly affect them.

The companion website at http://resources.corwin.com/EMPOWER-secondary contains two downloadables that may be helpful for you and your students when forming dialogic classroom spaces: a quick-reference chart for students that compares dialogue with debate, and a one-pager for teachers detailing nonviolent communication as dialogic procedural feedback. (Both could be used in PLC work, as well.)

Groundbreaking research from Applebee et al. (2003) found that dialogic discussion-based approaches led to impressive progress in academic achievement across student groups and settings of all kinds. The gains were found (1) when discussion was dialogic, thought-provoking, and academically demanding; (2) when discussion worked to build "envisionments" or mental models of understanding; and (3) when discussion led to curricular cohesion—that is, when the discussion fit an ongoing disciplinary conversation that students were pursuing over time (as in a guided inquiry approach).

PLC connection

Lesson study is a way to frame and support meaningful talk about teaching through co-planning and then reflecting on lessons. Analyzing student work together is another high-leverage discussion activity.

Principles of Effective Discussion

- Involves planning for specific kinds of conceptual learning related to the inquiry, and for specific kinds of strategic learning, particularly about speaking and listening (E-M)

- Requires students to read, write, and prepare in some concrete form pre-discussion (P-O)

- Prepares learners for success initiating, framing, and sustaining discussions (P-O)

- Motivates learners to share their unique ideas and insights with their peers (P-O)

- Uses discussion structures and scaffolds to promote engagement, inclusion of all involved, exploration, elaboration, personal inquiries, respect, understanding different perspectives, search for shared values and common ground, development of mental models and maps for problem solving, and high-road transfer (W-E)

- Promotes uptake, mirroring/summarizing, and asking thoughtful follow-up questions (W-E)

- Goes beyond pro/con, either/or, and all binary thinking to look for multiple paths forward; bridges the gaps; and works toward the capacity to articulate, understand, and even defend various positions simultaneously (E-R)

- Helps learners clarify and reflect on what they are coming to know by asking them to name their learning and monitor their growth and to set action plans for future applications (R)

- Works for continuous improvement by naming and deliberately practicing potential moves of dialogue (E-R)

- Promotes transfer of powerful conversational moves into future academic discussions and civic discourse (R)

PROMOTING DEEP DISCUSSION MOVE 1: CAROUSEL CONVERSATIONS

Carousel Conversations (also known as "speed dating") are a fun and enjoyable way to get students talking pointedly about a particular prompt, issue, process, or artifact with one peer at a time, moving through several paired discussions. Students form an inner circle and an outer circle (standing or in seats) and have a set amount of time—typically 60 seconds or so (we use a timer and adjust the amount of time to the task but always keep it short)—to present their thinking, micro-writing, or other knowledge artifact such as their explanation of a drawing regarding the topic of conversation. They then reciprocate by listening to their partner for the same amount of time. A third 60 seconds could be taken for both participants to uptake each other's comments. Then the outer circle switches seats by moving one position to the right or left. The learners now have a new partner. This can continue for several turns before asking the learners to reflect on what they learned from their various exchanges.

The model Carousel Conversation lesson described in this chapter's EMPOWER canvas combines a variety of techniques: priming through responding personally to controversial statements/prompts, orienting through oral rehearsal for micro-writing, the walk-through of composing micro-arguments using the mental model of claim-data-reasoning (CDR) or claim-reasons-evidence-warrant (CREW), and then sharing and responding to these arguments through various "speed dates" (which prepares students to respond to reservations in their arguments, extending CDR to CDR-R and CREW to CREW-R) and reflecting on what has been learned. A possible extension is to then spontaneously compose new micro-arguments together in Carousel Conversation pairs.

Carousel Conversations are fantastically flexible and can be used to share thinking about any topic or to share and respond to any kind of micro-writing, process, or knowledge artifact. You can focus and structure the discussions in any way that fits your purposes. Students can even discuss in role (e.g., the outer circle students play activists with a proposal for pursuing change, and the inner circle students play famous civil rights reformers responding to these proposals or play those with vested interests who might be threatened by change. (See roles for questioning in Chapter 11 and on the companion website, as well as drama discussion roles later in this chapter.)

PROMOTING DEEP DISCUSSION MOVE 2: DIALOGUE PREPARATION TOOLBOX

Before learners can fruitfully participate in a discussion, they need to be primed, oriented, and prepared. The following moves are designed to prepare students before a collaborative activity begins so that they come to the activity with ideas to get the sharing started.

(Continued)

(Continued)

QUICK WRITES

A quick write involves a teacher (or student) providing a provocative prompt (such as a controversial statement—see Chapter 8) to respond to, or a prompt that asks learners to name what they have learned and why it matters, make connections and see relationships, pose questions, or reflect on and extend the implications and applications of what is being learned. Teachers can also prompt students to use concepts or vocabulary from the unit (from anchor charts or word banks) in their responses. Quick writes can likewise be used as an entrance or exit ticket (see Chapter 14).

The first step is to find or generate an open-ended prompt related to threshold knowledge. Examples from our civil rights unit might include

- Based on our reading, what seems to be the most effective way of fighting for civil rights? What makes you say so?

- Dr. King wrote that the arc of history is long, but it bends toward justice. To what degree do you agree or disagree, and why? To what degree would various characters and historical figures we have studied agree or disagree, and what makes you say so?

Learners are given a short amount of time (two to five minutes) to compose a response. They follow up with a think-pair-share, then can proceed to a different think-pair-share, small group share, or full class share.

ENTRANCE TICKETS

Learners can show they are prepared to contribute to a discussion by completing an entrance ticket to the next class that is assigned in the previous class meeting. This ticket can ask students to write notes, bring questions to ask, list major points to make, complete a preparatory worksheet, prepare a visual response, and so on.

DISCUSSION ITEMS/JOURNAL ENTRIES

Reading and learning journals can be used to prompt students to identify discussion items (DIs). DIs are student generated and can be *real questions, substantive comments, points of important connection, significant quotations, or provocative statements* inspired by students' reading or the overall inquiry. Before class, we ask that students list three to five DIs that they would be interested in discussing. The DIs and journals can be used to initiate discussion or submitted to the teacher who can choose particular ones for small groups to discuss. (You'll find a downloadable guide for using journals and discussion items on the companion website, http://resources.corwin.com/EMPOWER-secondary.)

online
resources

QUICK DRAWS

A quick draw (Himmele & Himmele, 2009) and sketch to stretch (Burke, Harste, & Short, 1988) are similar techniques through which learners "draw" a visualization of their understanding of an abstract process (e.g., how mirrors or lenses reflect light) or concept/term (e.g., civil rights). The drawing should be focused on a big idea or threshold knowledge. Provide time for learners to explain their drawing to a partner and then a small group, get a response, and revise it. This exchange will constitute rich discussion that leads to mental mapping.

STUDENT WORK SAMPLES

Excerpts of student-generated think-alouds, questions, visual creations, or responses to artifacts (like an object or image related to the topic), data sets, YouTube videos, photos, and so on can be used as source material to stimulate discussion.

ANCHOR CHARTS/CHALKBOARD SPLASHES/SKETCHNOTES

These techniques are all ways to record and summarize the major points made in student quick writes, journal entries, quick draws, or other forms of preparation so that they are available to everyone in the classroom for use during discussion and reflection. As students share their responses, these can be copied onto chart paper, the whiteboard, or elsewhere using words, codes, and visuals (we typically have a student scribe do this work). Students can then be asked to work in pairs or triads to notice similarities, differences, ruptures, patterns, and reader responses among the ideas recorded, and use these insights to fuel discussion.

PROMOTING DEEP DISCUSSION MOVE 3: ACTIVE LISTENING TOOLBOX

Most human beings, and certainly most of our students, need deliberate practice in becoming what we call "careful listening friends." All of the following activities can promote active and respectful listening to the perspectives and messages of others.

It's important to recognize that our personal filters, perspectives, assumptions, judgments, and beliefs can distort what we hear. As a listener, our role is to understand what is being said—to comprehend the speaker (or author) in the terms in which he or she wants to be understood. This requires conscious effort and the capacity to strategically bracket our biases and to reflect, mirror, ask questions, and provide and receive procedural feedback.

In all dialogue and discussion activities, we provide learners with prompts for some kind of deliberate practice with active listening and response. We model and actively teach how to uptake, how to establish and monitor norms for effective discussion, and how to disagree or handle disagreements, and then ask learners to deliberately practice and monitor these moves. We highlight uptake as one of the following: agreement and an explanation why; agreement plus extension, refinement, and questions/wonderings; or respectfully and causally (e.g., with "because" statements) explained disagreement. We foreground that we cannot disagree with what we do not yet understand.

(Continued)

(Continued)

Here are some of our most effective active listening strategies that foster uptake:

- Clarifying questions: Learners should ask questions to clarify certain points. Generate, post, and use stems to assist learners: "What do you mean when you say . . . ?" "Can you tell me more about that/about what you mean when you say . . . ?"

- Mirroring/summarizing: Ask learners to periodically summarize the previous speaker's comments or deeper points—or to mirror the overall conversation thus far. Learners should then confirm with the speaker that they understand him or her the way he or she wants to be understood.

- Paraphrase passport: Ask learners to describe and then reflect on what has been said by paraphrasing: "What I'm hearing is . . . " "Sounds like you are saying . . . Is that correct?" Confirm from the speaker that this is what he or she meant. This can be used as the "passport" or requirement to sharing your own reflection or contribution.

- Following questions/mirror statements: Learners ask questions that mirror back to the speaker: "Tell us more about. . . ." "Can you or anyone else give us another example of that . . . ?" "I heard you say that you think X . . ." (e.g., "I heard you say that civil rights problems are best addressed in a local community rather than by the federal government"). Typically, even just a mirror statement elicits more elaboration from the original speaker.

- Cite your classmate: Actively encourage learners to cite their classmates both in discussion and in their writing. Highlight and celebrate this move when it happens, and explain how this kind of substantive uptake is essential to a community of practice.

- Enactive questions/mental map questions: This question type (Morgan & Saxton, 2006) focuses learners on future action (e.g., *What will we do now? To what new problems or issues could we apply what we've learned? What are we responsible for doing now that we understand/believe/are convinced of? What are the major takeaways, and how will we use them? What kind of mental model or map have we developed for moving forward with social action, or for our future reading, composing, and learning?*) For example, after reading a variety of fiction and nonfiction texts about how social institutions (including schools) enact repressive social policies, we asked: *What preemptive steps do our readings make us consider to protect us from the kind of rules that suppress civil rights? How can we keep suppression of rights from happening in our schools, our towns, and our wider culture? How can we enact one or more of our authors' visions of how to work for justice and against prejudice in our own classroom, school, and community?*

- Articulate critical standards and goals: Ask students to describe a person who is a good speaker or listener (or any other kind of expert you want them to emulate), identifying the person's stances, traits, and moves and even how they feel about such a person (usually the feelings are very positive). You can create an anchor chart that lists these expert moves and hang it in the classroom.

- Careful listening friends: Ask students to be "careful listening friends" to each other. This means they don't raise hands when others speak, but they do exhibit listening behaviors like maintaining eye contact and nodding. Learners can be asked to brainstorm the behaviors of careful listening friends, put these on an anchor chart, and use it to reflect on their listening behaviors.

- Policing your voice: Learners should be prepared before they speak, speak succinctly, be respectful, make their point, and then allow others to speak (Kay, 2018). We often time conversational turns and note this on discussion maps (described as follows).

- Discussion maps: The teacher or a student leader introduces the topic or issue under discussion. Students run the discussion, typically using a protocol to promote inclusion and uptake. The discussion is timed, and there is a deliverable identified: something to be achieved or created. A student (or the teacher) maps out the discussion on a whiteboard (though it can also be done on chart paper). The map typically has all the student names written around a circle and with lines and arrows drawn from one speaker to the next. These can be coded by color or symbol to show the kind of response (asked a clarifying question, added an idea, offered an alternative, asked a new question, etc.).

- Conversation points tracker: Learners track an ongoing conversation by recording the most important points made by others. All students can do this, but sometimes one student keeps a master conversation tracker on a whiteboard, sometimes through sketchnotes.

  Afterward, students are asked to look at the map of the discussion and to debrief, considering what the map reveals, what went well, how discussion could be improved next time, and so on.

As always, model how to use these tools, then mentor learners into deliberately practicing them in small and large group discussions.

PROMOTING DEEP DISCUSSION MOVE 4: SHORT RESPONSE AND REFLECTION GUIDES

Short response guides, like those listed here, can be used to prepare learners prior to discussion and also to guide or reflect on discussions. The learners respond to the prompts in the guide and then use their responses as the basis of discussion with others, ultimately sharing major insights with the class and reflecting on trends, comparisons, differences, and takeaways. As always, the teacher can first model a response, then have students help him or her create a response, and then have learners work in pairs or on their own using a guide to create a response. (Download a student-led discussion rubric/checklist from the companion website, http://resources.corwin.com/EMPOWER-secondary.)

online resources

(Continued)

(Continued)

6 *L*'S

Compose a response to one or more of the following (thanks to our Boise State Writing Project colleague Debra Smith for sharing this):

LIKED: Something you liked about the text (or data set, activity, or experience) and why you liked it

LEARNED: Something new you learned, in general, or about the inquiry, specifically, and why you think this learning could be important

LAUGHED: Something that made you laugh—with humor or recognition—and why you laughed

LIVED THROUGH: Something you were helped to think, feel, or experience and what the text/author did to create this thinking, insight, feeling, or experience

LED TO: How you might apply something you learned

LACKED: Anything you felt the text or experience lacked that could be added or revised, and why you think so

Use these responses as the basis for your sharing and ensuing discussion.

SUMMARY PROMPTS USING MENTAL MODELS

These quick guides reinforce using text structure and simple mental models for text types and literary elements like character to mirror back central moves and ideas so that they can be discussed and then responded to.

For narrative: SWBSS—Somebody (major character), Wanted (had a goal), But (conflict/complications), So (resolution), So what? (theme/generalization)

For character: GSAWSS—Goals, Stakes, Actions taken toward goals, World/context and how it affects character, Struggles = So what?

For informational text: DTPP—Details–Topic–Pattern–Point made about the topic by patterning of details (a main idea is a comment about a topic highlighted in the text)

For argument: CREW-R—Claim–Reasons–Evidence–Warrant–Respond to reservations

REFLECTION GUIDES

These guides can aid in reflection and discussion that cultivates a spirit of transfer after a learning episode.

What? So What? Now What?

What? Describe the experience; outline what happened that compelled you to deeper understanding, to think about and perhaps change your thinking and/or behavior (i.e., learn!).

So What? Describe what difference and significance the learning experience had for you (and why it should matter to others).

Now What? Describe what's in store for the future now that you've learned from this experience; outline how you are going to use what you have learned and what you will do to continue learning. (See "Self-Assessments" in Chapter 14 for more about student reflection.)

Learning Process Questions

- What was your most significant learning from today/this week/this unit?
- Why did you learn it? (For what purposes can learning be applied now and in the future?)
- How did you learn it? (What was the process of learning?)
- What were the challenges to learning? How did you overcome them?
- What helped your learning? How can you continue to use and cultivate these resources?
- How do you know that you learned it? (What is the proof positive of learning?)
- What did you learn about yourself? What did you learn about others and other perspectives? What did you learn about expertise?
- What will you do now to extend and explore your learning, to improve it, and to apply it?

QUESTIONING GUIDES

Of course, any questioning scheme (see Chapter 11) can be used to foster discussion. To extend the use of these schemes, we advocate having students monitor the types and patterns of questioning and response, and then to reflect on what went well and what the discussants could do differently next time.

PROMOTING DEEP DISCUSSION MOVE 5: DISCUSSION DRAMAS

There are a variety of drama discussion techniques that learners find highly engaging. Drama discussions encourage exploring multiple perspectives and make it safer for learners to speak because they are not necessarily speaking for themselves. Drama work provides an exploratory space that invites and extends learning. For more detail about each of the following techniques, see *Action Strategies for Deepening Comprehension* (Wilhelm, 2013a).

WRITING IN ROLE

Several drama techniques ask students to write in the role of characters or authors (or historical figures, objects, animals, forces, ideas, etc.); exchange ideas in the form of

(Continued)

(Continued)

letters, notes, action plans, public service announcements (PSAs), or other forms of writing; and respond to each other's creations. (This could also be done on a class Facebook page or in Google Docs.)

One of our favorites is the *postcard exchange*. In role, students create postcard visuals from various scenes, events, or ideas in a text and then on the flipside compose a postcard message about it to send to another character (a character/author/figure from the same text or another text or situation, or even to a student in the class). Students can then respond, in role, to the correspondence they receive.

In *correspondence activities*, students can also compose formal letters, telegrams, advertising circulars, PSAs, memos, arguments, fact sheets, applications/résumés, annotations, directions, op-ed pieces, letters to the editor, or any other form of communication. This technique provides a way for students to learn and practice using the features of different genres.

PROMPTS

To assist students or point them in the right direction, you can start a letter, note, or report with a prompt that they must complete. Here are two examples from *Number the Stars*:

> "Dear Annemarie, When you helped my family escape to Sweden, I did not know what life would hold in store for us . . ." —Ellen

> "Dear Uncle Henrik, When you said the war would end, I did not think that you were right because . . ." —Annemarie

FORUM DRAMAS

There are many different kinds of forum dramas. Forums are a kind of inside–outside exchange. The insiders (or participants) are the learners engaged in a role play. The outsiders (or spectators) observe—drama educators call this being "in the forum"—and then may choose to enter the role play to contribute. So they are spectators who can choose to become participants. A forum requires that there be a role player who presents a problem or asks questions—or there can be several participants who create a role play or drama of some kind of trouble or scenario that those in the forum are then invited to join. Role players are asked to actively invite those in the forum in, and may even suggest roles (e.g., by saying, "I wonder what the reporters present might want to ask?" or "The jury members may now ask questions").

Likewise, students can self-select and take on a variety of roles from which they can report on or talk about story events or ideas. When they enter the drama, they identify their role ("I'm Dr. Phil, and I just have to say . . ." or "I'm Reverend Sunly from the Baptist church, and I . . .") to provide their perspective, give advice, and so on. Students can choose roles that will offer perspectives that have not yet been heard. We often brainstorm with students the names of characters, popular culture figures, or local figures that would be interested in the subject of our discussion. Students can choose their role from the list, or be assigned.

Likewise, members of the forum can observe and reflect. Reflections can be done in role: Reporters can offer summaries, rival newscast companies can provide different perspectives from "the right" or "the left," jury members can judge the responsibility and culpability of various characters, and so on.

STRANGER IN ROLE

The stranger in role is an excellent technique for posing questions and stimulating students to explain what they know in a forum. The teacher generally plays the role of "stranger"—someone from a different culture, place, or planet who has no knowledge or understanding of the topic under study or the story being read (e.g., the naval officers at the end of William Golding's *Lord of the Flies* are strangers in role who can ask questions about what has happened on the island). Students can volunteer to take on the stranger role once they have seen it modeled. The stranger interviews the class or small groups about what is going on. This is a great way to get students to write summaries, explain important ideas to a listener with no background, or consider alternative courses of action and other possibilities that go beyond what has been read.

A variation is *expert in role* in which the teacher in role withholds important information, like the ending of a story or text. In this case, the teacher has special knowledge that the students need. But the students need to articulate the right kind of questions as they interview the teacher to elicit his or her special knowledge.

IF YOU HAD FIVE MINUTES WITH . . .

Students write out one or two questions that they would ask the president, Nelson Mandela, Dr. Martin Luther King, or some other expert pertinent to the inquiry. The class brainstorms possible answers, or may even role-play the conversation. Groups of students might also work together to craft what they think the expert's response would be. This could lead to a hotseat (Chapter 11), panel discussion, or radio show (Wilhelm, 2013a) with various characters.

POWERFUL PLANNING: DISCUSSION THAT PROMOTES RELATIONSHIPS

Dialogue and civic discourse: These are complex and necessary skill sets for learning and for life—for promoting our personal, professional, and civic relationships. They are necessary to making oneself known, to seeing others and their perspectives, and to working toward equity. As teachers, we must realize our role in explicitly teaching our learners to engage in appropriate, respectful, and meaningful discussions in and beyond the classroom. We can achieve this by providing structured opportunities for our students to deliberately practice dialogue, including uptake, procedural feedback, active listening, and more.

In our civil rights unit, we teach students to converse in ways that respect and even honor the perspectives and thinking of others who are different, to converse substantively about issues of civil rights, and to tie these conversations back to issues of silencing, opening, and supporting the civil rights of others. We all need to know how to engage in civil democratic discussions at play, at home, at church, in civic forums, and wherever we find ourselves. Dialogue is necessary to deep understanding and the use of all forms of threshold knowledge. We must teach students not just for school, but for all of life.

Transferring Our Learning: What to Remember When Designing Powerful Discussions to Extend Learning

- Consider your specific goals for each lesson, and how discussion helps meet those goals.

- Guide and structure discussion so students learn new ways of speaking and listening that deepen conceptual and procedural understandings.

- Create routines that support equal contributions and the sharing of all perspectives.

- Model a specific discussion, listening, or response strategy; how to use it; and how to monitor its successful use.

- Have students reflect on their progress and create action plans for future improvement.

Lesson: Carousel Conversation Dialogues

Unit: How do we protect and promote civil rights?

ENVISION the destination
(Where are learners going, and why?)

GOAL *What kind of thinking is targeted?*	EVIDENCE *What product(s) will serve as proof of learning?*	MEASURES OF SUCCESS *What's the standard and quality-assurance tool?*	STAKES *Why will learners buy in?* *What's the "why" behind the learning?*
X-2 Interpretation X-2 Explanation/reasoning ✓ Application of skill/strategy X-2 Perspective taking	✓ Performance assessment: Micro-argument shared several times, revisions based on feedback and response to others' micro-arguments ✓ Structured/unstructured observation	✓ **SIMPLE:** √–, √, √+ on discrete facts/skills X **CHECKLIST of Primary Traits:** Assess if product contains essential characteristics/features using a mental map for micro-argument such as claim-data-reasoning (CDR) or claim-reasons-evidence-warrant (CREW).	Use ESSENCE as a guide for buy-in. Your lesson should have one or more of the following: ✓ E-S: Emotional spark/salience (i.e., relevance) ✓ S-E: Social engagement (i.e., collaboration) ✓ N: Novelty (i.e., new concepts and skills) ✓ C-E: Critical/creative exploration opportunities
Understanding and developing evidentiary reasoning that forms the basis on a logical micro-argument Careful and responsive listening and uptake and responses to reservations	**Students** will compose **micro-arguments** with a claim, data (what makes them say so), and reasoning (so what? Evidence explanation). Respondents will **mirror** and **uptake** the elements of the micro-argument with points of agreement and explanations why, or will offer emendations or reservations to the argument and explain why.	The argument provider has a clear position on the controversial statement expressed in a debatable, defensible, and interesting/significant claim. He or she provides evidence from a text, the world, or life that answers the question, *What makes me say so?* (regarding position from the claim), and that is reasoned about (so what? Explaining the evidence to connect it to the claim). The listener can mirror the claim, data, and reasoning back; express reservations; and hear revisions and responses to these reservations, demonstrating active listening. The listener can provide procedural feedback to the arguer and can provide uptake.	**E-S:** Students respond to controversies that apply to the inquiry on civil rights. **S-E:** Carouseling requires active listening and collaborative uptake and revision. **N:** Carouseling/speed dating may be new to students, and so might controversial statements. **C-E:** Learners apply what is learned to their evolving conceptions and mental models about argument, and about the best ways to promote and protect civil rights in their own lives and communities.

MAP out the path to expertise/mastery
(How would an expert deconstruct and approach this task, step by step?)

TWITTER SUMMARY (3 bullets max)	MENTAL MODELS, PROCESS GUIDES, HEURISTICS	A MODEL OF GOOD WORK LOOKS LIKE . . .	DIFFERENTIATION AND LAYERING
Experts can develop positions and express them through arguments using claims, evidence, and reasoning. Active listeners can mirror back what they hear and respond through uptake.	CDR or CREW for argument Mirror and uptake for active listening Development of conceptual understanding through reflective listening and response to many perspectives	*CDR that connects the data to the claim through reasoning/responses to reservations; mirroring of same*	Learners will play the roles of both presenter and respondent several times. Learners will see different models of argument and of response and uptake. Learners engage in deliberate practice of argument, active listening, and response. Continual use of procedural feedback will occur.

(Continued)

POWER through your lesson
(What is the sequence of initial major must-make instructional moves?)

PRIME	ORIENT	WALK THROUGH (and check for understanding)	EXTEND AND EXPLORE	REFLECT
Provide students with controversial statements regarding the issue of civil rights. For example: • Kids can make no difference in the fight for civil rights. • An owner of a business has the right to choose whom he or she will serve and not serve. • We must stand up to authority to fight for civil rights. • Everyone is entitled to equal rights no matter what. • Human beings will always oppress those whom they can oppress. • Power corrupts, and absolute power corrupts absolutely. Teacher and learners can provide additional prompts. In pairs, then quads, students discuss their responses to these statements.	FRAME today's lesson: "Think of times when you had to quickly make a case or try to convince someone of something. Share with a neighbor. This was a kind of micro-argument. When do you foresee making micro-arguments in the future?" "As we have been discussing, an essential skill for all learners and citizens is being able to respond to issues, to use evidence to generate claims, and then to reason from evidence to show how it supports the claim, by explaining how rules or principles or values connect the evidence to the claim [warranting]. When it comes to complex issues like civil rights, we need to be able to make and respond to arguments." "Today, we'll practice responding to controversial statements and using our response to compose micro-arguments. This will give us practice in writing more complete arguments for our final projects, and will help us when we read and compose arguments later in school and throughout our lives."	MODEL: Teacher models his or her response to one of the statements, turning it into a micro-argument—for example, "Kids *can* make a difference in civil rights [claim]. I base this on the evidence of how the Parkland High School students organized Twitter campaigns, marches, and walkouts to protest gun violence in schools [safe evidence as it can be verified by news reports]. This supports my claim because it shows that kids can self-organize protests that heighten awareness and build support for civil rights issues like feeling safe and protected in school [reasoning]." Mentoring: Ask each student to write a micro-argument to one or more of the controversial statements by expressing a position of some level of agreement or disagreement with the statement (a claim), providing evidence in support of answering the question, *What makes me say so?* or *What do I have to go on?* (data/evidence); checking to see that data/evidence is "safe" (i.e., that it will be accepted by the audience); and then providing an evidence explanation of how it supports the claim (reasoning). CHECK FOR UNDERSTANDING: Ask students to share and label each other's claims, evidence, and reasoning. Have them check if the claim states a position: something they want others to believe or do. Does the evidence answer the question, *What makes me say so?* Explain how the evidence supports the claim by answering the question, *So what?* about the data. Students share micro-arguments in new pairs or triads and receive procedural feedback. Revise as necessary.	DELIBERATE PRACTICE/ ARTICULATE CONSCIOUS AWARENESS: In Carousel Conversations, half the class is put into an inner circle of desks or chairs facing outward. The other half of the class is seated in desks in an outer circle facing the desks in the inner circle. The inner circle students share their arguments. The outer circle students respond to the arguments by mirroring the claim, data, and reasoning, and then providing uptake by expressing any points of agreement or reservation and explaining how they respond to reservations. Discussion ensues. After 3 to 4 minutes, the teacher asks the outer circle students to move one chair to the right. The process is repeated 3 or 4 times. After a few turns, the inner and outer circles switch seats. GUIDED PRACTICE: Students can be asked to compose daily micro-arguments about topics that come up in class and readings. They can be asked to respond in the role of the author or characters or historical figures they have studied to the controversial statements, making micro-arguments from their points of view. DIFFERENTIATE: If some students are struggling, work with them or have other successful learners assist. Start with safe evidence, then add reasoning. Likewise, those advancing can be asked to include reservations and responses to them in their micro-writing. DEBRIEF: Share procedural feedback and use this to revise student micro-arguments throughout the unit.	Summarize what you learned about presenting, active listening, or argument. What is the mental model for basic argument? For active listening? When and in what situations does argument take place in school, in professions, and in politics and public policy? What makes an argument strong and compelling? What makes an argument weaker, and one we should have reservations about? When do you foresee using micro-arguments and more extended formal arguments in your learning and life? What makes good evidence? What makes powerful reasoning? How can we proactively respond to reservations? Self-score yourself on argument now. What did you learn this unit, this week, or today that affected your score? What do you want to work on next? What is your action plan for doing this work and continuing to improve? HOMEWORK EXTENSION: Use what you learned in another class, at home, or in your favorite activities. Watch an advertisement and tease out the implied micro-argument (e.g., "you should buy X" using evidence, implied reasoning, a rule, a value, a principle, etc.). Watch a speech or movie or read a story or newspaper article and summarize the articulated or implied argument being made. If these texts are about civil rights: TWOFER!

PART 5: REFLECTING

ENVISION   MAP   PRIME   ORIENT   WALK THROUGH   EXTEND/EXPLORE   REFLECT

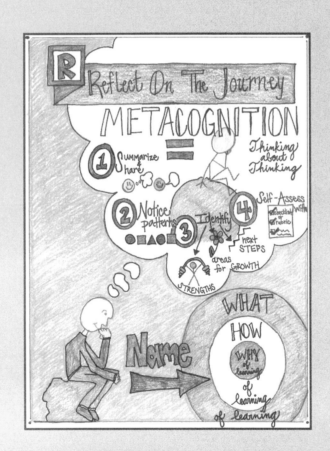

Chapter 14

MOVING INTO THE FUTURE

Reflecting Through Assessments *for* and *as* Learning

ESSENTIAL QUESTION
What kinds of assessments and feedback do the
most to promote engagement and learning?

Rachel recently attended an exhibit called *Student Voices* in which participants circulated the room and listened to prerecorded interviews of students talking about various projects they had been involved in. Many of the interviews started with students responding to the question, "What do you think of when you hear the word *assessment*?" Their responses included many of the things you would expect students to say (and were right in line with what we have heard teachers say); the word *assessment* made them think of words like *test, grade, stress, high-stakes, judgment, wrong answer*, and so on. As two teachers near Rachel discussed these responses and the long history of negative associations that come with the word *assessment*, one teacher said to the other, "If we know that the word *assessment* carries all this baggage, and that formative assessment is really about something else entirely, why don't we just call it something different?"

See
*Lesson Plan
Canvas*
on page
239

Well, there's the rub. How can we reframe assessment practices so that they are clearly in support of learning—a way of sharing critical standards, knowledge, and power *with* students, instead of exercising power *over* them? The term *assessment*, after all, comes from the Italian *assidere*, which means "to sit beside."

Assessment is commonly divided into the categories of summative and formative. Summative assessments usually are done at the end of a unit or series of lessons. A summative assessment determines the status of learning and is typically in the form of a grade or a benchmark of some type. Author Lorna Earl (2003) refers to this practice as assessment *of* learning, which can lead to an emphasis on performance (vs. progress) and, as illustrated by what students said in the *Student Voices* exhibit, is too often used to identify deficits or failure. Earl defines formative assessment under two categories. Assessment *for* learning is when data are analyzed to help inform the next phase of teaching and learning, and assessment *as* learning is when the assessment itself (like procedural feedback) assists in promoting learning. With assessment *as* learning, the role of the student in the process is essential. The student personally monitors what he or she is learning and uses the feedback from this monitoring to make adjustments, adaptations, and even major changes in understanding. Assessment *as* learning provides a more reflective constructive focus on productive struggle, progress, and continuous improvement.

This chapter explores how formative assessments can be embedded as a regular, natural, and necessary part of classroom instructional practice that apprentices and moves student learning forward. The forward movement is based on students' self-reflection and teachers' reflective willingness to adjust their plans based on the evidence of student progress toward focal learning goals. Formative assessment should happen often—ideally, *every single day*—as a regular part of classroom practice. If students are actively doing work, then their work samples provide a formative assessment. Every teaching strategy in this book makes student reading, composing, or thinking visible and available to the learner, his or her peers, and the teacher, which means it is material for formative assessment. Technology apps like Google Forms, Edmodo, and Kahoot! can be used for exit tickets and other kinds of formative assessment as well.

HOW FORMATIVE ASSESSMENTS FIT INTO EMPOWER

A major goal is for our students to monitor their own progress and, as D. Royce Sadler (1989) writes, to know how to "bridge the gap between where they are and where they are heading" (p. 22). It is through formative assessment that teachers and learners know when learning has been adequately *primed* and *oriented*, and that learners are therefore prepared for success with the new challenge. It is formative assessment that guides the *walk-through* and *extension*, indicating when it is time to go deeper, reteach, or move to the next step in the process of apprenticeship. Through gathering regular and varied evidence of student learning, teachers make reflective and informed decisions about when and how to move from "I do" to "we do" to "you do together or alone"—to use differentiated support, different materials and tasks, and then extensions and applications of all kinds. Through strategies that focus on assessment *as* learning, students *reflect* throughout all the stages of EMPOWER, and teachers use that reflection to guide and adjust their instructional planning at key moments. A powerful mental model of this kind of critical reflection is the DEAL model (shown in Figure 14.1), which reflects the process of doing, studying/reflecting, acting/revising, and then planning to reengage in the learning process with more conscious awareness and competence.

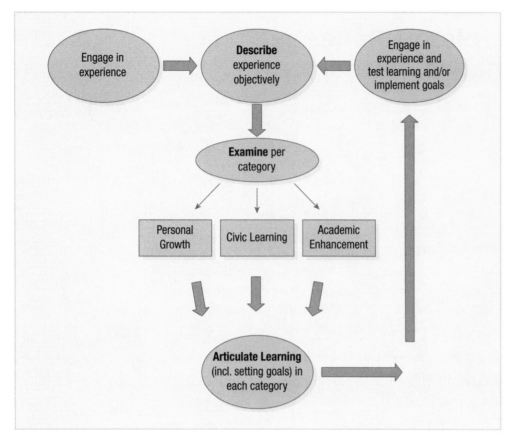

Source: Reprinted by permission from Springer Nature: Springer, *Innovative Higher Education*, "The Articulated Learning: An Approach to Guided Reflection and Assessment" (Ash & Clayton, 2004).

In this chapter, we include tools to assist teachers in providing assessment *as* and *for* learning. We show how formative assessments can personalize learning, act in service of meeting critical standards, prepare learners for summative assessments, provide proof of progress, and highlight areas of productive struggle—and how these areas can immediately inform the planning, revision, and differentiation of upcoming lessons. Finally, and most important, we explore how we can involve students in the assessment process so that they practice reflecting on and gain ownership of their own learning.

Principles of Reflective Formative Assessment

- Is planned to have a direct relationship to the major threshold learning goals. (E-M)

- Is valued as a cyclical process, informing teachers and students about what has been accomplished and what to do next; mirrors the notion that to teach for true understanding, you must continuously assess for understanding. (E-M)

- Is oriented toward future learning goals and culminating projects. Learners understand the purpose of each formative assessment *for* and *as* learning, and as it serves the goals and deliverables of the unit. (P-O)

- Is embedded in daily instruction as natural and continuous, and at friction points of potential progress or struggle so that it informs the next teaching/learning episode. (W-E)

- Foregrounds agency, involving articulation of what is being done and could be done next as a teacher and as a learner. (W-E)

- Is challenging in that it moves students beyond their current capacity. (W-E)

- Is transparent, accessible, and immediately usable for teachers and learners as part of the learning process of apprenticeship and continuous improvement. (W-E-R)

- Reflects a dynamic growth mindset of possibility and future orientation—focusing on learners' assets rather than deficits, and naming evidence of student progress along a continuum of learning (i.e., using the language of possibility to celebrate successes and naming power moves students attempt but haven't mastered *yet*), as well as potential ways forward. (W-E-R)

- Is modeled, shared, developed, and evaluated in a supportive learning environment so that students become independent at monitoring their own learning. (W-E-R)

- Has a direct impact on the teacher's instructional plan and the learners' action plans—either moving forward with a previous plan because the formative assessment indicates that is the right move, or adjusting the plan to fill a gap or move in a different direction. (R)

FORMATIVE ASSESSMENT MOVE 1: PEER ASSESSMENTS

When we recently asked a group of ninth-grade students what made feedback helpful to them, they generated this list:

1. Recognizes effort in trying out new strategies
2. Supportive and constructive
3. Immediately usable
4. Specific
5. Honest
6. On time

These principles closely match those proposed by Grant Wiggins (2012) that feedback must be (1) specific, (2) timely, (3) supportive, and (4) honest.

Our students often tell us that they want feedback that is immediate and useful. They *also* tell us that when feedback is given by adults, it feels like an authoritative command to change something. When given by their peers, however, feedback can become more about relationships and helping, exploring options, and exercising choice. Learners feel more able to reflect on the ideas; accept, revise, reject, or ask for more information; and so forth. The advantages of peer feedback extend to deliberately practicing feedback, developing deeper understanding of standards and mental models of expertise, developing articulated and usable knowledge, saving teacher time, distributing expertise, learning to be helpful to each other in the project of continuous improvement, building community and deepening relationships around significant work, and so on. It's important to note that the strategies included in Chapter 6 for setting up a sense of community and collaborative culture, especially preparing students to provide procedural feedback, are essential in preparing students to provide and receive feedback that is useful, can be heard, and moves their learning forward.

We need to set up the right classroom environment—the culture, protocols, norms, and strategies to support success and to ensure that students see the giving and receiving of feedback as a positive process that will enhance their learning. Peer assessment also directly prepares learners for the culminating project, and for extending and exploring, giving students adequate assistance (from teacher and peers) to achieve and demonstrate deep understandings (see Chapter 15). Frameworks for peer and self-assessment can help students develop the capacities of transfer and independent use.

PRAISE-QUESTION-WAYS FORWARD (P-Q-W) FRAMEWORK

One useful framework to engage and assist students in providing peer feedback with any performance or work sample is the Praise-Question-Polish (PQP) framework developed by Gloria Neubert and Sally McNelis (1990), which we have adapted into a Praise–Question–Ways Forward (PQW) framework to be more dialogic. This is a useful standard routine for a respondent to ask permission to provide feedback, and to get permission before providing it. When peers use this framework, it means that the feedback has been solicited and agreed to and creates more openness and a "culture of thinking" partnership. (Download a blank PQW guide for student use from the companion website, http://resources.corwin.com/EMPOWER-secondary.)

online resources

Questions in this protocol include items such as

- Praise: What was effective about my work sample/deliverable/presentation? What was a highlight of my work sample/deliverable/presentation, and why? What power moves did I make that stood out, and how did they help you to understand/help create meanings and effects?

(Continued)

- Questions: What clarifying questions do you have about my work sample/deliverable/presentation? What further questions do you have about my work sample/deliverable/presentation? About how I did something or its meaning? What were you thinking about as I shared/as you experienced it?

- Ways forward: What are one or two potential ways for moving forward that I could use next time I do this task or a similar project to revise, extend, explore, elaborate, and do the work more expertly? How could I revise and extend this work? I wonder what would happen if I/you . . . because . . .

Note the EMPOWER canvas here builds on the Carousel Conversation lesson from Chapter 13. In this lesson, students apply what they learned about writing micro-arguments in response to their reading of *Number the Stars*. The focus of the lesson is on peer-to-peer formative assessment of the micro-arguments through the application of the P-Q-W peer response protocol.

REAL FRIEND PEER REVISION

Another powerful protocol for peer response is the Real Friend Peer Revision Guide, shown in Figure 14.2. This guide highlights the five major revision moves of "keep, add, delete, move, and change." Again, this guide can be adapted for use with any kind of performance or work sample. (Find a downloadable version for student use on the companion website, http://resources.corwin.com/EMPOWER-secondary.)

■ FIGURE 14.2: REAL FRIEND PEER REVISION GUIDE

Getting started with peer response:

_____ Ask your partner if you have permission to help him/her.

_____ Ask your partner what kind of help he/she wants, what specific focus/foci there should be to the feedback, and what kind and form of feedback works best for him/her.

Providing the feedback:

Carefully read/view the work you've been given and consider how to give the following advice:

First, tell your partner at least one really strong move you want him/her to KEEP in the work, and tell your partner why by using a process or causal statement.

Now, make sure you give really good advice that will help your partner, and consider his/her requests for how to help and what to help with.

Provide your partner with at least 5 more pieces of SPECIFIC advice of any kind (move, add, delete, or change) from the following menu:

I wonder what would happen if you MOVED . . .

I wonder what would happen if you ADDED . . .

I wonder what would happen if you DELETED . . .

I wonder what would happen if you CHANGED . . .

If you can justify your advice as a process or causal statement, all the better.

(For example, "I wonder what would happen if you moved this part to the beginning because I think it might let the reader know your character and his problem sooner.")

Remember to phrase your advice in such a way that you are offering helpful advice, and you know that your partner is the BOSS of his/her own writing!

WRITER, if you accept the advice as helpful, you are done.

If you refuse a piece of advice, be prepared to explain why with a causal explanation: BECAUSE . . .

Source: Adapted from Wilhelm, Douglass, & Fry, 2014.

FEEDBACK ON THE FEEDBACK

In the Real Friend Peer Revision guide, we ask the writer to accept the feedback or to explain why the feedback is not going to be used. This leaves the composer or problem solver in charge of his or her own work but requires him or her to consider the feedback that has been given.

The person receiving feedback can rate the feedback he or she received through a *star rating system*. The stars awarded directly correspond to critical standards for feedback. So, for example, in a five-star rating system, one star means the feedback describes specific moves and text features the reviewer noticed, two stars describes specific effects and meanings of the moves made, three stars provides specific suggestions for moving forward, four stars denotes the feedback is causal and explains why a move worked or might work for you, and five stars says the feedback was immediately actionable and inspired action and revision. (Thanks to our colleague Troy Hicks for this idea.)

We also ask learners who have received feedback to build *a revision or action plan* for using the feedback to move forward. We ask learners to reflect on the feedback, think about what was learned from it, and consider how to use it. Sometimes we ask them to write their commitment to a revision/action plan as an exit ticket: *What are some strategies or moves you will try in order to move forward on this piece or in future compositions (or with this kind of task or problem-solving process)?* We have found that articulating and committing to an action plan makes it much more likely that learners will use the feedback.

FORMATIVE ASSESSMENT MOVE 2: SELF-ASSESSMENTS

Peer feedback is a useful precursor to self-assessment. The ultimate goal of all apprenticeship is to prepare students to apply what they have learned to reflect on and guide their own learning. In the case of assessment, the goal is for students to provide procedural feedback and feedforward to themselves. This self-monitoring and self-evaluation is part of social–emotional learning and should focus not only on how they might assess their own work but also on how they might become more conscious of themselves as learners, regularly checking in on their own understanding and adjusting their learning goals and strategies based on their self-assessments. Self-assessment involves reflection on big-picture goals for learning, as well as in-the-moment daily checks on learning.

Reflective sentence starters, or prompts, help students develop mental models for self-assessment. Figure 14.3 illustrates how sentence stems can be used to focus on specific types of self-assessment. (Download a version of this sentence stem self-assessment from the companion website, http://resources.corwin.com/EMPOWER-secondary.)

online resources

(Continued)

(Continued)

■ FIGURE 14.3: SENTENCE STEMS FOR SELF-ASSESSMENT

FOCUS OF SELF-ASSESSMENT	SENTENCE STEMS
Prior knowledge students bring to a new situation	This reminds me of . . .
Past experiences and work of relevance to the current challenge	I made a connection to/from . . .
Identifying what is involved in the learning process (i.e., what's the mental map for the task?) and how students can prepare for success, involving themselves in monitoring the process of task completion	The necessary steps for this task include . . . The process requires . . . Elements of the task that I have to remember next time are . . . I am wondering . . . The part I found the most difficult was . . .
Progress students have made	One thing I learned today . . . I now know . . .
Productive struggles and challenges, and strategies for working through them	I revised my thinking about . . . because . . . I navigated struggle/could navigate struggle by . . .
Learning what students still need to do and what might help them move forward	I'm confused about . . . One question I still have is . . .

To avoid a situation where students respond routinely but not substantively, it is important to mix things up. Sometimes, a prompt can make a great closing moment to a lesson, or be used at the start of a lesson. Teachers should also vary the types of responses students are asked to provide. The students could be asked to respond to a prompt in their journals or use it to prompt a discussion with a peer.

One strategy for reflecting on bigger-picture goals is to have students complete a more extensive reflection on their progress toward specific learning targets (ideally student-generated learning targets, co-negotiated based on standards and instructional goals). Figure 14.4 is an example of sentence stems for a learning target reflection; a downloadable version can be found on the companion website, too, http://resources .corwin.com/EMPOWER-secondary. (Also see the self-assessments specific to discussion in the "Reflection Guides" section of Chapter 13.)

■ FIGURE 14.4: LEARNING TARGET REFLECTION

My Learning Target

Name:

Date:

I have been focusing improvement on . . .

Milestones of success include . . .

The areas in which I still need to improve are . . .

My next learning target is to . . .

In order to achieve this target, I will need to (list steps) . . .

I will know that I have succeeded when . . .

EXIT TICKETS

Exit tickets provide information about what students learned in a lesson as well as challenges or questions they still have. Exit tickets focus on a specific skill or concept taught in a lesson and should articulate growth in understanding, productive struggle, and ways forward. Reading through these can quickly help a teacher identify next steps to take for individual students, groups of students, or the entire class. These can be adapted for any lesson or learning goal. (Note that we have already provided a specific example of one type of exit ticket in Chapter 6, the Gut Check.)

Follow this process to design an effective exit ticket prompt:

- Identify the focus skill(s) for the lesson.
- Engage students in a reading, composing, discussing, or problem-solving activity that uses the focus skill(s).
- Identify a micro-task students can complete relatively quickly that will elicit evidence of their current understanding and use of the focus skill(s).
- Reframe the focus skill(s) into a prompt that clearly names the task for students and how they should make use of what they have experienced in the lesson. For example, the prompt in Figure 14.5 starts by naming what they have experienced in the lesson ("after reading this source") and clearly names the task to complete (write an initial claim and use at least one piece of evidence from the source that supports the claim).

Figure 14.5 shows exit tickets from an early lesson in an argument unit that focuses on supporting claims with evidence. For this lesson, the teacher walks students through a think-aloud for a news article that presents a range of perspectives on homework, modeling the process for identifying the evidence the author uses to support his or her claims. To conclude the lesson, the teacher uses an exit ticket to gain evidence of students' progress on this focus skill.

■ **FIGURE 14.5: CLAIMS AND EVIDENCE EXIT TICKETS**

PROMPT FOR THIS EXIT TICKET: After reading this source, what is your initial claim about homework?
Include at least one piece of evidence from the text to support your initial claim.

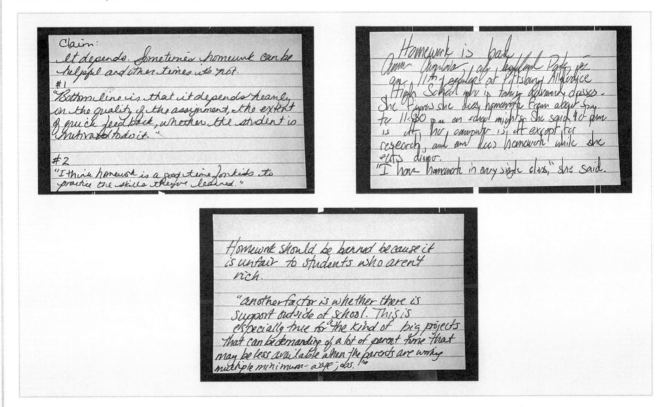

FORMATIVE ASSESSMENT MOVE 3: ANCHOR CHARTS

Anchor charts, which are co-created by the teacher and students, are used to gather evidence from the whole class about current thinking on key skills or concepts. They also serve a double purpose as a classroom artifact students can access for prompts and feedforward if they find themselves struggling during an assignment or activity. Anchor charts are displayed in the classroom where students can refer to them often and are updated throughout the unit as students engage in reading, composing, discussing, and problem-solving experiences. In our civil rights unit, we have anchor charts on the wall about issues and concepts related to civil rights, and on evidence, since evidence-based reasoning and argument is one of our focal goals.

Anchor charts can be used to articulate critical standards—in Figure 14.6, for example, about what constitutes good evidence. This in turn can be used to create semantic scales and other guides for monitoring the effectiveness of evidence in texts one is reading, as well as in one's own and peers' writing. See Chapter 10 (Figure 10.7, page 167) for an example of a semantic scale, and download a blank one for student use from the companion website, http://resources.corwin.com/EMPOWER-secondary. Semantic scales and anchor charts can be used with any major concept or strategy being taught in a unit; they also can invite and assess evolving understandings and expertise in assignments and culminating projects.

online resources

■ **FIGURE 14.6: EVIDENCE ANCHOR CHARTS**

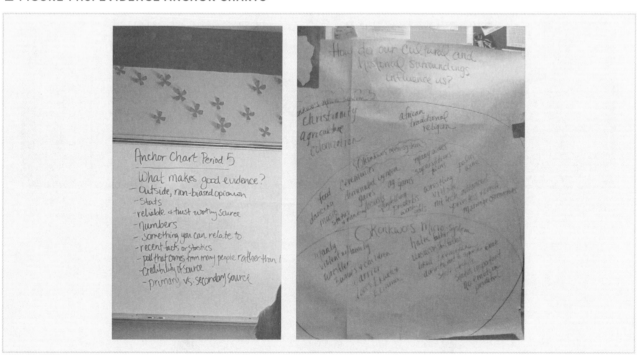

FORMATIVE ASSESSMENT MOVE 4: TEACHER-STUDENT CONFERENCES

Short, regular check-ins and conferences can be incredibly successful in moving students along in their learning—and they usually require much less time than written feedback. You can do a lot of work to help a student in just a one- or two- or five-minute conversation. Many of our "conferences" take 30 seconds or so, and it's amazing how they can build relationships and increase engagement and learning. Since apprenticeship classrooms involve lots of deliberate practice in the context of small group or individual reading, composing, and problem-solving activity, we can create significant slots of time to confer with students.

There are a variety of different conferences that serve different purposes. Of course, different purposes can be combined. Though we think it's important for teachers to personally conference with each learner, we also have peers quickly conference together at various times in a unit. In our civil rights unit, we conference about required reading and writing assignments but also about reading and composing that students are pursuing independently through their personalized learning agendas. (We're grateful to our colleagues Penny Kittle and Kelly Gallagher [2018] for helping us think about conferencing in ever richer ways.) The following is a list of types of conferences:

- Gut Checks/check-ins: Quick, personal queries into how things are going and what help might be needed with reading, composing, daily activities, the ongoing inquiry, culminating projects, etc.

- Comprehension: To check understanding of reading and the ongoing inquiry

- Nudge or challenge conferences: *Here's something new I want you to try that builds off what you already know and do . . . What is a next step you can think of to move forward? What's a potential action plan for your project?*

- Invitation conferences: *Here's a book I think you might enjoy/a kind of writing/ learning activity I think you'd like . . . that you might find challenging but satisfying . . .*

- Looking for trouble: *Let's find an area of challenge and look for a way through it.*

- Evaluation and reflection conferences: *Let's see how well you are meeting critical standards and reflect on how to keep improving and extending learning.*

- Connections to inquiry conference: *What are connections you are seeing to our inquiry in your life, current events, favorite movies and shows, free reading, and other subjects? What future applications do you see?*

- Reading life conference: *When and how much are you reading beyond class? How can I support you?*

- Writing life conference: *When and how much are you writing beyond class? What things are you trying? How can I support you?*

- Student-led conferences: For learners to present and justify their learning, and to celebrate progress and commit to a plan of next steps for

(Continued)

(Continued)

continuous improvement. We often have students do these for parents during parent–teacher conferences, or for roundtables of peers to teach others about their learning.

READING CONFERENCES

In reading conferences, we work to invite students to increase the (1) volume of their reading, (2) variety in their reading, (3) complexity, and (4) ways they identify with authors, genres, ideas, and favorite books. All of this is in service of building reading capacity, a growth mindset (Dweck, 2006), a reading identity, and the habits of expert readers. We ask things like *How is the reading going? What trouble is brewing in the book (all stories are about trouble)? What big ideas/themes might be emerging? Read aloud a favorite part—why is this a favorite? Read aloud a challenging part—why is this challenging? How might we navigate that challenge?*

We also prompt learners to tell us about how they are reading and responding, using Jeff's "Tell Me . . ." framework questions and prompts that reflect the dimensions of an expert reader's response from *"You Gotta BE the Book"* (2016):

Evocative: Entering the textual world, showing interest, relating to characters, visualizing, participating. For example: *Tell me what feelings you are experiencing as you read. What do you feel about character? Setting? Incident?*

Connective: Elaborating, connecting to life. For example: *Tell me what events from your life are similar to events happening to the characters. How does this text make you more aware of your own life? Of issues in the world?*

Reflective: Considering significance, recognizing conventions, recognizing reading as a transaction, evaluating the author and one's own reading. For example: *Tell me what kind of person you think the author is. Who would you recommend this book to? What is the most important thing you learned from reading this book?**

We like to have students name the moves and strategies they are using as readers and to endorse and build on these. We often share our own reading and always try to investigate processes of reading with students. This is inquiring into expert reading and how to do it.

WRITING CONFERENCES

In writing conferences, we use the notion of "order of operations" to focus on what is most important—in other words, first things first. We focus first on ideas and content, then on the form and organization of those ideas, then on voice, then on conventions and correctness issues. We ask students to read us a favorite part of their writing and then a challenging part (to explain the power moves or the challenges presented), and then work together to find ways forward. For specific ideas on what to prompt writers to talk about and to try, we use the strategies of narrative composing (see Fredricksen, Wilhelm, & Smith, 2012), the strategies of composing argument (Smith, Wilhelm, & Fredricksen, 2012, or the strategies for composing specific kinds of informational text structures (Wilhelm, Smith, & Fredricksen, 2012).

*For a complete list of over 100 "Tell Me . . ." questions, see "*You Gotta BE the Book*" (Wilhelm, 2016).

GENERAL PROMPTS FOR CONFERENCING

In conferencing, it's important to get the learner to talk. In apprenticeship, we try to get the apprentice to take over doing the work. As we tell our students, we've already passed seventh or ninth or eleventh grade. Now it is their turn!

The following prompts help to get students talking. It's important to get them to talk to us, to each other, and to wider audiences about their learning processes, and to share their learning in public spaces, like during parent–teacher conferences or learning celebrations (see Chapter 15).

- *Tell me about/talk to me about . . . something you are doing or thinking as a writer/reader/problem solver/citizen scientist, etc. Tell me about how you are working to meet this goal or standard of our unit . . .*

- *Tell me about the favorite part of your book/your writing/the inquiry . . . Why does that speak to you so much? Why do you find that so powerful?*

- *How does your reading/writing/inquiry connect to your deepest needs, desires, commitments, and goals?*

- *Mirroring: What I hear you saying is . . . Do I have that right?*

- *Say/tell me more about . . .*

- *Convince me of . . .*

- *What are some ideas you have for moving forward? What will you do next?*

- *How can we work together to address the challenge of organization/providing more detail/etc.?*

REFLECTING ON THE CONFERENCE

A crux move in making the most of student–teacher conferences is having students complete a written self-assessment, such as that shown in Figure 14.7, to promote reflection after any conference meeting.

■ **FIGURE 14.7: CONFERENCE REFLECTION**

Student–Teacher Conference Reflection

My conference was helpful and successful in these ways . . . because . . .

The power moves of the conference were . . .

For my next conference, I need to remember to . . .

One of the challenges of my conference was . . .

Ways to prepare for this kind of challenge in the future would be . . .

Things I have learned about my reading/my writing/myself from the conference are . . .

My action plan for using what I learned is . . .

If the conference is led by students, they can reflect:

Things that I have learned by preparing and holding a conference are . . .

If parents or other "keepers" were present:

The major insights my parents, peers, or other visitors learned about me and my learning from the conference are . . .

POWERFUL PLANNING:
USING FORMATIVE ASSESSMENT AND THE POWER OF *YET!*

Formative assessment drives learning forward. It is inquiring into what is understood, how it is understood, and what should be done next to further understanding and application. All teaching and learning in fact begins with formative assessment. At the beginning of a unit, we ask: *What do learners know already about the said topic or the required strategies?* This can be a question to inform the teacher of how to prime and orient and where to begin the unit, and to consider what prior knowledge needs to be activated or built before proceeding with a unit of study.

Introducing any new strategy or skill should be determined by students' present level of engagement, skill, knowledge, understanding, and performance—and what is available to them next. This is the power of *yet*. Note that many of the techniques described in previous chapters—think-alouds, student-generated questions, discussions, deliverables, and so on—constitute formative assessment because they show what students can do and cannot quite do *yet* but might if we assist them. This information guides the teacher to make plans *for* instruction that promotes learning in the zone of proximal development. Otherwise, we can waste a lot of time teaching what most students already know how to do, or pitching instruction in the zone of frustration.

In our civil rights unit, we focus on developing strategies for inferencing, for perspective taking and social imagination, and for evidentiary reasoning and composing arguments. It's the ongoing feedback we use to name and monitor learning progress in these areas that serves as the "thermometer of student understanding." It raises questions for us as teachers: *Are my plans moving too quickly or too slowly for the students? Do I need to regroup some students to meet specific needs versus assuming all students move at the same pace? Are there skills needed before they approach a task that I have not yet helped them to meet?*

Paul Black and Dylan Wiliam (1998) note that such assessments only become "formative assessments" *when the evidence is actually used to adapt the teaching to meet the needs of the students.* In other words, formative assessment only works if the teacher is open and flexible, willing to adjust his or her teaching plan for the next month, the next week, the next day, or even the next moment. A crux move is making sure that formative assessments work *for teachers* and *for learners*—that they are integrated throughout the lesson sequence to move students along in their continuum of learning, to motivate, and to name growth and possibility. Formative assessments can't be add-ons, be graded, or take up precious teaching time; rather, they need to support teachers and students in articulating evidence of learning and planning for next steps.

Transferring Our Learning: What to Remember When Designing and Implementing Formative Assessments That Foster Reflection

- Consider the most powerful ways to structure and deliver the formative assessment given the purpose.

- Consider how the formative assessment mirrors major learning goals and helps develop knowledge necessary for the culminating projects.

- Understand how the formative assessment is working *for* and *as* learning, providing data to assist teachers in planning the next lesson, and preparing and encouraging students to grow through their zones of proximal development.

- Consider how to introduce and model a specific strategy and help learners to monitor its successful use.

- Consider how the formative assessment helps students to reflect on their progress, reinforces a growth mindset, and leads to creating action plans for continuous future improvement.

Lesson: Praise–Question–Ways Forward (P-Q-W) Peer Response

Unit: How do we protect and promote civil rights?

ENVISION the destination
(Where are learners going, and why?)

GOAL *What kind of thinking is targeted?*	EVIDENCE *What product(s) will serve as proof of learning?*	MEASURES OF SUCCESS *What's the standard and quality-assurance tool?*	STAKES *Why will learners buy in?* *What's the "why" behind the learning?*
✓ Explanation/reasoning ✓ Application of skill/strategy	✓ Constructed (discrete task, long/short response, graphic organizer)	✓ **HOLISTIC:** Assess whole product or response against a generic 1–4 rubric.	Use ESSENCE as a guide for buy-in. Your lesson should have one or more of the following: ✓ E-S: Emotional spark/salience (i.e., relevance) ✓ S-E: Social engagement (i.e., collaboration) ✓ N: Novelty (i.e., new concepts and skills) ✓ C-E: Critical/creative exploration opportunities
After reading Chapter 16 of *Number the Stars*, students will apply what they learned about writing a micro-argument in response to statements by using evidence from the novel and their own experience. Students will evaluate a peer's use of claims and how they are connected to evidence through an explanation (evidentiary reasoning) to get at explanatory principles about what promotes and protects civil rights.	Student-generated micro-arguments about the essential question, using claims, evidence (from reading and experience), and reasoning Students' capacity to identify micro-argument elements of claim, data, and reasoning about data with explanations connecting it to a claim with a peer and complete a P-Q-W peer assessment	The peer responder completes the P-Q-W reflection, using specific references to moves the writer makes in his or her micro-argument. The procedural feedback is clear and specific enough and provides actionable items for the writer to move the piece of writing forward.	**E-S:** Students synthesize what they have learned so far through the inquiry on civil rights. **S-E:** The writer writes to an authentic audience (a peer), and the peer responder provides feedback to assist the writer in improving his or her writing. **N:** This is a unique approach to peer response, involving peers in the formative assessment process. **CE:** Learners apply what is learned to their evolving conceptions and mental models about argument, and about the best ways to promote and protect civil rights in their own lives and communities.

MAP out the path to expertise/mastery
(How would an expert deconstruct and approach this task, step by step?)

TWITTER SUMMARY *(3 bullets max)*	MENTAL MODELS, PROCESS GUIDES, HEURISTICS	A MODEL OF GOOD WORK LOOKS LIKE . . .	DIFFERENTIATION AND LAYERING
The P-Q-W protocol moves students toward independence in identifying strengths and possibilities (power moves and potential power moves) of a work sample and in applying critical standards to the work of oneself and others.	Claim–data–reasoning for argument Providing procedural feedback through description of specific moves and descriptions of what meanings and effects are or could be achieved through these moves	*Praise is specific, procedural, and causal by identifying what specific moves look like and what they achieve. Questions are specific and lead to action. Wonderings are specific, causal, and actionable.*	Expectations for P-Q-W can be differentiated, starting with just praise, or questions, then wonderings. Sentence stems and starters can be used to help descriptions be specific. More modeling and mentoring can be provided to those who need it, by teacher or by peers.

(Continued)

POWER through your lesson
(What is the sequence of initial major must-make instructional moves?)

PRIME	ORIENT	WALK THROUGH (and check for understanding)	EXTEND AND EXPLORE	REFLECT
FRAME THE LESSON: "Today's activity builds on the speed dating lesson in which we wrote micro-arguments in response to statements related to our inquiry question. In this lesson, you will apply what you learned about writing micro-arguments in response to statements to write a micro-argument in response to reading *Number the Stars*, especially Chapter 16. Then, you will use a P-Q-W peer response to provide procedural feedback to a peer on his or her micro-argument." "When have you given or received helpful feedback? Let's remind ourselves of what good feedback looks, sounds, and feels like. When have you been an effective thinking partner?" "When we can use procedural feedback for others in a specific case such as this, we demonstrate our own understanding and expertise, and we are helpful to our peers."	Teacher begins by providing the following directions for the writing task. "Given what you learned about writing micro-arguments, write a micro-argument in response to our essential question, *How can we best protect and promote civil rights?* Be sure to use evidence from the text (especially Chapter 16), personal experience, and our class discussions in your micro-argument." "Keep in mind that the goal for today is for you to articulate the key features of a successful micro-argument in response to a peer's writing so that you both can show your understanding of what makes an effective argument. You will be trading your micro-argument with a peer for feedback." "This will be hugely helpful as we work toward our culminating argument projects for the unit and as we continue to offer each other P-Q-Ws and other forms of peer feedback now and in the future."	MODEL/MENTOR: Teacher models the process for writing a P-Q-W response to a micro-argument (shared model, perhaps from another class period). After modeling the *P* response, the teacher calls on students to help write the *Q* response. MONITOR: Students work in pairs to write the *W* response for the shared model. MONITOR: Students trade micro-arguments and complete P-Q-W response: *Praise* What is strong and effective about the writing? What should be kept/not be changed? Why is this move/excerpt effective, and what meaning and effects does it achieve? *Question* As a reader or viewer, what are you left asking about? What do you not understand? *Ways Forward* What specific causal suggestions for ways forward or for extending and elaborating can you make?	After writing P-Q-W peer response, peers meet for a conference to discuss their responses. The writer asks questions about anything he or she needs clarified. Learners consider how the experience of providing and receiving peer feedback went, what they want to keep doing, and what they might change to make the experience more helpful. Learners consider when, where, and how this kind of feedback can be used in other classes and in their lives.	STUDENTS COMPLETE A FINAL REFLECTION ON THEIR OWN MICRO-ARGUMENT: The feedback that was most helpful to me was . . . because . . . One thing I still have a question about is . . . Action/Revision Plan: Here is a list of priorities for revising my micro-argument: 1. 2. 3. 4. Here is a list of priorities for providing effective peer feedback that can be heard and used: 1. 2. 3. 4.

Chapter 15

BRINGING IT ALL TOGETHER

Extending, Exploring, and Reflecting Through Culminating Projects and Assessments

> **ESSENTIAL QUESTION**
> How can culminating projects and summative assessments promote our students' ongoing engagement, understanding, and high-road transfer?

Jeff can remember the many years that he lovingly graded and commented on student work. When he would return these tests and papers, learners would typically look at the grade, crumple the papers up, and throw them away! His evaluation process was a heartbreaking waste of time. Now, every unit concludes with celebrations where students share and justify their work both in class and then after school. In small groups, they share their writing by reading excerpts aloud. They present their collaborative multimedia projects and report on service learning connections. They explain how they personalized their learning by extending and exploring what was learned together as a class and then making it their own. They share with peers, family, and friends, and receive reflective feedback from a wide variety of responders who acknowledge their efforts and name what they have learned and potential ways to apply and extend the work. They archive their work and ask "keepers" such as friends and family to reflect and comment on their work. Units conclude with learners reflecting on what they have learned from their learning journey, from their reflections, and from feedback and move on to create action plans for how to build on that learning through the future.

See *Lesson Plan Canvas* on page 257

Reflection is necessary *throughout* any teaching and learning process. If we want our teaching to *matter*, immediately and throughout our students' lives, the major goal of any specific unit is always an expression of *high-road transfer*. This kind of transfer requires that learners continually *reflect* on what they are learning, why they are learning it, and how to extend and apply it.

We want our students to extend their learning in service of actualizing their full capacities personally, academically, in their future field of chosen work, and in the domain of democratic citizenship and civic engagement. This book has been about teaching with intent and mindfulness toward these kinds of goals, and ongoing reflection is necessary to achieving this.

The end of any inquiry or apprenticeship is the time to create what cognitive scientists call a *knowledge artifact*, also known as a *culminating project*—to compose something that is usable; that is of service to self, community, and environment; that is extensible and transferable; and that shows proof positive of achievement or growth toward significant threshold knowledge goals and standards. These threshold knowledge goals from the envision phase of unit and lesson planning are now actualized in accomplishment. Now is the time for sharing and celebrating clear and internally persuasive "proofs positive" of progress and achievement.

Not only is it important for students to present and justify their learning; they need to be involved in assessing their own learning. As Bob Fecho (2011) argues: "If assessment is always something done *to* us rather than *with* us or *by* us, it will rarely ever be *for* us. Nor will it provide us with the skills to call our own abilities into focus. We remain, for the most part, at the mercy of the judgment of others" (p. 32). And as Brian Huot (2002) puts it: "Unless we teach students how to assess, we fail to provide them with the authority inherent in assessment" (p. 64).

WHAT'S AT STAKE: STANDARDS, INTERNAL PERSUASION, AND HIGH-ROAD TRANSFER

When it comes to such projects and summative assessment, learners need to have internalized the capacity to develop and articulate critical standards, and to apply these critical standards to themselves, their own work, the work of peers, the work of others, and a variety of real-world tasks and policies. As Rick Stiggins (1987) maintains: "If you do not have a clear sense of the key dimensions of a sound performance—a vision of poor and outstanding performance—you can neither teach students to perform nor evaluate their performance" (p. 37); nor can students consciously pursue an outstanding performance.

This means that *throughout our instruction* we need to involve learners in the processes of developing standards, apprenticing them into ways to describe and evaluate performance in terms of standards. This process is dialogic, growth mindset, and future oriented (Dweck, 2006). Internal persuasion occurs through open inquiry and dialogic testing of all perspectives. The understanding that results is personally compelling, vested, and internalized. The learner's way of knowing and composing is accepted by the community of practice. Learning is independently extended not because it is required by authority but *because the learner deeply understands and is convinced and compelled by this way of knowing* (Bakhtin, 1991).

Grading, in contrast to our goals, is a form of authoritative discourse that is monologic and past oriented. Grading, a judgment placed on a learner by a teacher or another outsider without the learner's participation, reflects an authoritative information-centered theory and practice. Any information-driven test, with multiple-choice items (mystical guess?) or fill-in-the-blank items or even essays that only reflect back content, does not demonstrate or promote understanding or the capacity to use and extend what has been learned. As the psychometrician Paul Dressler was fond of maintaining: A grade is a gross estimation based on a biased evaluation from a partially informed observer about an ill-defined amount of learning of an indeterminate amount of material based on a very small slice of evidence about a learner's progress . . . and so on!

It's also important to remember that all next-generation standards highlight the movement *from assessment of information to assessment of performances*. Performances require conceptual understanding that is applied in a specific context to do the work that experts do. In our civil rights unit, learners know from day one that they are going to compose multiple advocacy pieces that will be—or become—arguments of policy or arguments of problem–solution. They also know that they will use their evolving understandings to implement some kind of service learning project that is reciprocal in serving their own needs and those of others and a community. When students become familiar with the inquiry process, we actively involve them in planning units, identifying culminating projects, bringing in interesting materials, and even planning daily lessons. (Download a ready reference guide to backwards planning culminating projects from the companion website, http://resources.corwin.com/EMPOWER-secondary. See also Chapter 3, page 43, about planning culminating projects as part of mapping.)

In our civil rights unit, learners know that these deliverables will require meeting major unit goals about developing and expressing social imagination, taking the perspectives of others and addressing their felt needs, seeing complex implied relationships in data to make inferences, and writing arguments with defensible and debatable claims, generated from evidence and reasoning about the evidence. They know that everything we do during the unit will be focused on developing these strategies and putting them to use in creating the culminating projects.

To this end, from the onset of the unit, learners are involved in reviewing examples of culminating projects from previous years and are coached to use these models to articulate critical standards for their own projects. Every day, we reflect on our progress toward these goals and create daily deliverables that can be used to show that progress, and perhaps be used in the projects.

HOW CULMINATING PROJECTS AND ASSESSMENTS FIT INTO EMPOWER

First point: If we want our instruction to be coherent and to maximize student engagement and learning, then we must *envision* and *map* out our units so that *instruction and assessment practices work together synergistically*, continually promoting motivation and reinforcing how to meet major goals, threshold knowledge, and standards-based achievements.

Second, because we are always apprenticing, learners should be *primed* to value and use their prior experience and current needs and be *oriented* toward moving forward to the major goals and projects. They should be involved in monitoring the unit instructional sequence so that they understand the goals and how every activity is working toward these goals. They are involved in monitoring and assessing their own progress as well as that of their peers who represent a community of practice in the classroom. Knowledge must be continually enacted and made visible. Critical standards should be expressed as performance standards and be worked toward in the daily deliverables. This transparency also allows learners to bring in materials and insights from their experience and culture that are helpful to the community.

To provide a useful *walk-through* and work toward *extending* and *exploring*, daily deliverables, formative assessments, and student reflections on learning should be a part of each day's lesson. Assessment must be ongoing, multimodal, and from various perspectives. Assessment should be descriptive (not numbers or letters) and provide visible signs of growth and accomplishment over time, and reinforce principles of expert practice, mental models, and maps that can continue to evolve and contribute to future learning and living. Learners continually *reflect* on their growth toward standards and expertise. (What have I learned? How do I know I've learned it? How can I expand and transfer this knowledge?)

■ FIGURE 15.1A: TEACHER'S EXPERT MENTAL MODEL FOR ASSESSMENT

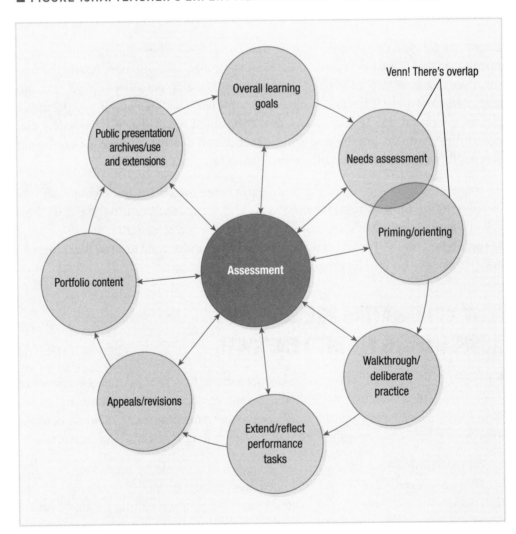

Assessment is a collaborative process that is most effective when it involves reflections from the self, from peers, *and even from other stakeholders working together.*

Finally, it should always be remembered that all reflection, and especially assessing and reporting student learning, is a caring, sensitive process requiring teachers' professional judgment so that students will have a continuing impulse to engage and learn, and will see how to proceed with future learning.

MENTAL MODELS OF ASSESSMENT

Like any expert practice or process, we need to develop and use a mental model for pursuing it. In Figure 15.1, we provide a teacher's expert mental model for assessment

■ FIGURE 15.1B: STUDENT'S MENTAL MODEL FOR MAKING USE OF ASSESSMENT

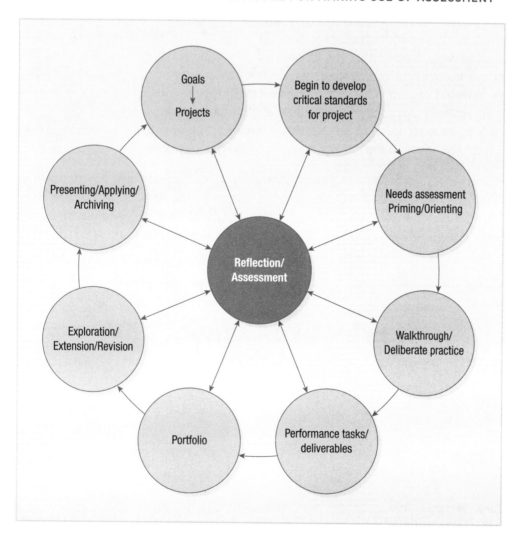

and a student's mental model for making use of assessment. The major difference is in the perspective:

- Teacher's goals: What should students know and be able to do? How are the goals being met/how well have they been met based on the critical standards? How are students helped to reflect on learning and rehearse for transfer?

- Student's goals: What do I want to learn? How will I show that I've learned it? How can I use what I am learning in other situations now and in the future?

Bottom line: All assessment should always be tied to our highest goals for deep understanding and transfer!

PLANNING FOR ASSESSMENT: WHY, WHEN, AND HOW TO ASSESS?

In apprenticeship, all reflection and assessment is meant to focus on increasing engagement and understanding. In George Hillocks's (e.g., 1986a, 1986b) research reviews of feedback and evaluation procedures, he found that all the time teachers spend responding to completed student work leads to insignificant or even no increases in motivation or learning. The kinds of reflection and assessment that *do* lead to learning are done in the context of the learning process, can be immediately used and applied to improve the learning process and products, and foreground accomplishment and evolving competence. *The central move here is not to evaluate, per se, but to provide information that will promote reflection about the effects of actions as related to goals.*

Bottom line: Years of research show that providing more feedback in a context of immediate use promotes deeper engagement and learning (Bransford, Brown, & Cocking, 2001; Hattie, 2008; Hillocks, 1986a, 1986b). It's crucial that our planning, teaching, student learning activity, and ongoing assessment be connected and work together coherently for the same purposes and goals.

Principles of Effective Culminating Projects and Assessments

Culminating projects should be planned and introduced to

- Reflect progress toward real-world expertise and applications

- Be knowledge artifacts or service projects that can be extended and revised by oneself or others

- Be archival—usable, revisable, and extensible by others over time (E-M-P-O)

The assessments/feedback we provide along the journey of learning and at the final presentation of the culminating project (formative and summative) need to be explicit, be reflective and count and lead to action in these ways:

- Be goal (and standards) referenced

- Be performance based

- Be reflective of our teaching (it is unethical to assess learners on something we have not helped them to learn over time)

- Pay personal attention to the individual learner and his or her efforts, activity, and evolving understandings

- Be transparent, concrete, specific, and easy to understand by learners and other stakeholders

- Be actionable/immediately usable and user-friendly

- Be timely, provided at the point of need when it can be immediately used (not afterward)

- Be consistent and ongoing

- Be principled and transferable—learners learn principles of expert practice and mental maps they can use in the future

- Be shared and used by learners to reflect, self-assess, and provide feedback to peers and self to monitor progress and explore ways forward (W-E-R)

BRINGING IT ALL TOGETHER MOVE 1: RANKING MODELS TO ARTICULATE CRITICAL STANDARDS

The use of models and modeling is integral to guided inquiry/cognitive apprenticeship. Vygotsky (1978) called modeling the teaching tool of all tools. Teachers must provide concrete models of success, show students how to develop and use new knowledge and strategies in contexts of actual use, then coach and mentor learners to help them mirror the model, work with others to do it, then do it on their own.

Although we are addressing reflection at the end of this book, *reflection is something that must occur throughout the whole learning process.* We typically use this particular strategy very early in any unit, by having students review exemplars of the assigned culminating projects. We collect examples from year to year so that we can use them to introduce the next year's students to strong culminating projects completed by fellow students. But if we are doing a project for the first time, we find models on the internet or out in the world.

(Continued)

Here are the steps for using examples to model and help students reflect on quality work:

Step 1: Ask learners to consider an area of competence and expertise in their lives, and how they know they have been successful at a task in this domain. Discuss critical standards of success. Inform learners that they will participate in articulating critical standards for one of our culminating unit projects.

Step 2: Select three examples of a culminating project (we always select strong ones, as we want these exemplars to become the baseline for the work).

Step 3: Make sure the three examples are different in various ways so that the students will see that there are creative options for completing this kind of culminating project.

Step 4: Ask students to individually experience and review the three projects, and to take notes about the strengths of each.

Step 5: Ask students to individually rank the projects in terms of quality, with 1 being the best, 2 the second best, and 3 the third best.

Step 6: Ask students to individually identify the reasons for their ranking in terms of data and reasoning—that is, values/rules/principles/standards of quality they are applying to the data: What makes 1 the best? What makes 2 strong but not quite so strong as 1?

Step 7: Ask students to meet in a learning group with the goal of trying to come to consensus. The deliverable goal here is to come up with reasons for their ranking—that is, to identify and then articulate the critical standards exemplified by an excellent example of the performance task. So even if the group cannot come to agreement, they should try to agree on evidence and standards of excellence.

Step 8: Have the groups share their thinking, and the class then boils down and chunks their observations on quality to three, four, or five critical standards that must be met on their own culminating projects.

This can become the basis of a student-generated assessment guide (rubric, semantic scales, checklist, etc.). The teacher may work with students to add curricular standards that must be met if these haven't yet come up.

BRINGING IT ALL TOGETHER MOVE 2: UNPACKING AND TRANSLATING STANDARDS WITH STUDENTS

Reflection needs to occur before, during, and after learning for that learning to become conscious and transferable competence. For that reason, every strategy in this chapter could be used at the beginning or in the process of a unit. This strategy is very useful for teachers to do during envisioning and mapping, and then with students during priming and orienting phases of a unit.

Standards are clearly defined dimensions of expertise. The process and achievement of standards are something learners need to be able to identify and explain. In the world outside of school, all assessments are performance-based assessments: We are asked to use and perform what we know to get work done. Standards-based assessments give teachers a wealth of information about how well students are progressing toward major goals, and give that same information to other stakeholders like the students, their parents, other teachers, community members, and policy makers. This kind of assessment can inform and help us reexamine our thinking about instruction, differentiation, grouping, and much more.

Just as we ask students to generate critical standards for success, we also involve them in composing usable benchmarks that describe progress toward or achievement of the standard in actual performance, in ways that can be understood and used by students, parents, community mentors, and others. Growth mindset language that foregrounds growth and possibility (e.g., *approaching proficiency, partially proficient, proficient,* and *extending proficiency*) is compulsory in this regard (Dweck, 2006).

To consider standards-based assessment throughout a unit, ask

- What daily performances (micro-writing/deliberate practice, etc.) can be used for formative assessment *as* and *for* learning?

- What other behaviors and products can be observed as evidence of growth and learning?

- What focal standards are to be met in the unit, and how will these be assessed in daily deliverables and culminating projects? What other threshold knowledge (i.e., other content-area concepts and strategies) will be assessed?

- What are the purposes of the different ongoing assessments (e.g., to name strengths, productive struggles, or ways forward; to check progress; to inform grouping for differentiated instruction; to inform instructional planning; or to convey information to students about what to keep doing and what to do next)?

- What are the most important criteria of success/critical standards for success? (Name just a few; focus on what matters most.)

- What does meeting each criterion/critical standard look like in actual accomplishment? Describe. This is benchmarking—and *this is the hard work!*

TRANSLATING BENCHMARKS INTO STUDENT-FRIENDLY LANGUAGE THROUGH "I CAN . . ." STATEMENTS

Students can be asked to translate standards into performance descriptions such as "I can" statements. An extension is to use "I'll know I can when . . ." or "I know I can

(Continued)

(Continued)

because . . ." statements and even "I can continue to improve by . . . because," which helps students not only to understand the standard and what it requires of them but also to provide self-assessment in terms of procedural feedback and feedforward. This process not only helps teachers and students understand the standards more deeply, but it also prepares both for on-point instruction, deliberate practice, and procedural feedback.

For example, take a Common Core standard such as Reading Standard 1 for eighth grade:

CCSS.ELA-LITERACY.RL.8.1

> Cite the textual evidence that most strongly supports an analysis of what the text says explicitly as well as inferences drawn from the text.

Ask students what this standard means in actual accomplishment and performance. Have students brainstorm in small groups and then share and discuss their ideas. The teacher can help with phrasing, fairly quickly coming up with something like the following:

> **I will be able to/can** notice and identify the most important key details in a text. **I can** justify how I know these are the most important key details using rules of notice. I can figure out what these details directly express, both on their own and together as a pattern, and what they indirectly imply about a central topic or problem taken up by the text. I can cite evidence by explicitly referring back to the text and using page numbers so a reader can find and confirm the evidence.

Confirm that all students understand what the standard means. Retranslate and simplify as needed. Sometimes it is useful to enumerate what must be done to meet the standard:

> When I meet the standard, I can . . .
>
> 1. *Notice and identify the most important key details*
>
> 2. *Explain how I know these are the most important details, using rules of notice*
>
> 3. *Figure out what these details directly express and mean about a central topic*
>
> 4. *Figure out what individual details suggest or imply by making inferences*
>
> 5. *Figure out what patterns of details suggest or imply by making inferences*
>
> 6. *Refer to and correctly cite the key details I use in my analysis of what the text means so that a reader can find the evidence and confirm it as "safe"*

This lays all of the groundwork for students to meet other standards, like Reading Standard 2 about identifying main ideas and themes (e.g., *I can explain how the key details work together to express a theme, generalization, or "topic comment"*).

The process also helps teachers to see how standards are sometimes complex and ask quite a bit of students (although the different moves are generally part of the same organic and complex process) and helps students to see the same. Unpacking standards lets teachers know what they must help students to learn and deliberately practice. Of course, the same process can be taken with all math, science, and other kinds of standards. If the next-generation standards truly reflect expertise (and we think that they do), then it can be very useful to unpack the standards and translate them into performance moves.

The process also leads to understanding how the standard can focus procedural feedback and procedural feedforward (e.g., the way that you cite [directly cited major key details such as . . .] demonstrates how you determined what the text said literally, and the way that you [explained what different details implied and patterns of details implied] helped us understand your inferences and conclusions because this process . . .).

BRINGING IT ALL TOGETHER MOVE 3: REFLECTING WITH PORTFOLIO CONTENTS ENTRY LETTERS

A major purpose of assessment is for our students to articulate and internalize critical standards and apply them to their own (and others') work, both now and in the future. Another major purpose of all reflection including assessment is to promote students telling agentive stories about themselves as learners. Agentive stories foreground that students are learners, that they are continually learning how to learn, and that they are developing and can apply ever more expert concepts and strategies through their deliberate practice with expert strategies. This kind of reflection develops a powerful learner identity and sense of self-efficacy.

One way to involve students in telling this agentive story is to have them keep an ongoing portfolio through the year (or through their school career or life!) that tells the story of their learning and offers proof of productively navigating struggle and proof of progress and achievement over time. Such portfolios are easily made digital with electronic documents, photos, and scans, though many of our students prefer a hard copy in a binder. Portfolios are an expert strategy of showing one's development over time, and of showing the scope of one's work. From architects to teachers and professors, many professionals keep formal port-folios throughout a career, and many other professionals and hobbyists keep informal ones.

To aid in this process, we often prompt students to reflect on what examples of recent work demonstrate productive struggle, experimentation, progress, or mastery. We usually do this at least once a week. We also directly suggest to students that certain pieces of work—whether a daily deliverable or something more substantial—should be included in the portfolio.

To help learners identify and reflect on what the work sample demonstrates, we provide a general form that they can adapt as needed (see Figure 15.2); find a downloadable version of this Portfolio Contents Entry Sheet on the companion website, resources .corwin.com/EMPOWER-secondary.

online resources

(Continued)

(Continued)

FIGURE 15.2: PORTFOLIO CONTENTS ENTRY SHEET

Student name/date:

Title of work sample:

I have chosen the following piece for inclusion in the portfolio because:

☐ It demonstrates mastery of _____ (standard or learning goal) because _____

☐ It shows growth when I compare it to _____ because _____

☐ It demonstrates a stage/various stages I used to complete my work by _____

☐ It demonstrates how I productively struggled to _____ by using this form of deliberate practice:

_____

A strength of my work is _____ because _____

(repeat as necessary)

I knew I was finished with this work when _____

because _____

I can foresee using these same strategies of this kind of task in the future when _____

Next time I try this or a similar task, I will try to personalize my learning, try something new, and explore or extend and elaborate

by _____

_____

Following are notes from peers, parents, keepers (community mentors), and teachers who have reviewed the

portfolio: _____

_____

_____

_____

online resources 🔎 Available for download at **http://resources.corwin.com/EMPOWER-secondary**

Periodically, perhaps quarterly, students could write responses to the following prompts in their portfolio:

> *What I currently most enjoy composing is . . . because . . .*
>
> *What I currently most enjoy reading is . . . because . . .*
>
> *I find time to read and write by . . .*
>
> *Something I am very good at outside of school is . . .*
>
> *Something I am good at in school is . . .*
>
> *Something I am improving on is . . . because . . .*
>
> *Something I want to get better at is . . . because . . .*
>
> *I am working to get better by . . .*
>
> *Comments from peers, parents, keepers, and others about the work samples include . . .*

COVER LETTERS

At the end of units and the year, we have students review their portfolio and write a cover letter outlining the major trajectories of their learning journey, and pointing us to work samples they want us to notice and explanations of what they think these samples demonstrate. All of this naming of learning promotes reflection and in turn names the student as an agentive learner who deliberately and mindfully improves over time.

BRINGING IT ALL TOGETHER MOVE 4: REFLECTING WITH PROCESS ANALYSIS

A process analysis is another way to reflect on any task and it can also be included in a portfolio (such as a culminating project). A process analysis is a way of reflecting before, during, and soon after any process of reading, composing, solving any problem, or navigating any kind of task. The process analysis describes how the learner went about completing the task, what decisions were made and why, what struggles were navigated and how, and what options were considered and discarded or could be used in the future. It captures the mental model and map for doing this task.

The process analysis can be composed in many ways: multimodally with a flow chart; another kind of map; a "choose your own adventure" story; a slide show; or other means. Try to avoid being too directive in what is required for a process analysis; it should work for the learner, which often requires flexibility. Following are tips for writing a process analysis.

Before

- What is the task? (What are you doing/working on?)

- How is it similar to other tasks you've completed in the past? How might this prior experience help you?

- How will the task involve reading, composing, or problem solving?

- How are you feeling about the task? If needed, how can you reframe your feelings to be more productive?

- How will you get started? What steps will you need to take? How will you schedule your time and create due date milestones? How will you divide up and manage the work if this is a group project?

- What is the purpose of the task? How will you know you have been successful? In what contexts will the product be shared and used? In what situations will it be useful in the future?

During

- Consider what you are doing, the decisions you are making, what seems to be working and not working, and why. Perhaps talk/think out loud about it or make some quick notes if you are able so you'll have some reminders afterward when you compose your process analysis.

(Continued)

(Continued)

- How did you get the "stuff" you needed to get started with the composing, meaning making, or problem solving?

- How did you go about structuring task completion, the composition, or knowledge artifact on the macro level?

- What moves did you make to structure task completion, the composition, or knowledge artifact at the micro level/sentence and word level?

- What were the challenges, and how did you productively struggle through them?

After

- What did you do, and in what order?

- Why did you do what you did? And why did you do it in that order?

- What worked? Why did it work?

- What did not seem to work? Why not? What did you do about this?

- How did you feel at various points in the process? How did you reframe if needed?

- What options did you have that you did not play out? What could or will you do differently the next time you have this task or are faced with similar challenges?

- To what degree were you successful? How do you know?

- How can you be even more successful next time?

Action Plan/Cultivating a Spirit of Transfer

- Where to now?

- How will you further explore and extend your learning?

- How will you apply this learning now and in the future?

BRINGING IT ALL TOGETHER MOVE 5: APPEAL LETTERS

Early in our teaching careers, we often gave challenging assignments and never actually helped our students prepare for success. We assigned and evaluated, but we did not teach or apprentice them into expert practice. Therefore, we spent our weekends grading lots of crappy assignments and the next week dealing with angry students and sometimes parents.

These days, our lives are much better. We respond to student work daily during class time, in quick hits, in ways that learners can immediately use, and through daily formative assessments, procedural feedback, and lessons based on observed common or individual needs. We have many fewer major assignments to assess as we work over time to help students deliberately practice mastering the concepts and moves of experts. Therefore, when it comes time for high-stakes projects or compositions to be assessed, they are usually quite good. When students fall short of a standard or criterion, they usually agree that this is so, and we can brainstorm strategies that have been taught and practiced that will aid in improvement. We always allow students to redo work (until a "drop dead" deadline like the end of a grading period) because this is in keeping with growth mindset and apprenticeship (Dweck, 2006). But if a student persists in insisting that he or she has met a standard (and we disagree), then we turn the responsibility back to the student in the form of an appeal letter.

In the appeal letter, the student

- Uses a formal letter format

- Composes a micro-argument(s) in which he or she
  - Claims to have met the questioned standard (or standards)
  - Provides evidence from his or her work that he or she has done so
  - Explains how the work samples provided demonstrate the standard has been met, as articulated by benchmarking in the assessment guide

- Hand delivers the letter (If possible, we read the letter in the student's presence so that we can converse.)

Typically, the result is either that the student receives the credit (if he or she is convincing enough) or that the student sees what he or she can do to meet the standard and then proceeds to revise. This strategy can work beautifully: It puts the responsibility on students, assists them to explain the standard and how they have met it, and encourages them to be an agent who self-advocates through their writing. Plus, they've been tricked into writing another argument and received more deliberate practice with standards.

POWERFUL PLANNING: PROMOTING REFLECTION AND AGENCY FOR ALL

When it comes to assessment, the job of teachers is to pursue it *in careful and sensitive ways that promote ongoing reflection, motivation, deep engagement, and the continuing impulse to learn.* Assessment and instruction are *inseparable,* and *inseparable from reflection,* because effective assessment reflectively informs teaching and learning. It is important to move toward criterion-referenced, standards-based evaluation with a future orientation. It is essential to do authentic intellectual work—to eliminate busy work and make sure all activities meet the correspondence concept (i.e., the real-world expert test).

You cannot formally assess everything students do. If you try, the students will not be doing enough creating and composing, and you will be tired (if not exhausted!) and grossly misusing your time. Modeling an assessment of one student example and then asking students to peer assess for the same moves is much more efficient and promotes student reflection, agency, and expertise.

In our civil rights unit, students are involved in reflecting on and assessing their own and each other's work nearly every day and monitoring progress toward the big-picture goals and the capacity to complete culminating projects. They share how they are learning and how they can navigate challenges. After learners write a summary of the day's reading or activity, or a micro-argument about how effectively a historical figure promoted civil rights, we provide model feedback to one example. Learners then use the model to provide procedural feedback based on critical standards of the task. This process can be done in just a few minutes and involves all of us: each individual, all peers, and the teacher working together to inquire into learning and how to make it best happen for all.

Transferring Our Learning: What to Remember When Designing and Implementing Culminating Projects and Assessments That Foster Reflection

- Determine general goals for students, now and in the future, by articulating the specific goals for a unit and by considering how the ongoing assessment plan works toward those goals.

- Consider how daily formative and final summative assessment practices are designed to motivate, create a continuing impulse to learn, extend conceptual and procedural understandings, and apply critical standards of success.

- Share what skills learners will need to engage effectively in self-assessment, peer assessment, and assessment of professional texts and knowledge artifacts.

- Introduce and model assessment strategies; show how to use each strategy; highlight the purpose, process, and problem-solving moves; and then monitor successful use.

- Support learners to reflect on their progress, demonstrate growth and accomplishment, and create action plans for continuing to mindfully develop and extend their critical capacities and assessment processes.

- Remember that thinking and reflecting is the glue that holds knowing and doing together and leads to 3D learning and deep understanding!

Lesson: Ranking Models to Reflect On and Articulate Critical Standards

Unit: How do we protect and promote civil rights?

ENVISION the destination
(Where are learners going, and why?)

GOAL *What kind of thinking is targeted?*	EVIDENCE *What product(s) will serve as proof of learning?*	MEASURES OF SUCCESS *What's the standard and quality-assurance tool?*	STAKES *Why will learners buy in?* *What's the "why" behind the learning?*
X-2 Interpretation X-2 Explanation/reasoning ✓ Application of skill/strategy X-1 Self-assessing/reflecting	✓ Performance assessment: articulating and explaining critical standards for a culminating project such as a written composition or a collaborative multimedia composition, or a service learning project that applies what has been learned throughout the unit	✓ **SIMPLE:** √−, √, √+ on discrete facts/skills ✓ **CHECKLIST:** Assess if product contains essential characteristics/features.	Use ESSENCE as a guide for buy-in. Your lesson should have one or more of the following: ✓ E-S: Emotional spark/salience (i.e., relevance) ✓ S-E: Social engagement (i.e., collaboration) ✓ N: Novelty (i.e., new concepts and skills) ✓ C-E: Critical/creative exploration opportunities
Learners will be able to rank the effectiveness of three strong work samples of culminating projects from most to least effective, and will be able to explain and justify their ranking with critical standards. The overall goal is to articulate critical standards for a culminating project that are internally persuasive, that can guide learning, and that can be revised and extended throughout a unit to reflect growing understandings.	Students generate micro-arguments that articulate critical standards (reasoning and warrants of value) and cite evidence of how their top-ranked project meets these critical standards. Students will be able to mirror what they hear peers say about the dimensions of expert performance, then will provide uptake in the form of points of agreement, elaboration, reservation, or possible revision or disagreement along with an explanation why. Learners will come to agreement on 3–5 critical standards and put these in a rubric, semantic scale, primary trait checklist, or other kind of assessment guide.	Speakers can articulate a claim about which model is the best example, then provide justification in terms of data and reasoning from that exemplar. The reasoning will include values and standards of expertise and will justify the significance of these to an expert performance. Listeners will be able to mirror these elements of an argument back. Groups will be able to agree on 3–5 most important critical standards of expertise on this kind of project, and can explain why these are the most important standards to achieving success on this kind of project.	**E-S:** Students respond to successful models of a task they will need to complete. **S-E:** Learners work together to articulate critical standards that will guide their work. **N:** Ranking may be new to students, and ranking requires reasoning using values, rules, or standards to justify the ranks. **C-E:** Learners apply what is learned to their evolving conceptions and mental models about expertise with argument (or whatever composition or project they will do), about social imagination and perspective taking, and about the best ways to promote and protect civil rights in their own lives and communities.

MAP out the path to expertise/mastery
(How would an expert deconstruct and approach this task, step by step?)

TWITTER SUMMARY (3 bullets max)	MENTAL MODELS, PROCESS GUIDES, HEURISTICS	A MODEL OF GOOD WORK LOOKS LIKE . . .	DIFFERENTIATION AND LAYERING
Experts possess clear models of an expert performance that they can use to guide problem solving, reflect on progress, and assess outcomes.	Claim–data–reasoning for argument Critical standards are an articulation of the dimensions of expert performance that fulfills a specific purpose and can be used to guide problem solving.	A rubric, semantic scale, or checklist of 3–5 critical standards and an indication of what meeting each will look like	Learners will see different models of success and of argument and response. Learners will develop and use various guides that articulate critical standards for expert performance.

(Continued)

POWER through your lesson
(What is the sequence of initial major must-make instructional moves?)

PRIME	ORIENT	WALK THROUGH (and check for understanding)	EXTEND AND EXPLORE	REFLECT
Learners are prompted to consider an area of personal competence or expertise, then to name processes and dimensions that are part of a competent performance. Students make notes and then discuss in pairs or triads. How do they know that they are making progress on a task? What is the proof positive? How do they know they have achieved success or an exemplary performance? Students engage in large group discussion of critical standards, dimensions of expert performance and how these inform deliberate practice, and ongoing reflections like procedural feedback and assessment.	Learners are invited to participate in articulating critical standards for a culminating unit project. Their input is needed to identify the dimensions of an effective or even expert performance, and to discuss various ways of meeting these kinds of critical standards. Make it clear that students have skin in this game and that critical standards will evolve as we learn throughout the unit. The articulated critical standards will guide our practice in understanding the issues of civil rights, sharing and applying our understandings, and arguing for particular individual practices and social policies through composing powerful arguments in school and throughout our lives. The critical standards will be used for self-, peer, and teacher evaluations of work.	Teacher shares three different examples of strong and successful models of expert performance on a culminating project. Learners individually read/view and rank the models from most to least effective and then articulate a micro-argument justifying their top choice with evidence from that example and reasoning tying this evidence to critical success standards that they must articulate. Learners meet in small groups to come up with 3–5 most important standards and to articulate benchmarks describing what success on each standard looks like. CHECK FOR UNDERSTANDING: Learning groups articulate 3–5 standards, justify each one, and provide a first-draft benchmark for each. This is then shared in the large group to inform a class learning guide.	DELIBERATE PRACTICE/ ARTICULATE CONSCIOUS AWARENESS: In the whole class group, learners agree on 3–5 most important critical standards for success. The whole class participates in creating a first-draft rubric, a checklist of primary traits, or semantic scales to guide deliberate practice toward expertise. Learners will be told that the learning guide can be revised at any time throughout the unit as we learn more about standards of success. DIFFERENTIATE: If some students are struggling, work with them to assist, or have other successful learners assist. Different models can be provided, and different groupings or more time can be provided. DEBRIEF: Return to the learning guide and ask for revisions at least once a week.	Summarize what you learned. What is the mental model for successful performance on this task? What makes this kind of project useful, strong, and compelling? What will I need to learn throughout the unit to be prepared for success? Why does success matter, and how can my project be used, extended, archived, etc., to do work or inform work that matters in the world? Why do critical success standards matter in the world? HOMEWORK EXTENSION: Find other examples of this or a similar kind of performance out in the world and assess its success according to your criteria. Provide procedural feedback or feedforward for improvement. Practice articulating critical standards for other tasks in another class, at home, or in your favorite activities.

Concluding Thoughts

WHAT'S NEXT? AN EMPOWERED VISION OF OUR FUTURE TEACHING AND LEARNING

> ## ESSENTIAL QUESTION
> How can we set up our systems for continuous improvement?

Aristotle typically evaluated any object, person, or process with respect to its *telos*—its ultimate purpose, goal, or end. The telos of a knife is to cut, so a knife that does not cut well is not a good knife. We've been arguing in this book that the telos of any educational enterprise is learning how to learn. More specifically, the end is learning how to deeply engage, understand, and expertly use what has been learned, and we've further argued that this learning should be in service of democratic citizenry and social justice.

Learning happens when a learner (whether student or teacher) *is transformed*. Learning happens when learners change their frame of reference by critically reflecting on their prior assumptions. Learning happens when learners consciously make and implement plans that bring about new ways of defining their social worlds, and new ways of being and of undertaking action in these worlds (Mezirow, 2000). The shift into deeper learning happens when learners can see why and how their understanding has changed and how this change in understanding can be put into action. This kind of transformation is hugely motivating: Developing expertise is empowering. Every human being wants to be more competent and powerful, and being so is especially significant when this serves personal growth and is helpful to others or the environment.

When we engage in guided inquiry—whether with our students into essential questions like *What makes me me?* or *How can we most effectively protect and promote civil rights?* or *How can we remediate stormwater pollution in our community?* or with our colleagues as teacher researchers into issues like how to more effectively teach reading or to use grouping structures and collaborative activities—both reflectivity *and* reflexivity must be used.

Reflectivity—the use of personal values, experiences, and habits to make meaning—is essential to all learning. But so is *reflexivity*—the privileging of the perspective, history, and values of others—of considering different ways of understanding, being, and performing knowledge. Reflexivity means suspending our own assumptions and exercising social imagination in order to understand what someone else brings to our learning and practice, whether this someone else is a student, a colleague, or an expert from the field.

Guided inquiry requires and rewards collaborative, dialogic, active, thoughtful, engaged learners and community members who have a dynamic mindset toward solving problems together. Guided inquiry requires and rewards both reflectivity and reflexivity.

It's essential that schools teach skills like critical thinking, problem solving, collaborating, information and data gathering, reflecting, and participatory planning. These are the stances and strategies of disciplinary expertise and democratic work. They include values such as respect for human dignity, equity, freedom, and social responsibility. Guided inquiry curricula not only strongly support academic learning but also robustly support collaborative, dialogic sharing—between teachers, between teachers and students, and between students—that leads to improved problem solving, rewarding interpersonal relationships, and deepened understanding. A guided inquiry approach such as cognitive apprenticeship is exceptionally powerful in promoting engagement and learning because it "integrates academic and social practices that position inquiry as (1) dynamic and dialogic, (2) attentive, probing, and thoughtful, (3) agentive and socially responsible, (4) relational and compassionate, (5) reflective and reflexive, and (6) valuing multiple and interdisciplinary perspectives" (Jennings & Mills, 2009, p. 1583).

These capacities are certainly worth cultivating in our students and in ourselves as teachers, learners, and democratic citizens. This is what EMPOWER guides us to do daily as we apprentice learners and each other into more powerful and transformative ways of learning, relating, and being—of democratic working and living.

EMPOWER also helps us to teach specific kinds of threshold knowledge, and to do so ever more deeply over time by helping learners internalize mental maps and models of expert performance. We don't teach argument and evidentiary reasoning only once; we don't teach students how to read for main idea only once; we don't teach for social imagination and the capacity to see multiple perspectives only once. We teach these kinds of central processes over and over again, lesson after lesson, unit after unit, and year after year. These are throughlines of all curricula and of next-generation standards. EMPOWER helps us to teach these kinds of threshold knowledge in ways that can be named, used, built on, and extended in the future.

EVERYONE MEANS EVERYONE; ALL MEANS ALL

It is one of our deepest beliefs that every committed teacher can become an expert planner of instruction who apprentices all learners toward deeper engagement and expertise. It is likewise our belief that every learner can outgrow his or her current self and become a more competent and even expert reader, writer, mathematician, or citizen scientist—no matter one's background. It is our deep commitment to make this vision possible. When we say that every teacher has the potential to be highly effective and that every learner can become a competent reader and writer, "all means all." We are compelled by the research on human potential (Bloom, 1976; Vygotsky, 1978), the research on motivation and engagement (Csikszentmihalyi, 1990; Smith & Wilhelm, 2002, 2006), and the research on the development of expertise (Ericsson & Poole, 2016) that this is within our reach.

This is too important a project to leave to chance.

That is why we use EMPOWER as the way to enact the research and practical knowledge of expertise in teaching and learning. It is our calling to actualize the full potential of ourselves and all our learners. This is why inductive and restorative practice, along with restorative justice, is so necessary: When things go awry with learning or behavior, we need processes for bringing the learner(s) back into the community and its work. This is an issue of civil rights and social justice.

EMPOWER works for inclusion, equity, and social justice. It does so by creating a classroom community that learners find worth belonging to—one that serves their greatest hopes and values, makes compelling personal connections to all learning, is culturally relevant, creates a sense of belonging, requires their active participation from the start, makes the path to expertise clear to all, and provides the necessary assistance and differentiation for all to walk that path. We have found that struggling students often up their game to amazing levels when they are actively supported into the stances and practices of the expert community (Smith & Wilhelm, 2006).

Here's another major point. EMPOWER offers a way to integrate and situate almost all of the most pressing concerns of schools through our actual instruction. *Only in a context of collaborative guided inquiry* can many powerful features of motivation, flow experience and engagement, social connection and relational learning, social-emotional learning (SEL), executive functioning (EF), culturally responsive teaching (CRT), inductive and restorative practice, growth mindset and agentive identity (Dweck, 2006), and more be truly achieved. These conditions, attitudes, and capacities must be situated, integrated, and actively cultivated in our daily teaching and learning activity. These are not goals that can be achieved separately from relationships, complex tasks, and a meaningful context of use. In fact, we argue that guided inquiry is a context that *necessarily* requires and rewards meeting all of these goals for learners, and that informational teaching does not meet any of them.

Many schools frame their efforts to meet these goals as separate siloed programs and often as a form a remediation. By integrating these efforts through EMPOWER, we create curricular coherence, and naturally create situations that co-create and support success.

We know that improved teaching is the most powerful avenue to learner engagement and learning (e.g., National Writing Project & Nagin, 2003).

Therefore, as teachers, we must consciously and consistently serve the following roles:

- A constant provider of radical invitations to connect to purposeful learning that matters to learners (and to colleagues) right now and in the future
- A constant provider of radical invitations to engage in collaborative and accountable inquiry that serves the self, peers, community, and environment

- A collaborative participant creating community and caring

- A fellow learner in a community of practice

- A thinking partner who makes others and their developing capacities and potential visible

- A thinking partner who apprentices learners into expert ways of making meaning, doing the disciplines, working together, being reciprocal and compassionate, and so much more

MOVING FORWARD: JUST GET GOING!

If students (or colleagues) need to learn ways of collaborating, repairing relationships, cultivating social–emotional capacity, reading, composing, or problem solving, or any kind of learning or way of being, then it is up to us to help them. It is up to us to teach. Ours is the most powerful profession in the world because our job is to express faith in the future and work always toward transformation. Our mission is to actualize all potential: to make what is possible come into being. What could be more powerful and wonderful than that?

The research on teacher change and development shows that we do not change our theories and then change our practices (Wilhelm, Baker, & Dube-Hackett, 2001). We change our practices, and by reflecting on our innovations, we then change our theories, which in turn fuels future change.

So we need to get off the dime and continually change our practice. In a powerful article, "Four Postulates for Teacher Change," Stephen Leinwand (1994) offers four insights, which we recast here:

- We must teach in distinctly different ways from how we were taught. Therefore, we must be mindful about what works and have a map for moving forward.

- The traditional curriculum was designed to meet societal needs that no longer exist. We must therefore design new curricula and instruction that helps learners "learn how to learn."

- If you don't feel somewhat uncomfortable and inadequate, you're probably not doing the job. Just as we need students to lean into productive struggle and move through new zones of proximal development and into a transformed future, so do we. We need to get started on doing what we can't do yet, and use thinking partners and tools like EMPOWER to help us.

- Continually revising and refining our instruction demonstrates our professional commitment to growth. It's important to take the next step in the journey. Try something. Every educational experiment is doomed to success (except perhaps for afternoons in February or the day before a vacation!) because something is going to be learned and new ways forward will emerge.

Here's our suggestion: start by planning a lesson using EMPOWER. You'll find that it not only helps your planning but will also help with implementing the plan, reflecting and making decisions while teaching, reflecting afterward, and naming ways to improve the lesson the next time you teach it. Then you can plan a unit using EMPOWER. Once you do so, it will become easier to plan the next unit, and you'll find yourself thinking about how to make the "must-make moves" even before you sit down to plan. It's also helpful to have thinking partners. Just like having a running partner improves your commitment to and practice of an exercise routine, so does having a colleague to plan and reflect with. This works well for us even when we plan with someone who teaches a different grade or subject.

Every journey starts with the first step. Decide which step to take next. Every journey continues because we agree to take the next steps, to make the road by walking, joining arms with our fellow thinking partners and learners. By planning the journey, taking the first steps, trying new moves, studying and reflecting on what happened, and then reflecting on and using what we have learned to take more next steps, we engage in the powerful journey of continuous improvement.

REFERENCES AND RESOURCES

Applebee, A. N., Burroughs, R., & Cruz, G. (2000). Curricular conversations in elementary school classrooms: Case studies of interdisciplinary instruction. In S. Wineberg & P. Grossman (Eds.), *Interdisciplinary curriculum: Challenges to implementation* (pp. 93–111). New York, NY: Teachers College Press.

Applebee, A. N., Burroughs, R., & Stevens, A. S. (2000). Creating continuity and coherence in high school literature curricula. *Research in the Teaching of English, 34*(3), 382–415.

Applebee, A. N., Langer, J. A., Nystrand, M., & Gamoran, A. (2003). Discussion-based approaches to developing understanding: Classroom instruction and student performance in middle and high school English. *American Educational Research Journal, 40*(3), 685–730.

Ash, S., & Clayton P. (2009). The articulated learning: An approach to guided reflection and assessment. *Innovative Higher Education, 29*(2), 137–154.

Autor, D. H., Levy, F., & Murnane, R. J. (2003). The skill content of recent technological change: An empirical exploration. *The Quarterly Journal of Economics, 118*(4), 1279–1333.

Autor, D., & Price, B. (2013, June 21). *The changing task composition of the US labor market: An update of Autor, Levy, and Murnane (2003).* Retrieved from https://economics.mit.edu/files/9758

Bakhtin, M. M. (1991). *Dialogic imagination: Four essays by M. M. Bakhtin* (C. Emerson & M. Holquist, trans.). Austin: University of Texas Press.

Barab, S., & Hay, K. (2001). Doing science at the elbows of experts: Issues related to the science apprenticeship camp. *Journal of Research in Science Teaching, 38*(1), 70–102.

Bereiter, C. (2004). Reflections on depth. In K. Leithwood, P. McAdie, N. Bascia, & A. Rodrigue (Eds.), *Teaching for deep understanding* (pp. 8–12). Toronto, ON: OISE/UT and EFTO.

Black, P., & Wiliam, D. (1998, October). Inside the black box: Raising standards through classroom assessment. *Phi Delta Kappan*, 139–148.

Bloom, B. (1976). *Human characteristics and school learning.* New York, NY: McGraw-Hill.

Bransford, J. D., Brown, A. L., & Cocking, R. R. (Eds.). (1999). *How people learn: Brain, mind, experience, and school.* Washington, DC: National Research Council.

Bransford, J., & Johnson, M. (1972). Contextual prerequisites for understanding: Some investigations of comprehension and recall. *Journal of Verbal Learning and Verbal Behavior, 11*, 717–726.

Bridgeland, J. M., DiIulio, J. J., Jr., & Morison, K. B. (2006). *The silent epidemic: Perspectives of high school dropouts.* Washington, DC: Civic Enterprises.

Britton, J. (1983). Writing and the story of the world. In B. M. Kroll & C. G. Wells (Eds.), *Explorations in the development of writing: Theory, research, and practice* (pp. 3–30). New York, NY: Wiley.

Brown, J., Collins, A., & Duguid, P. (1989). Situated cognition and the culture of learning. *Educational Researcher, 18*(1), 32–42.

Bruner, J. (1986). *Actual minds, possible worlds.* Cambridge, MA: Harvard University Press.

Bryk, A., Gomez, L., Grunow, A., & LeMahieu, P. (2017). *Learning to improve: How America's schools can get better at getting better.* Cambridge, MA: Harvard University Press.

Burke, C., Harste, J., & Short, K. (1988). *Creating classrooms for authors and inquirers.* Portsmouth, NH: Heinemann.

Burley-Allen M. (1995). *Listening: The forgotten skill*. New York, NY: Wiley.

Carlone, H. B., & Johnson, A. (2007). Understanding the science experiences of successful women of color: Science identity as an analytic lens. *Journal of Research in Science Teaching, 44*(8), 1187–1218.

Christenbury, L., & Kelly, P. (1983). *Questioning: A path to critical thinking*. Urbana, IL: National Council of Teachers of English.

Collins, A., Brown, J. S., & Newman, S. E. (1992). Cognitive apprenticeship: Teaching the crafts of reading, writing, and mathematics. In L. B. Resnick (Ed.), *Knowing, learning and instruction: Essays in honor of Robert Glaser* (pp. 453–494). Hillsdale, NJ: Erlbaum.

Connelly, F., & Clandinin, D. (1988). *Teachers as curriculum planners: Narrative of experience*. New York, NY: Teachers College Press.

Cook, C., Fiat, A., & Larson, M. (2018). Positive greetings at the door: Evaluation of a low-cost, high-yield proactive classroom management strategy. *Journal of Positive Behavior, 20*(3), 149–159.

Cousins, G. (2006). An introduction to threshold concepts. *Planet, 17*(1), 4–5.

Csikszentmihalyi, M. (1990). *Flow: The psychology of optimal experience*. New York, NY: Harper & Row.

de Bono, E. (1985). *Six Thinking Hats: An essential approach to business management*. Boston, MA: Little, Brown.

de Bono, E. (1986). *CoRT thinking: Breadth*. New York, NY: Pergamon Press.

De Pree, M. (2003). *Leading without power: Finding hope in serving community*. New York, NY: Wiley.

Delpit, L. (2006). *Other people's children: Cultural conflict in the classroom*. New York, NY: Norton.

Dewey, J. (1916). *Democracy in education*. New York, NY: The Free Press.

Dweck, C. (2006). *Mindset: The new psychology of success*. New York, NY: Random House.

Earl, L. (2003). *Assessment as learning: Using classroom assessment to maximize student learning*. Thousand Oaks, CA: Corwin.

Edmiston, B. (1991). *What have you travelled? A teacher researcher study of structuring drama for reflection*. Unpublished doctoral dissertation, Ohio State University, Columbus.

Ericsson, A., & Poole, R. (2016). *Peak: Secrets from the new science of expertise*. New York, NY: Houghton-Mifflin Harcourt.

Erikson, E. (1963). *Childhood and society* (2nd ed.). New York, NY: Norton.

Fecho, B. (2011). *Teaching for the students: Habits of heart, mind, and practice in the engaged classroom*. New York, NY: Teachers College Press.

Fehr, B. (2008). Friendship formation. In S. Sprecher, A. Wenzel, & J. Harvey (Eds.), *Handbook of relationship initiation* (pp. 29–55). New York, NY: Psychology Press.

Fredricksen, J., Smith, M., & Wilhelm, J. (2012). *So, what's the story?: Teaching narrative to understand ourselves, others and the world*. Portsmouth, NH: Heinemann.

Freire, P. (2013). *Education for critical consciousness*. London: Bloomsbury Academic.

Freire, P. (2014). *Pedagogy of the oppressed* (30th anniversary ed.). New York, NY: Bloomsbury.

Gee, J. (2003). *What video games have to teach us about learning and literacy*. New York: Palgrave Macmillan.

Grossman, P. (1990). *The making of a teacher: Teacher knowledge and teacher education*. New York, NY: Teachers College Press.

Haberman, M. (2010, October). The pedagogy of poverty versus good teaching. *Phi Delta Kappan, 92*(2), 81–87.

Hall, J. (2018). How many hours does it take to make a friend? *Journal of Social and Personal Relationships, 36*(4), 1278–1296.

Haskell, R. (2000). *Transfer of learning: Cognition, instruction, and reasoning*. San Diego, CA: Academic Press.

Hattie, J. (2008). *Visible learning*. Thousand Oaks, CA: Corwin.

Heath, C., & Heath, D. (2017). *The power of moments: Why certain experiences have extraordinary impact*. New York, NY: Simon & Schuster.

Hillocks, G., Jr. (1986a). *Research on written composition: New directions for teaching*. Urbana, IL: ERIC and National Conference for Research in English.

Hillocks, G., Jr. (1986b). The writer's knowledge: Theory, research, and implications for practice. In A. Petrosky & D. Bartholomae (Eds.), *The teaching of writing* (85th Yearbook of the National Society for the Study of Education, Part II) (pp. 71–94). Chicago, IL: National Society for the Study of Education.

Hillocks, G., Jr. (1995). *Teaching writing as reflective practice*. New York, NY: Teachers College Press.

Hillocks, G., Jr. (1999). *Ways of thinking, ways of teaching*. New York, NY: Teachers College Press.

Himmele, P., & Himmele, W. (2009). *The language-rich classroom: A research-based framework for teaching English language learners*. Alexandria, VA: ASCD.

Huot, B. (2002). *(Re)articulating writing assessment for teaching and learning*. Logan: Utah State University Press.

Immordion-Yang, M. (2016). *Emotions, learning and the brain: Exploring the educational implications of affective neuroscience*. New York, NY: Norton.

Jennings, M., & Mills, H. (2009). Constructing a discourse of inquiry: Findings from a five-year ethnography at one elementary school. *Teachers College Record, 111*(7), 1583–1618.

Jensen, E. (2006). *Brain-based learning: The new paradigm of teaching*. Thousand Oaks, CA: Corwin.

Johannesen, R. L. (1996). *Ethics in human communication* (4th ed.). Prospect Heights, IL: Waveland Press.

Johannessen, L. R., Kahn, E., & Walter, C. C. (1982). *Designing and sequencing prewriting activities*. Urbana, IL: NCTE and ERIC.

Johnston, P. (2012). *Opening minds*. Portland, ME: Stenhouse.

Joiner, T. (2005). *Why people die by suicide*. Cambridge, MA: Harvard University Press.

Joiner, T. (2010). *Myths about suicide*. Cambridge, MA: Harvard University Press.

Kahnemann, D. (2011). *Thinking fast and slow*. New York, NY: Farrar, Straus & Giroux.

Kay, M. (2018). *Not light, but fire: How to lead meaningful race conversations in the classroom*. Portland, ME: Stenhouse.

Kittle, P., & Gallagher, K. (2018). *180 days: Two teachers and the quest to engage and empower adolescents*. Portsmouth, NH: Heinemann.

Knowles M., Holton III, E., & Swanson, R. (1998). *The Adult Learner* (5th ed.). Houston, TX: Gulf.

Lapp, D., & Flood, J. (2005). Exemplary reading instruction in the elementary school: How reading develops, how students learn, and how teachers teach. In J. Flood & P. Anders (Eds.), *Literacy development of students in urban schools: Research & policy* (pp. 153–179). Newark, DE: International Reading Association.

Lave, J., & Wenger, E. (1991). *Situated learning: Legitimate peripheral participation*. New York, NY: Cambridge University Press.

Leinwand, S. (1994, September). Four postulates for change. *Mathematics Teacher, 87*, 392–393.

Lieberman, M. (2013). *Social: Why our brains are wired to connect*. New York, NY: Crown.

Maslow, A. (1943). A theory of human motivation. *Psychological Review, 50*(4), 370–396. http://dx.doi.org/10.1037/h0054346

McCann, T. (2014). *Transforming talk into text: Argument writing, inquiry, and discussion, grades 6–12*. New York, NY: Teachers College Press.

McCann, T., Johannesen, L., & Kahn, E. (2006). *Talking in class: Using discussion to enhance teaching and learning*. Urbana, IL: NCTE.

McLaughlin, M., & Allen, G. (2002). *Guided comprehension: A teaching model for grades 3–8*. Newark, DE: IRA.

McLaughlin, M., & DeVoogd, G. (2004). *Critical literacy: Enhancing students' comprehension*. New York, NY: Scholastic.

McTighe, J., Seif, E., & Wiggins, G. (2004). You can teach for meaning. *Phi Delta Kappan*, 62(1), 26–31.

Mezirow, J. (2000). *Learning as transformation: Critical perspectives on a theory in progress*. San Francisco, CA: Jossey-Bass.

Moll, L., Amani, C., Neff, D., & Gonzalez, N. (1992). Funds of knowledge for teaching: Using a qualitative approach to connect homes and classrooms. *Theory Into Practice*, 31(2), 132–141.

Moll, L., & Gonzales, N. (1994). Lessons from research with language minority children. *Journal of Reading Behavior*, 26, 439–456.

Moore, C. (2016). *Creating scientists: Teaching and assessing science practice for the NGSS*. New York, NY: Taylor & Francis.

Morgan, N., & Saxton, J. (2006). *Asking better questions* (2nd ed.). Markham, ON: Pembroke.

National Assessment of Educational Progress. (2002). *The nation's report card: Writing 2002*. Washington, DC: National Center for Education Statistics.

National Writing Project & Nagin, C. (2006). *Because writing matters: Improving student writing in our schools*. San Francisco, CA: Jossey-Bass.

Neubert, G., & McNelis, S. (1990). Peer response: Teaching specific revision suggestions. *English Journal*, 79(5), 52–56.

Newmann, F. M., & Associates. (1996). *Authentic achievement: Restructuring of schools for intellectual quality*. San Francisco, CA: Jossey-Bass.

Newmann, F. M., Carmichael, D. L., & King, M. B. (2016). *Authentic intellectual work: Improving teaching for rigorous learning*. Thousand Oaks, CA: Corwin.

Newmann, F. M., & Wehlage, G. G. (1995). *Successful school restructuring: A report to the public and educators by the Center on Organization and Restructuring of Schools*. Madison: Board of Regents of the University of Wisconsin System and Document Service, Wisconsin Center for Education Research.

Noguera, P. (2018, May 23). *Teaching for transformation*. Keynote at Transformative Teaching Summit. King of Prussia, PA: American Reading Co.

Nystrand, M. (with A. Gamoran, R. Kachur, & C. Prendergast). (1997). *Opening dialogue: Understanding the dynamics of language and learning in the English classroom*. New York, NY: Teachers College Press.

Osman, M., & Hannafin, M. (1992, June). Metacognition research and theory: Analysis and implications for instructional design. *Educational Technology Research and Development*, 40(2), 83–99.

Paley, V. (1993). *You can't say you can't play*. Cambridge, MA: Harvard University Press.

Perkins, D. N. (1986). *Knowledge as design*. Mahwah, NJ: Erlbaum.

Perkins, D., & Salomon, G. (1988). Teaching for transfer. *Educational Leadership*, 46(1), 22–32.

Raphael, T. (1982). Question answering strategies for children. *Reading Teacher*, 36(2), 186–190.

Richtel, M. (2010, June 6). Attached to technology and paying a price. *New York Times*. Retrieved from https://www.nytimes.com/2010/06/07/technology/07brain.html

Ritchhart, R., & Perkins, D. N. (2000, Spring). Life in the mindful classroom: Nurturing the disposition of mindfulness. *Journal of Social Issues*, 56(1), 27–47.

Rogoff, B., Matusov, B., & White, S. (1996). Models of teaching and learning: Participation in a community of learners. In D. Olson & N. Torrance (Eds.), *The handbook of cognition and human development* (pp. 388–414). Oxford, UK: Blackwell.

Rose, D., & Meyer, A. (2002). *Teaching every student in the digital age: Universal design for learning*. Alexandria, VA: Association for Supervision and Curriculum Development.

Rose, D., Meyer, A., & Hitchcock, C. (Eds.). (2005). *The universally designed classroom: Accessible curriculum and digital technologies*. Cambridge, MA: Harvard Education Press.

Sadler, D. R. (1989, June). Formative assessment and the design of instructional systems. *Instructional Science, 18*(2), 119–144.

Schon, D. (1987). *Educating the reflective practitioner*. San Francisco, CA: Jossey-Bass.

Seligman, M. E. P. (2002). *Authentic happiness: Using the new positive psychology to realize your potential for lasting fulfillment*. New York, NY: Free Press.

Short, K., & Harste, J. (1996). *Creating classrooms for authors and inquirers* (2nd ed.). Portsmouth, NH: Heinemann.

Shulman, L. (1986). Those who understand: Knowledge growth in teaching. *Educational Researcher, 15*(2), 4–14.

Shulman, L. (1987). Knowledge and teaching: Foundations of the new reform. *Harvard Educational Review, 57*(1), 1–22.

Smagorinsky, P., Johannessen, L. R., Kahn, E., & McCann, T. (2011). *Teaching students to write essays that define*. Portsmouth, NH: Heinemann.

Smith, M. W., & Wilhelm, J. D. (2002). *"Reading don't fix no Chevys": Literacy in the lives of young men*. Portsmouth, NH: Heinemann.

Smith, M. W., & Wilhelm, J. D. (2006). *Going with the flow: Improving literacy learning for boys (and girls too!)*. Portsmouth, NH: Heinemann.

Smith, M. W., & Wilhelm, J. D. (2009). *Fresh takes on teaching the literary elements: How to teach what really matters about character, setting, point of view, and theme*. New York, NY: Scholastic.

Smith, M., Wilhelm, J., & Fredricksen, J. (2012). *Oh yeah? Putting argument to work both in school and out*. Portsmouth, NH: Heinemann.

Sousa, D. (2001). *Brain-based learning: How the brain learns* (2nd ed.). Thousand Oaks, CA: Corwin.

Sparks, S. D. (2017, May 16). Children must be taught to collaborate, studies say. *Education Week*. Retrieved from https://www.edweek.org/ew/articles/2017/05/17/children-must-be-taught-to-collaborate-studies.html

Stiggins, R. (1987). NCME instructional module on design and development of performance assessments. *Instructional Topics in Educational Measurement*. Portland, OR: Northwest Regional Educational Laboratory.

Stone, D., & Heen, S. (2014). *Thanks for the feedback: The science and art of receiving feedback well*. New York, NY: Viking.

Taylor, M. (1976). *Roll of thunder, hear my cry*. New York, NY: Dial.

Tharp, R., & Gallimore, R. (1988). *Rousing minds to life*. Cambridge: Cambridge University Press.

TNTP. (2018). *The opportunity myth*. Retrieved from https://tntp.org/assets/documents/TNTP_The-Opportunity-Myth_Web.pdf

Toulmin, S. (1958). *The uses of argument*. Cambridge, UK: Cambridge University Press.

Van Manen, M. (1977). Linking up ways of knowing with ways of being practical. *Curriculum Enquiry, 6*(3), 205–228.

Vygotsky, L. (1978). *Mind in society: The development of higher psychological processes*. Cambridge, MA: Harvard University Press.

Weglinsksy, H. (2004). Facts or critical thinking skills. *Phi Delta Kappan, 62*(1), 32–35.

White, B. (1995). Effects of autobiographical writing before reading on students' responses to short stories. *Journal of Educational Research, 88*, 173–184.

White, B. (2004). Preparing students for difficult texts and concepts. In P. Gantt & L. Meeks (Eds.), *Teaching ideas for 7–12 English language arts: What really works* (pp. 15–29). Norwood, MA: Christopher-Gordon.

Wiggins, G. (2012). Seven keys to effective feedback. *Educational Leadership, 70*(1), 10–16.

Wiggins, G., & McTighe, J. (1998). *Understanding by design.* Alexandria, VA: ASCD.

Wiggins, G., & McTighe, J. (2006). *Understanding by design.* Washington, DC: Association for Supervision and Curriculum Development.

Wilhelm, J. (1995). *Standards in practice, 6–8.* Champaign, IL: NCTE.

Wilhelm, J. (2007). *Engaging readers and writers with inquiry.* New York, NY: Scholastic.

Wilhelm, J. D. (2012). Cultures of collaboration: Leveraging classroom potential. *Voices From the Middle, 20*(2), 60–62.

Wilhelm, J. (2013a). *Action strategies for deepening comprehension* (2nd ed.). New York, NY: Scholastic.

Wilhelm, J. (2013b). *Enriching comprehension with visualization strategies* (2nd ed.). New York, NY: Scholastic.

Wilhelm, J. (2013c). *Improving comprehension with think alouds* (2nd ed.). New York: Scholastic.

Wilhelm, J. D. (2014, May). Moving towards collaborative cultures: Remixing classroom participation. *Voices From the Middle, 21*(4), 58–60.

Wilhelm, J. D. (2016). *"You Gotta BE the Book": Teaching engaged and reflective reading with adolescents* (3rd ed.). New York, NY: Teachers College Press.

Wilhelm, J. D. (2016, March). Working toward conscious competence: The power of inquiry for teachers and learners. *Voices From the Middle, 23*(3), 58–60.

Wilhelm, J. D., Baker, T. N., & Dube-Hackett, J. (2001). *Strategic reading: Guiding the life-long literacy of adolescents.* Portsmouth, NH: Heinemann.

Wilhelm, J. D., Douglass, W., & Fry, S. W. (2014). *The activist learner.* New York, NY: Teachers College.

Wilhelm, J., & Friedemann, P. (1998). *Hyperlearning: Where inquiry, projects and technology meet.* York, ME: Stenhouse.

Wilhelm, J., & Novak, B. (2011). *Teaching literacy for love and wisdom.* New York, NY: Teachers College Press.

Wilhelm, J., & Smith, M. W. (2014). *Reading unbound: Why kids need to read what they want and why we should let them.* New York, NY: Scholastic.

Wilhelm, J., & Smith, M. W. (2016). *Diving deep into nonfiction: Transferable tools for reading ANY nonfiction text.* Thousand Oaks, CA: Corwin.

Wilhelm, J., Smith, M., & Fredricksen, J. (2012). *Get it done! Writing and analyzing informational texts to make things happen.* Portsmouth, NH: Heinemann.

Wilhelm, J., Wilhelm, P., & Boas, E. (2009). *Inquiring minds learn to read and write.* Oakville, ON: Rubicon.

World Economic Forum. (2016) *The future of jobs.* Retrieved from http://reports.weforum.org/future-of-jobs-2016/chapter-1-the-future-of-jobs-and-skills/

Zacaraian, D., Alvarez-Ortiz, L., & Haynes, J. (2017). *Teaching to strengths: Supporting students living with trauma, violence and chronic stress.* Alexandria, VA: ASCD.

Zeichner, K., & Tabachik, P. (1981). Are the effects of university teacher education "washed out" by school experience? *Journal of Teacher Education, 32*(3), 7–11.

Zelazo, P. D., Blair, C. B., & Willoughby, M. T. (2016). *Executive function: Implications for education* (NCER 2017–2000). Washington, DC: National Center for Education Research, Institute of Education Sciences, U.S. Department of Education. This report is available on the IES website at http://ies.ed.gov

INDEX

general processes, 158 (figure), 158–160
literal level, 173–174, 176
teacher-student conferences, 235, 236
visual strategies, 131
See also Questioning strategies; Think-aloud strategies
Real Friend Peer Revision Guide, 230 (figure), 230–231
Reflection
agentive stories, 251
civil rights unit, 46
as conference purpose, 235
on conferences, 237, 237 (figure)
DEAL model, 226, 227 (figure)
in EMPOWER model, 22–23
at ends of units, 241
guides, 216–217
importance, 241–242
on learning targets, 232, 232 (figure)
ongoing, 46, 255
process analysis, 253–254
on standards, 248–249
on task demands, 65
See also Assessments; Formative assessments
Reflexivity, 259–260
Regression, task, 64, 66–69, 67 (figure), 68 (figure), 69 (figure)
Relationships. *See* Collaborative classroom culture
Roll of Thunder, Hear My Cry (Taylor), 207–208
Romeo and Juliet, 72
Rules of notice
in civil rights unit, 149–150
for text cues, 155, 162–165, 163–164 (figure)
types, 163
for visual texts and images, 122, 131, 134–136

Sadler, D. R., 226
Say something prompt, 197
Scenarios
ranking, 123–124, 124–125 (figure)
role plays, 121
Science
Next Generation Science Standards, 33, 69, 110
texts, 143, 152
Scientific inquiry, 100 (figure)
See-Think-Wonder, 122, 122 (figure), 123 (figure)
SEL. *See* Social–emotional learning
Self-assessments, 231–233, 232 (figure), 242
Semantic scales, 166, 167 (figure), 234
Sentence stems, for self-assessment, 231–232, 232 (figure)
Shakespeare, William
Hamlet, 142, 143
Romeo and Juliet, 72
Short response guides, 215–216
Silent Discussion, 200–201, 201 (figure)
6 L's (Liked, Learned, Laughed, Lived Through, Led to, Lacked), 216
Sketchnotes, 213
Sketch to stretch, 212–213
Smith, Debra, 216
Smith, M. W., 162
Social–emotional learning (SEL), 192, 231, 261

Social relations. *See* Collaborative classroom culture
Speed dating. *See* Carousel Conversations
SQs. *See* Subquestions
Standards
assessing performance, 20, 242, 243, 244, 247–251
generating essential questions from, 110–111
Idaho, 33
next-generation, 20, 33, 69, 110, 132, 243, 251
reflection on, 248–249
science, 33, 69, 110
threshold knowledge and, 110, 111
Stay and Stray. *See* Gallery Walks
Stiggins, R., 242
Stranger in role technique, 219
Student-centered discovery learning, 20
Student work samples, 213
Subquestions (SQs), 99, 101, 110
Summary prompts, 216
Summative assessments, 225, 242
See also Assessments
Surveys, 81, 115–116, 117–119, 118–119 (figure)
Symbolism, 155–156, 170–171

Talkback think-alouds, 165–168, 166 (figure)
Tasks
accessing, 64, 65, 76
assessing, 64, 74–75
compressing, 64, 70–74
regressing, 64, 66–69, 67 (figure), 68 (figure), 69 (figure)
Teacher-student conferences, 235–237
Teaching
change in, 27–28, 262
differentiation strategies, 36, 36 (figure)
goals, 26
informational, 27, 28, 30, 31–32, 32–33 (figure), 34–35 (figure)
pedagogy of poverty, 25, 28, 30, 31 (figure)
rock climbing vignettes, 6–8
roles, 261–262
See also Transformational teaching
"Tell Me . . ." framework, 236
Templates, 71–74, 73 (figure)
Texts
genres, 183
orienting moves, 162
structures, 183
summary prompts, 216
visual, 131–132, 134–135, 148
See also Reading; Visualization strategies
Things Fall Apart, 139, 139 (figure)
Think-aloud strategies
cued, 154–156, 156–157 (figure), 170–171
effective, 154
in EMPOWER model, 153
free response, 158–160, 160–162 (figure)
goals, 152
rules of notice, 155, 162–165, 163–164 (figure)
talkback, 165–168, 166 (figure)
tips, 169

Because...

ALL TEACHERS ARE LEADERS

PLANNING POWERFUL INSTRUCTION

Specifically for Grades 2–5, the authors present your go-to guide for transforming student outcomes through stellar instructional planning.

FLASH FEEDBACK

Offering solutions to burnout, *Flash Feedback* takes teachers through the process of crafting strategic feedback to student writing and developing a realistic plan for structuring classroom culture.

NO MORE FAKE READING

Discover how to transform your classroom into a vibrant reading environment. This groundbreaking book combines the benefits of classic literature with the motivational power of choice reading.

GRAMMAR KEEPERS

This kid-friendly cache of 101 lessons and practice pages helps your students internalize the conventions of correctness once and for all.

To order your copies, visit **corwin.com/literacy**

Impact your students' literacy skills tomorrow

DEVELOPING WRITERS OF ARGUMENT

Complete with guidance on applying the lessons' techniques in a broader, unit-wide context, *Developing Writers of Argument* offers a practical approach for instructing students in this crucial aspect of their lifelong development.

READ, TALK, WRITE

Laura Robb lays out the classroom structures that create the time and space for students to have productive talk and written discourse about texts.

THESE 6 THINGS

Take a deep breath and refocus on six known best practices—establish and strengthen key beliefs, then build knowledge and increase reading, writing, speaking and listening, and argumentation in every content area, every day.

DISCIPLINARY LITERACY IN ACTION

ReLeah Lent and Marsha Voigt present a framework for teachers that keeps their subjects at the center and shows them how to pool strengths with colleagues in ongoing communities of professional learning around content-specific literacy.

A SAGE Publishing Company

Helping educators make the greatest impact

CORWIN HAS ONE MISSION: to enhance education through intentional professional learning.

We build long-term relationships with our authors, educators, clients, and associations who partner with us to develop and continuously improve the best evidence-based practices that establish and support lifelong learning.